D1280951

The Five-Book Prelude

WILLIAM WORDSWORTH

The Five-Book Prelude

Edited by
Duncan Wu

BLACKWELL
Publishers

Copyright © Blackwell Publishers Ltd, 1997
Redaction, introduction and notes copyright © DuncanWu, 1997

First published 1997

Reprinted 1997

Blackwell Publishers Ltd
108 Cowley Road
Oxford OX4 1JF, UK

Blackwell Publishers Inc
350 Main Street
Malden, Massachusetts 02148, USA

British Library Cataloguing in Publication Data
A CIP catalogue record for this book is available from the British Library

Library of Congress Cataloging in Publication Data
Wordsworth, William, 1770–1850.
[Prelude.   Selections]
The Five-Book Prelude / William Wordsworth : edited by Duncan Wu.
p.   cm.
Includes bibliographical references and index.
ISBN   0–631–20548–9 (hc.) — ISBN   0–631–20549–7 (pbk)
I. Wu, Duncan. II. Title.
PR5864.A3   1997   96–43608
821'.7—dc20   CIP

Typeset in 10½ on 12½pt Galliard
by Ace Filmsetting Ltd, Frome, Somerset
Printed and bound in Great Britain
by T. J. International Limited, Padstow, Cornwall

This book is printed on acid-free paper

Contents

Acknowledgements

For assistance and advice at the Wordsworth Library I am grateful to Jeff Cowton, Librarian, and Robert Woof, Director of the Wordsworth Trust; I am also grateful to the Chairman and Trustees of the Trust for permission to publish from manuscripts in their possession. During work on the present text I have been indebted to previous editors: Ernest de Selincourt, Helen Darbishire, Stephen Gill, J. C. Maxwell and W. J. B. Owen. This edition would not have been possible without the scholarship of Jonathan Wordsworth and Mark L. Reed. It is a pleasure, once again, to acknowledge the help and encouragement of my editor at Blackwell Publishers, Andrew McNeillie.

The author and publishers wish to thank the following for permission to use copyright material: The Trustees of Boston University for material from Joseph F. Kishel, 'The "Analogy Passage" from Wordsworth's Five-book Prelude', *Studies in Romanticism*, 18:2 (Summer 1979); Oxford University Press for material from Jonathan Wordsworth, 'Into a Populous Plain: The Five-Book Prelude' in *The Borders of Vision*, Clarendon Press (1982), pp. 235–46. Copyright © Jonathan Wordsworth 1982; and Mary Jacobus, 'Providence, Signs, and the "Analogy Passage"' in *Romanticism, Writing and Sexual Difference*, Clarendon Press (1989), pp. 276–86. Copyright © Mary Jacobus 1989; Yale University Press for material from Kenneth R. Johnstone, 'The Five-Book Prelude of January–March 1904' in *Wordsworth and the Recluse* (1984), pp. 106ff. Every effort has been made to trace the copyright holders, but if any have been inadvertently overlooked the publishers will be pleased to make the necessary arrangement at the first opportunity.

Abbreviations

Grasmere Journals	Dorothy Wordsworth, *The Grasmere Journals*, ed. Pamela Woof (Oxford, 1991)
Griggs	*The Letters of Samuel Taylor Coleridge*, ed. E. L. Griggs (6 vols., Oxford, 1956–71)
Jarvis (1981)	Robin Jarvis, 'The Five-Book *Prelude*: A Reconsideration', *JEGP* 80 (1981), 528–51
JEGP	*Journal of English and Germanic Philology*
Masson	*The Collected Writings of Thomas De Quincey*, ed. David Masson (14 vols., London, 1889–90)
McKenzie (1981)	D. F. McKenzie, 'Typography and Meaning: The Case of William Congreve', in *Buch und Buchhandel in Europa im achzehten Jahrhundert*, ed. G. Barber and B. Fabian, *Wolfenbütteler Schriften zur Geschichte des Buchwesens*, 4 (Hamburg, 1981), pp. 81–125
Moorman	Mary Moorman, *William Wordsworth: A Biography* (2 vols., Oxford, 1957–65)
MY	*The Letters of William and Dorothy Wordsworth: The Middle Years*, ed. Ernest De Selincourt, *i: 1806–11*, rev. Mary Moorman (Oxford, 1969); *ii: 1812–20*, rev. Mary Moorman and Alan G. Hill (Oxford, 1970)
N&Q	*Notes and Queries*
Norton *Prelude*	*The Prelude: 1799, 1805, 1850*, ed. Jonathan Wordsworth, Stephen Gill and M. H. Abrams (New York, 1979)
Notebooks	*The Notebooks of Samuel Taylor Coleridge*, ed. Kathleen Coburn et al. (4 vols., London, 1957–90)

Observations on the Lakes	William Gilpin, *Observations relative chiefly to Picturesque Beauty, made in the year 1772, on several parts of England; particularly the Mountains and Lakes of Cumberland and Westmoreland* (2 vols., London, 1786)
OET *Prelude*	*The Prelude or Growth of a Poet's Mind*, ed. Ernest de Selincourt, rev. Helen Darbishire (2nd edn, Oxford, 1959)
Owen *WC*	W. J. B. Owen, 'Understanding *The Prelude*', *WC* 22 (1991), 100–9
PQ	*Philological Quarterly*
Prose Works	*The Prose Works of William Wordsworth*, ed. W. J. B. Owen and Jane Worthington Smyser (3 vols., Oxford, 1974)
Reed	Mark L. Reed, *Wordsworth: The Chronology of the Middle Years, 1800–1815* (Cambridge, Mass., 1975)
Romanticism	*Romanticism: An Anthology*, ed. Duncan Wu (Oxford, 1994)
Romanticism: A Critical Reader	*Romanticism: A Critical Reader*, ed. Duncan Wu (Oxford, 1995)
Shaver	Chester L. and Alice C. Shaver, *Wordsworth's Library: A Catalogue* (New York, 1979)
Stillinger (1989)	Jack Stillinger, 'Textual Primitivism and the Editing of Wordsworth', *Studies in Romanticism*, 28 (1989), 3–28
Stillinger (1994)	Jack Stillinger, *Coleridge and Textual Instability* (New York, 1994)
Thompson	T. W. Thompson, *Wordsworth's Hawkshead*, ed. Robert Woof (Oxford, 1970)
Ward	Thomas De Quincey, *Confessions of an English Opium-Eater, and Other*

	Writings, ed. Aileen Ward (New York, 1966)
WC	*The Wordsworth Circle*
Woof	Robert Woof, 'Presentation of the Self in the Composition of *The Prelude*', in *Presenting Poetry: Composition, Publication, Reception*, ed. Howard Erskine-Hill and Richard A. McCabe (Cambridge, 1995), pp. 138–62
Wordsworth (1977)	Jonathan Wordsworth, 'The Five-Book *Prelude* of Early Spring 1804', *JEGP* 76 (1977), 1–25
WR i	Duncan Wu, *Wordsworth's Reading 1770–1799* (Cambridge, 1993)
WR ii	Duncan Wu, *Wordsworth's Reading 1800–1815* (Cambridge, 1995)

Introduction

The *Five-Book Prelude* is by any standards a remarkable work. Dating from March 1804, it contains much of Wordsworth's finest blank verse, including the spots of time, the infant babe, the discharged soldier, the infant prodigy, the Winander boy, and the climbing of Snowdon; it thus incorporates most of the *Two-Part Prelude* of 1799, alongside some of the most impressive poetry composed for the thirteen-Book poem of 1804–5.

Its roots lie in the final months of 1798, when the Wordsworths found themselves stranded in Goslar in Germany during what they understood to be the coldest winter of the century. The preceding year had been one of the most important of the poet's life. His close association with Coleridge had begun in July 1797, when the Wordsworths had moved from Racedown Lodge in Dorset to Alfoxden House, a few miles from Nether Stowey. Between them, Coleridge and the Wordsworths had an extraordinarily productive relationship; interestingly, its fruits registered first in the work of the younger man, with composition of 'This Lime-Tree Bower my Prison' in July 1797 – a poem displaying a Wordsworthian love of Nature.

Wordsworth himself wrote surprisingly little in the latter half of 1797, but presumably learnt a great deal from his new friend. One topic of conversation must have been Coleridge's plan for *The Recluse*, the poem that would herald the millennium, Christ's thousand-year rule on earth, of which the revolutions in America and France were regarded as harbingers. Coleridge had distinct notions of what it should say; he would later characterize it as 'the *first* and *only* true philosophical poem in existence'.[1] By 'philosophy' he probably had in mind an explanation of how universal betterment and brotherhood would come about – something that would almost certainly have entailed an elucidation of his own philosophical system, a cocktail of ideas derived from the writings of David Hartley, Joseph Priestley, and Bishop Berkeley, among others.[2] This would have required some explaining – and, even then, Wordsworth may not fully have appreciated it (or at least that seems to be the implication of Coleridge's disappointment with *The Excursion* years later[3]). In Wordsworth's defence, it might be said that *The Recluse* was probably so ambitious and, finally, so idealistic, as to have been unwritable.[4]

Coleridge was persuaded that Wordsworth was not merely a great man, but a great poet, and in the heady atmosphere at Alfoxden in 1797–8 he convinced him that he was the only person capable of writing *The Recluse*. By January 1798, Wordsworth had adopted the scheme as his own, and produced a number of blank verse poems and fragments that he decided would contribute to it.[5] They are composed with a conviction he would never have again, leading one to suspect that this was probably the only point at which he could ever have written the poem. But perhaps there were already problems with the scheme; Wordsworth's instincts may have told him that the project was not for him. In the event it was quickly dropped – temporarily, he supposed – for *Lyrical Ballads*, which would help pay their way to Germany. There, he would attempt to continue *The Recluse* and to finish it as soon as he could. But Germany turned out to be a disappointment. The Wordsworths had set out believing it to be the intellectual hub of Europe, thanks perhaps to the influence of Germanists such as Dr Beddoes of Bristol,[6] with whom Coleridge and Wordsworth were acquainted. As such, it would be, they thought, the ideal location in which to compose the great philosophical

[1] *Romanticism*, 573.

[2] See Peter Mann's Introduction to Coleridge's *Lectures 1795 on Politics and Religion*, ed. Lewis Patton and Peter Mann (Princeton, 1971), pp. lviii–lxvii.

[3] See *Romanticism*, 572–4, 595–6.

[4] Jonathan Wordsworth provides an exemplary account of the poem in 'The Light That Never Was', the Epilogue to *Borders of Vision*.

[5] Among these were *The Ruined Cottage*, *The Pedlar*, and the two fragments Jonathan Wordsworth has published as 'In storm and tempest' and 'Not useless do I deem' (*The Music of Humanity* (London, 1969), pp. 172–3, 269–72).

[6] For more on Beddoes, see John Edmonds Stock, *The Life of Thomas Beddoes* (1811), and my '*Lyrical Ballads* (1798): The Beddoes Copy', *The Library*, 15 (1993), 332–5.

poem of the age. Goslar, the walled city in which the Wordsworths found themselves immured during the harsh winter of 1798–9, was in the event uncongenial, to say the least, as Wordsworth wrote in February 1799: 'Goslar was once the residence of Emperors, and it is now the residence of Grocers and Linen-drapers who are, I say it with a feeling of sorrow, a wretched race; the flesh, blood and bone in their minds being nothing but knavery and low falsehood.'[7] Cold, isolated, and distinctly uncharmed by the locals, Wordsworth found little inspiration for a poem that was to proclaim universal brotherhood. In despair one day he found himself writing, on a page of one of his notebooks,

> Was it for this
> That one, the fairest of all rivers, loved
> To blend his murmurs with my nurse's song,
> And from his alder shades and rocky falls,
> And from his fords and shallows, sent a voice
> To intertwine my dreams?[8]

This plaintive questioning turned out to be the start of *The Prelude*. Not surprisingly, the admission in verse that he was failing to write *The Recluse* unlocked Wordsworth's creative energies, and composition of blank verse continued apace. It was not the millennial epic proposed by Coleridge, and flowed unhindered for precisely that reason – it was dependent not on philosophical disquisition, for which Wordsworth had little talent, but on his own memories of the past, about which he could write with complete confidence. Having written one and a half books of the two-Part poem, he realized that the work should address itself to Coleridge – he may have seen that his failure to honour his friend's high hopes had been his inspiration all along – and in a new manuscript made a number of revisions to this effect.[9] At an early stage, therefore, *The Prelude* became the poem to Coleridge, and it contains frequent allusions to his poetry and *The Recluse*, of which Coleridge was in a sense the co-author, and which Wordsworth still believed he could write. On completion of the two Books of what he had come to regard as the

---

[7] *EY* 249.

[8] 'Was it for this', quoted from *The Prelude: The Four Texts (1798, 1799, 1805, 1850)*, ed. Jonathan Wordsworth (London, 1995).

[9] For this insight and others, I am indebted to Woof, esp. pp. 151–3.

poem on his life, Wordsworth in fact made a concerted effort to return
to *The Recluse*, the main results being the 'Prospectus' to *The Recluse*[10]
and 'Home at Grasmere' – an intermittently impressive, but ultimately
unconvincing, work that eventually stalled, and remained unfinished.

The next few years cannot have been easy for someone who knew he
had an epic to write but no belief in his ability to do so. Having Coleridge
on the case cannot have made matters easier: depressed, hopelessly in
love with Sara Hutchinson, and badly addicted to opium, Coleridge had
relinquished his own poetic ambitions and transferred them to
Wordsworth. For Coleridge it was imperative, for both their sakes, that
Wordsworth fulfil their joint aspirations by embarking on the great
work he had planned; in mid-January 1804 he told Richard Sharp:
'Wordsworth is a Poet, and I feel myself a better Poet, in knowing how
to honour *him*, than in all my own poetic Compositions, all I have done
or hope to do – and I prophesy immortality to his *Recluse*'.[11] It is a
poignant irony that, at the time Coleridge penned that pious tribute to
the author of his pet project, Wordsworth was in Grasmere fretting over
his inability to compose it. Coleridge was in increasingly poor health
and about to depart for Malta; that in itself may have concentrated
Wordsworth's mind on the continuing failure to press on with *The
Recluse*, dependent as it was on his friend's guidance. 'I am very anxious
to have your notes for the Recluse', he told Coleridge on 6 March.[12]
Perhaps it was renewed guilt; or perhaps, having read the second Part
of the *Two-Part Prelude* to Coleridge on 4 January, he felt a new
surge of inspiration. For whatever reason – and any of these factors may
have played a part – the millennial epic was deferred, once again, by
recourse to the poem on his life. This was the beginning of the *Five-
Book Prelude*.

Wordsworth conspicuously did not require Coleridge's notes in
order to continue work on the poem on his life; no doubt that gave it an
added attraction. All the same – perhaps because *The Recluse* still seemed
to be within his reach, and he felt so uneasily aware that the byway
down which he was straying meant abandonment, however temporary,
of his duties as its author – Coleridge's presence is powerfully felt in the

[10] Presented in an early version, *Romanticism*, 246–8.
[11] Griggs, ii. 1034. See also the letter to Poole of 14 October 1803, in *Romanticism*,
566–7.
[12] *EY* 452.

materials composed during February[13] and March 1804. As Robert Woof felicitously puts it, *Five-Book Prelude*, Books III–V, are pervaded by 'a certain loving-kindness for Coleridge – an awareness of his poor health; sorrow that they missed each other at Cambridge, with the wondering possibility that perhaps, had they met earlier, Coleridge's disastrous undergraduate failure might have been avoided.'[14] These preoccupations may even have informed Wordsworth's reorganization of the existing drafts. The first thing he did was to place 269 lines before the original opening question, 'Was it for this', the first 54 of which were a fragment written 18–19 November 1799, while on a two-day walk from Ullswater to Grasmere to arrange the renting of Dove Cottage. The remainder date largely from January 1804, and ruminate on the various subjects available to someone wishing to write an epic poem. The tone seems dilatory and indecisive, dogged by the kind of uncertainty that Wordsworth must have felt about *The Recluse*.[15]

The second major act of rearrangement entailed the removal of three of the spots of time from Part I of the two-Part poem, along with a passage composed contemporaneously with, but not incorporated into, it ('There was a boy'[16]), and their positioning at strategic points within the five-Book scheme. 'There was a boy' thus provides a crucial resolution to the central section of Book IV,[17] as a counterbalance to the delicious satire of the infant prodigy, whose erudition makes country people 'pray for God's good grace', and which grieves 'Grandam Earth' at finding him impervious to Nature. The boy of Winander, by contrast, is so integrated with natural forces that he enjoys with them 'a concourse wild / Of mirth and jocund din'. He is the recipient of a natural 'education' far healthier than the sterile knowledge of the prodigy.

This was followed by the spot of time describing the drowned man of Esthwaite, concluded by new lines in which the experience is claimed to have been 'hallowed' by a spirit allying it to 'the works / Of Grecian art

---

[13] Though, as Mark L. Reed has observed, composition is likely to have stopped *c.*20–4 February, when Dorothy was seriously ill (Reed, 637).

[14] Woof, 153–4.

[15] A particularly shrewd discussion of the opening of *The Prelude* is offered by A. D. Nuttall, *Openings: Narrative Beginnings from the Epic to the Novel* (Oxford, 1992), ch. 4.

[16] The passage had, of course, been published in *Lyrical Ballads* (1800); see Cornell *LB* 139–41.

[17] Book IV, ll. 472–505, below.

and purest poesy'.[18] This distinctly aesthetic context should not surprise us too much, as in the two-Part poem the experience was introduced as having effected 'the growth of mental power / And love of nature's works'.[19] None the less, it does seem callous to adduce the man's death as further evidence for Wordsworth's suitability as the poet of *The Recluse* – a lapse that serves only to highlight the doubts he must have had as to whether he was up to it.

After this episode in the earlier poem, he went on to say what spots of time are and provided another two examples. The master-stroke of the new scheme was to move these materials to the end of the poem – the conclusion of Book V. Wordsworth thus provided the work with a logic distinct from the earlier one: recalling the archetypal sequence of fall and redemption, Books III–V were designed to demonstrate 'fallings-off', 'an abasement in my mind', from which he would be able to claim deliverance through the restorative and enduring power of Nature as represented by the spots of time. So it is that in Book III, the experience of loss is represented by the aimlessness of the poet's undergraduate career:

> Rotted as by a charm, my life became
> A floating island, an amphibious thing,
> Unsound, of spongy texture, yet withal
> Not wanting a fair face of water-weeds
> And pleasant flowers.[20]

Jonathan Wordsworth describes the simile as 'eccentric' – as indeed it is; it is also characteristically dense. If Wordsworth drifts, without direction, through an undistinguished student career, he is none the less blessed by the fair face of weeds and flowers that prove his earlier fostering by Nature, which will one day provide the means by which his imagination is to be restored. There is something reassuring about the way he uses the image of the floating island of Esthwaite[21] (where he grew

---

[18] Book IV, ll. 562–3, below.

[19] *Two-Part Prelude*, i. 257–8.

[20] Book III, ll. 340–4, below.

[21] Although commentators usually note that the floating island Wordsworth has in mind was the one on Derwentwater, the identification seems to me dubious. It is more likely that he was thinking of the one on Esthwaite, having seen it, probably on a daily

up) to describe his youthful waywardness. The island may float aimlessly, but it is a thing of Nature – a symbolic guarantee of the powers that will redeem the undergraduate poet. In Book V the threat to that inner power is even stronger, and comes in the form of the mechanistic habits of the picturesque, when he found himself pleased by Nature

> Not worthily, disliking here, and there
> Liking, by rule transferred from mimic art
> To things above all art.[22]

Rulebound in a manner that reduces the natural world to the level of an artefact, the perceiving mind becomes soulless in its confusion, 'a meagre, untaught eye / And nothing more, yet without delight'.[23] Only one response may be offered, and it turns out to be the last two spots of time – the Penrith beacon and waiting for the horses episodes[24] – which retain, from their appearance in the earlier *Prelude*, 'A fructifying virtue'; that is, the power to restore the mind even after its vigour has been depleted by excessive rationalism or intellectual rigidity. A characteristic of all four episodes is that Nature's ability to renew imaginative vision is affirmed by reference to the experience of death: the Winander boy's death is far from anticlimactic, his final integration with the elements being a just reward for the closeness of his relationship with them during his life; the drowned man of Esthwaite provides the young poet with an important lesson in his educational development; the visionary dreariness of the scene around the Penrith beacon is juxtaposed with the mouldered gibbet-mast and its gruesome history; and the waiting for the horses episode is inextricably associated with the premature demise of the poet's father. In other words, all these experiences, whether attributed to the poet or to someone else, embrace the apparently opposed realms

---

basis, while at Hawkshead. And that, rather than the one on Derwentwater, provided the subject of Dorothy's poem years later; see *Romanticism*, 501–2.

[22] Book V, ll. 218–20. Nicola Trott provides a comprehensive account of Wordsworth's engagement with the picturesque in her 'Wordsworth and the Picturesque: A Strong Infection of the Age', *WC* 18 (1987), 114–21. Jonathan Wordsworth writes about its impact on the poetry of 1798–1800 in 'Wordsworth and the Ideal of Nature in 1800', in *The Lake District: A Sort of National Property* (London, 1986).

[23] Book V, ll. 229–30, below.

[24] Book V, ll. 290–389, below.

of life and death; against the view that those worlds are unbridgeable, each experience operates as a reminder that through the replenishing virtue of Nature, the barrier that divides them can be broken down. As he had put it in *Descriptive Sketches* (1793), 'An unknown power connects him with the dead' (l. 543). Perhaps the possible early loss of Coleridge was on his mind, and the ensuing anxieties concerning how he might continue with *The Recluse*. In any case, the entire poem is framed by the spots of time – from the early experiences of woodcock-snaring and birds nesting in Book I to the waiting for the horses episode in Book V. The drafts give no clue as to when this plan was conceived, but it is likely that Wordsworth was working to it from the outset.

Of the new passages composed for the five-Book poem there are many important episodes offering variations on the theme of imagination impaired and restored, but none have attracted more critical notice than the climbing of Snowdon. It may seem surprising, at first, to find that the culmination of the *Thirteen-Book Prelude* was composed so early – well before most of the last seven Books. But the technique of beginning with the conclusion and working backwards is common to other poems, including *The Ruined Cottage* and 'The Idiot Boy'; the knowledge that, with the ending safely committed to paper, he could retrace his steps at leisure, evidently gave Wordsworth a feeling of security.

The climbing of Snowdon was copied into the manuscript by Mary Wordsworth, and it is surrounded by sometimes very rough draft in her husband's hand for the rest of Books IV and V. This would suggest that it was composed before them. It may even have been one of the first passages Wordsworth worked on in preparation for the new, expanded poem; at all events, it is likely that he embarked on the five-Book scheme with the structure of the final Book already determined. Beginning with the Snowdon episode, it outlines the final 'abasement of the mind' – the mechanistic tendencies discussed earlier – before concluding with the spots of time, the power of which has preserved his abilities as the poet of *The Recluse*. The structure is masterful; in a poem structured to celebrate the ultimate triumph of a mind repeatedly threatened by the detrimental effects of erudition and indolence, a climax is provided by the climbing of a mountain – an experience revealing 'The manner in which ofttimes Nature works / Herself upon the outward face of things'.[25]

---

[25] Book V, ll. 68–9, below.

Thus, in its original context, the climbing of Snowdon provides the evidence for which the prospective author of *The Recluse* yearns – that Nature can be relied on to restore him for the massive task of its composition. The blue chasm he recalls seeing at the summit is an image, finally, of hope – focused on a poem, still largely unwritten, for which Coleridge has the all-important notes.

After the Snowdon passage was copied into the notebook, Wordsworth drafted a series of analogous scenes, drawn both from his own experience and from books. These lines, which comprise what has come to be known as the 'analogy' passage, have attracted much attention, and are presented in Appendix I. Perhaps because time had intervened between them and composition of the Snowdon episode, he seems to have lost heart in them and broken off, resuming with a discussion of 'higher minds'. The decision cannot have been easy – the draft is much corrected, and part is recopied – but Wordsworth's instincts were right. After the episode describing the moonlit horse, the passage loses steam as it moves on to Columbus, Gilbert, Park and Dampier.

If the climbing of Snowdon was one of the first passages to be composed for the five-Book poem, those connecting it with the spots of time were evidently the last. They survive in the notebook, sometimes in very rough shape, none the less following a discernible line of argument. It is not clear whether Book V was completed, in so far as no extant fair copy of the poem is to be found, and the surviving drafts are at times too rough and sketchy to be regarded as finished copy. Even so, it looks as if Wordsworth understood the overall structure of the work from the start, and the manuscripts, whatever the shortcomings of individual drafts, are sufficient to indicate what that was. Wordsworth had abandoned the poem by 12 March, probably within six weeks of starting, by which time he was at work on further rearrangement and revision of the materials he had so far assembled. Although much has been said about the *Five-Book Prelude*, detailed analysis of its contents has been hindered by the absence of a text; in fact, the task of reconstruction has occasionally been described as impossible.[26] This is not so. The poem may be retrieved, and the present text reveals it, despite its brief life, to be more than a mere curiosity, a stepping-stone to the much

---

[26] See, for instance, James Averill, *Wordsworth and the Poetry of Human Suffering* (Ithaca, NY, 1980), p. 252.

greater achievement of the thirteen-Book poem. Its structure, while necessarily less ambitious than that of later versions, embodies one of the
central arguments of the larger work, along with much of its most important poetry. But it is as a product of early 1804, when Coleridge's
departure and ill health made completion of *The Recluse* more doubtful
than ever, that the *Five-Book Prelude* is most distinctive, for it articulates
a number of concerns of the moment. More so than in any other version, its predominant tone is self-justificatory. As Wordsworth reiterates
the pattern of abasement and restoration, he looks repeatedly for evidence that the natural education provided by the spots of time was not
in vain – that it would prepare him for the task of composing *The Recluse*. Guilt and self-doubt pervade the verse and its argument, and at
every turn there is the baleful reminder of the enemies of promise:

> petty duties and pressing cares,
> Labour and penury, disease and grief,
> Which to one object chain the impoverished mind
> Enfeebled and defeated, vexing strife
> At home, and want of pleasure and repose,
> And all that eats away the genial spirits . . .[27]

These lines appear in no other version of the poem, and although it
would be wrong to argue that they typify its mood, they certainly clarify
the tensions that impel it. The topos is familiar, with an important model
in Virgil's *Georgics*, iii. 66–7, a brief digression in the midst of a discourse on the need for good breeding stock in cattle. Wordsworth translated it at Cambridge while an undergraduate:

> The pleasant time, the glistering hour of life
> Flies first: a Ghastly train succeeds
> Of Dire diseases, pain-faded care
> And withering age.[28]

Virgil's lines obviously made an impression on him, because he reworked
them again in spring 1789, then in 1791–2 for *Descriptive Sketches*, and
once again in 1793 for *Salisbury Plain*. By the time they are echoed by

[27] Book V, ll. 150–5.
[28] DC MS 6, 5r.

the poet of *The Prelude*, they are integral to his understanding of human life, as reflected in the portrayal of suffering in *The Ruined Cottage*, *The Brothers* and *Michael*, among others. But what is so distinctive about the admonition they deliver in March 1804 is the additional echo, at line 155, of the poem Coleridge had chosen to publish on Wordsworth's wedding-day two years before:

> My *genial spirits* fail,
> And what can these avail
> To lift the smoth'ring weight from off my breast?[29]

Coleridge too has a source,[30] but given the circumstances it would be extraordinary had Wordsworth not had *Dejection* in mind as he worked. Perhaps he suspected that Coleridge's lack of poetic ambition, depression, and even to some extent his bad health, stemmed partly from the loss of self-confidence that had followed his own appointment as author of *The Recluse*. That responsibility can only have made him more than usually aware of the importance of maintaining his own health – a preoccupation that no doubt came easily to someone described by Coleridge as a hypochondriac.[31] The foes that thwart the aspirations of the poet had done their worst in Coleridge's case, and the persistent failure to write *The Recluse* may well have made Wordsworth feel much more susceptible to them than he would have done otherwise.

Today it is not easy, at a time when Wordsworth is renowned for *The Prelude*, to realize how close to failure he may have felt as he composed it. In 1804 he was known only for *Lyrical Ballads*, which, despite steady sales, could not be said to have established him in the eyes of either the critics or the public as the great poet he believed himself to be.[32] Most of his best verse to date – *The Ruined Cottage*, *The Pedlar*, *Peter Bell*, *Home*

---

[29] *Dejection: An Ode*, 40–2 (my emphasis), as published in the *Morning Post*, 4 October 1802 (*Romanticism*, 560–4).

[30] Milton, *Samson Agonistes*, 594: 'my genial spirits droop'.

[31] Coleridge to Richard Sharp, 15 January 1804: 'In spite of Wordsworth's occasional Fits of Hypochondriacal Uncomfortableness – from which more or less, and at longer or shorter Intervals, he has never been wholly free from his very childhood – in spite of this hypochondriacal *Graft* in his Nature, as dear Wedgwood calls it, his is the happiest Family, I ever saw' (Griggs, ii. 1032; emphasis original).

[32] The market fortunes of *Lyrical Ballads* are charted by W. J. B. Owen, 'Costs, Sales, and Profits of Longman's Editions of Wordsworth', *The Library*, 12 (1957) 93–107.

at Grasmere and *The Two-Part Prelude* – remained in manuscript, and there were no immediate plans to publish. That might have made little difference to him had it not been for the fact that to none of those works did he and his circle attach anything like the importance of the great work in prospect – *The Recluse.* His continuing truancy accounts for the tone of self-doubt that seems to permeate the *Five-Book Prelude*, leaving its mark even on the last lines he composed for it, probably around 10 March 1804. It ought, finally, to be an optimistic work, as it concludes with the two spots of time that confirm the poet's sense of imaginative renewal. But Wordsworth cannot leave them alone. The last of the episodes described in the analogy passage had described how Dampier and his men, cold and hungry after braving a storm in their Nicobar canoe, had seen the ill portent of an overcast dawn sky.[33] Writing within a few days, perhaps hours, of composing those lines, Wordsworth interpolates into the spots of time a brief comment that turns Dampier's prognostication of danger into something equally ominous for himself:

> The days gone by
> Come back upon me from the dawn almost
> Of life; the hiding-places of my powers
> Seem open; I approach, and then they close.

> (ll. 337–40)

The narrow gaps in the clouds that enabled Dampier to glimpse sunlight are translated here into an image of the poet's waning vision. There is a note of desperation in the implicit understanding that he has only a limited time left in which to write the great verse for which his early life has prepared him. And that, as much as the other pressures I have mentioned, must account for the tremendous burst of creative energy with which, in six weeks between late January and early March 1804, Wordsworth composed this remarkable poem.

---

[33] Appendix I, below, ll. 136–40.

Textual Matters

The *Five-Book Prelude* is distinct from any other version of Wordsworth's poem in so far as it exists in no complete manuscript text. There are, in fact, only two extant manuscripts relating directly to it: MS WW, a series of loose, dismembered cardboard folia razored out of a sketchbook, containing rough drafts towards Books III and V, and MS W, which contains some fair copy and some drafting towards Books IV and V. There are no extant manuscripts of Books I and II, and only rough drafts towards Book III in MS WW. No complete extant fair copy draft survives relating to any of the Books, and there are certainly none for the entire poem. In view of all this, how do we know the poem existed at all?

A principal source of information must be the poet's letters. He first mentions the *Five-Book Prelude* in a letter to John Thelwall of mid- to late January 1804: 'I am now after a long sleep busily engaged in writing a Poem of considerable labour, and I am apprehensive [lest] the fit should leave me, so that I wish to make the most of it while it is upon me'.[34] In late January or early February he was even more specific in a letter to Francis Wrangham: 'At present I am engaged in a Poem on my own earlier life which will take five parts or books to complete, three of which are nearly finished'.[35] He continued working throughout February, and in a letter dated 5 March reported to Hazlitt that he had completed 'about 1200 lines of the Poem on my own life'.[36] On 6 March he told De Quincey that he had 'just finished that part in which I speak of my residence at the University' – Book III, presumably – and in the same letter he claims that the poem as a whole is 'better [than] half complete: viz 4 books amounting to about 2500 lines'.[37] On the evening of 6 March he told Coleridge: 'I finished five or six days ago another Book of my Poem amounting to 650 lines. And now I am positively arrived at the subject I spoke of in my last. When this next book is done which I shall begin in two or three days time, I shall consider the work

---

[34] *EY* 432.
[35] *EY* 436.
[36] *EY* 447.
[37] *EY* 454.

as finish'd'.[38] That point was further off than Wordsworth thought. At about the time he was writing to Coleridge, Mary Wordsworth was copying into MS W the beginning of *Five-Book Prelude* Book V, the base text of which begins:

> Once (but I must premise that several years
> Are overleaped to reach this incident) . . . (MS W, 36r)

As Jonathan Wordsworth observes,[39] the poet is anxious about having skipped two years between the summers of 1789 and 1791 – years memorable for the long vacation in France. Within days, that unease was to develop into the knowledge that five Books were inadequate to express everything he had to say about the development of the imagination that was prepared to compose *The Recluse*, and the five-Book scheme was dropped in favour of something more ambitious. This had almost certainly occurred by 12 March, when he wrote to William Sotheby with the news that 'I have been very busy during the last six weeks, and am advancing rapidly in a Poetical Work, which though only introductory to another of greater importance, will I hope be found not destitute of Interest'.[40] By 18 March the complete text of Books I–V, in a form similar to that of the completed thirteen-Book poem, had been sent to Coleridge in MS M. We do not know when, precisely, the five-Book plan was rejected; nor can we be sure when the larger poem was first envisaged, but the realization that five Books were inadequate to the task must have come at some point between 6 and 12 March.

On the basis of this evidence a certain number of facts may be deduced. The most important is that, by late January or early February, Wordsworth was working on what he thought of as a five-Book version of *The Prelude*. During that time he was at work on Books III and IV of the *Five-Book Prelude*, and had brought them to completion by 6 March. At some time between about 8 and 12 March he composed much of Book V – and at least what survives in MS W.

The central problem for the editor is assessing what degree of completion the *Five-Book Prelude* drafts in MS W can be said to have reached, and whether the poem ever developed beyond that. Over the years vari-

---

[38] *EY* 452.

[39] Wordsworth (1977), 24.

[40] *EY* 456.

ous judgements have been offered. At one extreme, Robin Jarvis has questioned whether, given the state of the extant drafts, 'it can rightly be called a "poem" or *Prelude* "version" at all'.[41] At another, Jonathan Wordsworth argues that it 'was either finished or within easy striking distance of completion'.[42] Mark L. Reed agrees that Books I–II probably reached fair copy, but remains undecided as to whether Books III–V ever reached any stage of completion beyond the surviving drafts. He is sufficiently unsure about the nature of the materials to refrain from editing the poem in his Cornell Wordsworth edition of the *Thirteen-Book Prelude*.

Jarvis's arguments are carefully formulated, based on a close analysis of the manuscripts, as any judgement about the poem must be. He aims to demonstrate the 'disjointed' relationship of the various drafts, admitting that it is possible to retrieve text of the 'opening third or so' of Book V,[43] while arguing that MS W 'degenerates into more and more haphazard draft'.[44] It is certainly correct to point out the rough, sketchy nature of one or two of the drafts in MS W, which cannot serve as the basis for a reading text of this work, and the absence of a number of leaves makes it impossible to depend on this manuscript alone; but it is an exaggeration to say that because the relationship between the drafts is not always obvious, they are therefore 'haphazard'. That is not true to the way in which Wordsworth tended to work; the sequence posited by Jonathan Wordsworth does have a logic, and is plausible within the context of the notebook. To some extent, of course, this is a matter of opinion – as editorial decisions frequently are. And in situations such as this, where the textual witnesses are not always reliable, it would be wrong to claim access to some ultimate, objective grounds on which final judgement may be determined. But I am bound to wonder, particularly in the light of the vigorous debate that has in recent years surrounded the editing of works by Romantic authors, how much that really matters.[45]

This is no place for extended theoretical debate, but, as the question

[41] Jarvis (1981), 550.
[42] Wordsworth (1977), 24.
[43] Jarvis (1981), 544.
[44] Ibid., p. 550.
[45] I refer to the debate summarized in my article, 'Editing Intentions', *Essays in Criticism*, 41 (1991), 1–10, and extrapolated in a Wordsworthian context in 'Acts of Butchery: Wordsworth as Editor', *WC* 23 (1992), 156–61.

is begged, it would be wrong not to acknowledge the central issues. The facts so far adduced focus in a particularly compelling way on the nature of intentionality. It is clear from the poet's letters that he planned a five-Book version of *The Prelude*, and manuscript evidence indicates that it was largely executed. But did Wordsworth 'intend' to bring it to a further stage of completion? More importantly, what are we to make of the 'intentions' indicated by an unhelpful manuscript? Intentionality remains an important factor in the editing of texts, as it always will. But in opposition to the notion of a single, unified concept of intention embodied within the consciousness of a single person (the author), recent commentators offer another model that may be understood against a background of human conventions, expectations, practices and procedures, such that the elucidation of intended meanings occurs through the study of linguistic, stylistic and symbolic conventions in place at the time and place where the work was composed.[46] This bears powerfully on the way in which we approach the editing of a work, for textual criticism is not merely informed by, but provides the reader with, an interpretive experience – as Jerome J. McGann puts it, 'producing editions is one of the ways we produce literary meanings'.[47] Those meanings arise out of the collaborative relationship between the editor and whatever textual witnesses can be rounded up; indeed, they will vary depending on the witnesses available. In the case of the *Five-Book Prelude* there are two notebooks that can testify at first hand as to the poem's possible, or probable, contents. That they do this inexactly is a given of this particular situation. But what is to prevent the editor from attempting to reconstruct the probable, or possible, contents of the work, on the basis of a study of intentions within the context just outlined?

There are commentators besides Jarvis who would demur. I have in mind Jack Stillinger, whose provocative essay, 'Textual Primitivism and the Editing of Wordsworth', attacks the Cornell Wordsworth Series for the manner in which it seeks to standardize texts he describes as 'editorial constructs'. Stillinger defends Wordsworth's revisions on the grounds that they embody 'some degree of the poet's intention and authority'.[48]

---

[46] Most notably, McKenzie (1981), 91.

[47] *The Textual Condition* (Princeton, 1991), p. 33.

[48] Stillinger (1989), 27. This argument has been elucidated in Stillinger's useful book on the versioning of Coleridge's poetry (Stillinger (1994)); see esp. ch. 4, 'A Practical Theory of Versions'.

More recently, Zachary Leader has commented that as reviser Wordsworth was 'respectful of original meanings, which he sought to clarify or more fully realize, to perfect'.[49] He goes on to argue that 'ignoring or denying authorial agency and intention means ignoring or denying one's responsibility to persons'.[50] The problem with this line of argument will always be the same: who is the person whose intentions and authority are being invoked? And where are these totems to be found? The theoretical arguments behind such questions are well-known;[51] the crux is how they relate to the work of editors. That issue is relevant to Jarvis's concluding remarks:

> We cannot take for granted that, as he struggled with lines on the most difficult subject he had yet attempted, he had any clear idea of the shape of a Book or the orchestration of a whole poem; the nature of the *Prelude* manuscripts show that this was not his method. In short, it seems certain that there was never a completed version of the *Prelude* in five Books and we cannot now manufacture one.[52]

Although he is arguing for a position of doubt, you could hardly be more certain than is Jarvis of the existence of a controlling, auctorial intelligence. No one denies the existence of the poet in historical time, or, indeed, the validity of intentionality as a concept. The problem with Jarvis's argument is that its application is too limited: the crucial element here is the way in which he, like Leader, assumes the existence of a single, objective entity, which he authorizes as embodying intention.[53] The author, in short, is a convenient fiction – or, more precisely, a theoretical construction – which enshrines any or all of those emotionally-derived stances which its creators require.

From even a brief examination of the poet's fair copies, and most of his printed texts, it becomes evident that such notions are unsustainable: at every point of the production process, from composition to

---

[49] *Revision and Romantic Authorship* (Oxford, 1996), p. 75.

[50] Ibid., p. 77.

[51] See, e.g., Michel Foucault, 'What is an Author?', in *Textual Strategies: Perspectives in Post-Structuralist Criticism*, ed. Josué V. Harari (London, 1979), pp. 141–60.

[52] Jarvis (1981), 550.

[53] Incidentally, despite his advocacy of auctorial intention, Leader offers a persuasive and passionate defence of Taylor's editing of Clare, hitherto criticized as insensitive and detrimental; see *Revision* ch. 5: 'John Taylor and the Poems of Clare'.

publication, Wordsworth collaborated with others. Even his readers' tastes were crucial in determining how he presented his published work.[54] Mary Wordsworth composed lines 15–16 of his most famous poem, *Daffo-dils*, and he contributed the central narrative event, and a number of lines, to *The Ancient Mariner*.[55] Perhaps the most frequently cited example is that of Humphry Davy, whom Wordsworth had not met in July 1800 when he was invited to punctuate the text of *Lyrical Ballads* (1800).[56] As Davy did so, he was engaged, like all editors, in the generation of meanings that would allow him to perform the task he had been set. Which is to admit that the evidence assembled by the editor towards the construction of the text leads inevitably to *re*construction; as D. F. McKenzie points out, 'that body of evidence built up, like the generalisation it yields, cannot be independent of judgement, cannot be other than an interpretative model'.[57] Such recognitions are instructive for the reading and editing of all texts, and Jarvis's negative tones are suggestive in this regard: 'We cannot take for granted . . . we cannot now manufacture. . . .' Against the critical nescience of this position, I would argue that it is an essential element of the editor's task to take certain things for granted, and at times to make decisions about such elements as orthography, punctuation, even the choice of substantive readings, either against the stated wishes of the author or where no auctorial preference is discernible. This, after all, is what textual criticism is all about. As a skilled editor himself, Stillinger quite frankly admits that all texts are constructs, in the generation of which the exercise of editorial choice is basic.[58] All editors are in the business of 'manufacturing' texts, to use Jarvis's word, and in so doing, it is not always possible, or desirable, to make decisions governing their production conditional upon auctorial approval.

This is not to say that editorial practice should be divorced from the

[54] For instance, his desire, in the 2nd edn of *Lyrical Ballads*, to counterbalance the 'strangeness' of *The Ancient Mariner* with 'some little things which would be more likely to suit the common taste' (*EY* 264).

[55] See *Romanticism*, 168, n. 3.

[56] 'You would greatly oblige me by looking over the enclosed poems and correcting any thing you find amiss in the punctuation a business at which I am ashamed to say I am no adept': Wordsworth to Davy, 29 July 1800 (*EY* 289). Full consideration is given to Davy's part in the production of the ill-punctuated text of *Lyrical Ballads* (1800) in Cornell *LB* 27–8.

[57] McKenzie (1981), 91.

[58] See esp. Stillinger (1989), 15, and Stillinger (1994), 139–40.

historicity of literary works. On the contrary; every detail of the formal and physical presentation of the work in its historical context should contribute to the generation of the text. But it would be wrong to expect that act of interpretation always to produce the same results. Hayden White observes that the main traditions of literary history direct us

> to the historical context, the audience, the artist, and the work itself as elements constituting the literary field. And thus, we might want to say that any comprehensive study of the changes occurring in the field would have to take account of transformations in the relationships obtaining among those elements thus differentiated.[59]

White's comments explain why one editor might choose not to reconstruct a given text when another might have no hesitation in doing so, having formed different judgements about the nature of the materials.[60] Moreover, White accounts for the fact that different editors will always construct – or reconstruct – differently. From a Wordsworthian point of view the most important culprit in this regard is the poet himself, revising his work, not invariably for the best, from a perspective in constant flux. And if the present-day editor of the *Five-Book Prelude* is in doubt concerning the need to resort for a section of text to the *Two-Part Prelude*, he or she need only reflect that this is precisely what the poet himself would have done. The catch-words provided by the poet in the manuscript – 'One Christmas-time', for the concluding episode – indicate to his copyist where the spots of time were to be inserted, cannibalized from drafts of different, but related, works. In short, Wordsworth's methods of composition required that his amanuenses engage in editorial reconstruction.

Mark L. Reed and Jonathan Wordsworth, to whom any editor of the poem must be indebted for their pioneering surveys of the relevant, and very difficult, manuscript drafts, agree that the poem was not merely projected by the poet but that it reached some stage of completion. Jonathan Wordsworth argues that it was finished, perhaps in fair copy,

---

[59] Quoted in McKenzie (1981), 92.

[60] See, for instance, the reading text of *The Pedlar* in Jonathan Wordsworth's *The Music of Humanity* (1969), and the absence of one in James Butler's Cornell Wordsworth edition of *The Ruined Cottage and The Pedlar* (1979). See also the exchange on the matter between these editors in *WC* 10 (1979), 244–6.

prior to the plan for a much extended work on 12 March. The absence
of a final fair copy is no argument against this: 'Wordsworth had only to
tidy up 200 or so lines of existing draft; and it is worth pointing out that
if he had gone on to do so, evidence would probably not survive'.[61] Reed's
analysis of MS W leads him to suggest that the poet determined upon a
much extended poem – in effect, the *Thirteen-Book Prelude* – during
composition of Book V, and that his change of mind is reflected in the
MS W drafts. Reed's inference is therefore that the five-Book poem may
not have reached completion, and this explains in part the absence of a
text in his edition.

In one sense it hardly matters whether Wordsworth completed the
poem or not. The justification for reconstructing it and analysing it is
simple: for six weeks in early 1804, the poet conceived of it as
representing *The Prelude* in its ultimate form. That is to say, its structure
and contents had an imaginative reality for him during that time. For
that reason alone, it is vital to our understanding of the poem's evolution. A text, imperfect as it must be, is badly needed. In the absence of
further testimony, we cannot know whether it reached a stage of completion comparable to that attained by *The Two-Part Prelude*; what we
can say is that, on the basis of the surviving drafts, it is possible to reconstruct the poem in a form roughly approximating how the completed
work would have appeared in spring 1804. That is what this edition
aims to provide.

Granted that the question is irresolvable, my judgement of the drafts
in MS W and MS WW is that they none the less imply completion; that
is to say, that they make up the penultimate stage of composition, and
had the poet and his copyists wished to compile a fair copy from them,
they would have done so with little trouble. Some polishing would have
been necessary, and no doubt Mary and Dorothy would have taken
Wordsworth's advice as to the ordering of some passages in Book V; but
the notebooks contain sufficient materials for the construction of a version of the work. The rapidity with which *Thirteen-Book Prelude*, Books
I–V, was sent to Coleridge – within a week of the abandonment of the
five-Book scheme – is in itself indicative of the advanced stage at which
the poem had arrived. It is on this basis – that the surviving materials,
however sketchy they may sometimes be, stand only one step from com-

[61] Wordsworth (1977), 23.

pletion – that I have proceeded. The order in which copy was entered, and the position within the notebooks of missing leaves, are crucial to the design of the present text, and they have generally been given precedence over such considerations as where analogous passages appear in drafts of the *Thirteen-Book Prelude*.[62] Wherever possible, copy-text is provided by draft, however rough, in MSS W and WW; only when it is barely coherent, or absent from the notebook, have I resorted to corresponding passages elsewhere. In all such cases I have drawn on entries made as close as possible in time to composition of the present poem. For this reason the reader will find that Books I–III, though resembling the equivalent text in the *Thirteen-Book Prelude*, none the less differ in numerous details: they derive from MS M, the copy sent to Coleridge on 18 March 1804, less than a week after abandonment of the five-Book project. A complete schedule of manuscripts used in the construction of the text is provided in Appendix II.

The result is a reconstruction, and the ordering of some of its contents, particularly towards the end of Book V, must remain hypothetical. But such will always be the case where uncertainty compels us to conjecture. Other editors, no doubt, would argue for different configurations, just as I have differed in some of my decisions with those who have preceded me. Such is the nature of indeterminacy – although this edition provides an opportunity to argue that textual *aporia* may be the occasion not for deconstruction, but reconstruction. This situation, though it may appear strange on the surface, ought to be familiar; as the study of manuscripts becomes more common, partly through increased availability in facsimile form, critics have become more aware of the potential for a new variation on the Barthean and Derridean *jeu*, which, one may assume, need not necessarily be used to expose that 'central knot of indeterminacy', but rather to integrate it into the logic of the work.[63] It is a strength, rather than a weakness, in our work as students

---

[62] I have in mind the various drafts in MS W providing, in the present text, Book V, ll. 98–230, the analogous lines of which in the *Thirteen-Book Prelude* are arranged differently.

[63] One early, and provocative, product of this approach is George Kane and E. Talbot Donaldson's edition of *'Piers Plowman': The B Version* (London, 1975), in which the editors fabricate a text that answers our expectation for 'perfectibility' in the alliterative line. See, among other responses, David C. Fowler, 'A New Edition of the B text of *Piers Plowman*', *Yearbook of English Studies*, 7 (1977), 23–42.

of Wordsworth, to recognize that the text must remain 'open, unstable, subject to a perpetual re-making by its readers, performers, or audience'.[64]

Reception

As befits a work that has remained unread till now, Wordsworth's *Five-Book Prelude* has a peculiar reception history. Commentators have tended to discuss the one section of the poem which they have been able to read – paradoxically, the very lines which Wordsworth rejected: the analogy passage.[65]

The place of the poem within the evolution of the thirteen-Book poem was outlined first by Ernest de Selincourt in the Introduction to his 1926 edition, and his remarks were brought up to date by Helen Darbishire in her revised edition of 1959.[66] These were early days in scholarly terms, and neither editor fully realized the implications of MS W; nor did they have the benefit of the important drafts in MS WW. In 1964 J. R. MacGillivray gave the matter further consideration in his seminal essay, 'The Three Forms of *The Prelude* 1798–1805'.[67] While not correct about its probable contents, he came closer than any previous scholar to perceiving that the poem was 'about the development of the imagination under the dual influence of nature and books'.[68] Little more seems to have been written about it until Richard Schell's 1975 article, 'Wordsworth's Revisions of the Ascent of Snowdon'.[69] Schell

---

[64] D. F. McKenzie, *Bibliography and the Sociology of Texts* (London, 1986), p. 45.

[65] It is no part of my task here to account for the considerable body of critical comment concerning parts of the *Thirteen-Book Prelude* that originated in the five-Book poem. There is, therefore, no notice of the extensive debate surrounding, for instance, the Snowdon episode, except where critics have placed their observations within the context of the earlier work.

[66] *The Prelude*, ed. Ernest de Selincourt (Oxford, 1926), pp. xxxvi–xxxvii; rev. Helen Darbishire (Oxford, 1959), pp. l–li.

[67] In *Essays in English Literature from the Renaissance to the Victorian Age Presented to A. S. P. Woodhouse 1964*, ed. Millar MacLure and F. W. Watt (Toronto, 1964) (hereafter MacGillivray), pp. 229–44; repr. in *Wordsworth: The Prelude*, ed. W. J. Harvey and Richard Gravil (London, 1972), pp. 99–115.

[68] MacGillivray, p. 241.

[69] *PQ* 54 (1975), 592–603.

begins by reproaching Geoffrey Hartman and Jonathan Wordsworth for failing to attend, in respective accounts of the Snowdon episode, for its origins in the five-Book poem and development towards its climactic position at Book XIII of the larger work. He finds that its context as 'a singular tribute to Nature's "ministry" in the *Five-Book Prelude* is more appropriate than its later manifestation, which he regards as 'a distortion of sorts, not only of the incident as originally perceived and interpreted, but of the poem as a whole'.[70]

A comprehensive outline of the entire work as revealed by the extant manuscripts was still wanting; though not concerned with observations of a critical nature, Mark L. Reed provided a thorough account of them in his *Chronology of the Middle Years* in 1975.[71] And two years later, in his article, 'The Five-Book *Prelude* of Early Spring 1804', Jonathan Wordsworth made the most exhaustive attempt thus far to identify the drafts and surmise their probable order within the five-Book structure. His pioneering work of scholarship revealed far more about the poem than had hitherto been known, and laid the foundations for reconstruction of the present text. With an overall plan in place, Jonathan Wordsworth was able to make a number of observations on its author's aims. For the first time he relates it to anxiety over *The Recluse* and Coleridge's precarious state of health.[72] All subsequent critical statements refer to this article, usually supplementing it with the draft materials published in the Norton *Prelude* two years later (which also includes a brief but informative summary of the poem's evolution).[73]

Only at this point did extended critical discussion open up, as critics now had some notion of the poem's structure, gained by reference to parallel passages in the thirteen-Book poem. The first attempt to discuss it as a whole came with Jonathan Wordsworth's *William Wordsworth: The Borders of Vision* (reprinted pp. 166-79), which analysed the thematic patterns described in his earlier article. The portrayal of imaginative impairment at Cambridge in Book III was inadequate to Wordsworth's purposes, he argues, and this accounts for the attempts to

[70] Ibid., p. 602.
[71] See Reed, 635–44. It should also, perhaps, be pointed out that Reed is here much more cagey about the MS W drafts in relation to the five-Book poem than he was to be in Cornell *13-Book Prelude*.
[72] Wordsworth (1977), 24–5.
[73] *Norton Prelude*, 496–500, 516–17.

repeat it in Books IV and V. Wordsworth's problem 'was not that he didn't see the university as a temptation . . . but that he couldn't feel that he himself had yielded'. For the first time, too, Jonathan Wordsworth discloses the extent of the debt to Milton in Wordsworth's description of his imaginative 'fall'. But it is the analogy passage (see Appendix I) that has attracted most critical attention, perhaps because of its availability in print. In 'The "Analogy Passage" from Wordsworth's Five-Book *Prelude*' (reprinted pp. 153–65), Joseph F. Kishel speculates that 'the composition of the analogy passage played a significant role in Wordsworth's decision to rethink his entire poetic effort'; for him, the analogies betoken a lack of self-confidence on the poet's part as he 'began to question his own imaginative strength'. This persuasive reading informs that of James H. Averill in his volume *Wordsworth and the Poetry of Human Suffering*. Like Kishel, Averill regards the analogy passage as a 'troubled compromise', deferring the important theme of *The Recluse* – that love of Nature leads to love of mankind. James K. Chandler's volume, *Wordsworth's Second Nature*, set out to expose the political undercurrents within the poetry. Chapter 5, 'Rousseau and the Politics of Education',[74] is preoccupied with the infant prodigy[75] and the way in which he is really 'a delusive fantasy of moral perfectionism'[76] rather than the prodigy himself. In making this observation, Chandler makes comparison with Rousseau's *Emile* of which, he suggests, the prodigy is 'a reasonably coherent satire'.[77]

In *Wordsworth and The Recluse* (see pp. 180–5), Kenneth R. Johnston returned to the analogy passage to find that the explorers it mentions are 'metaphors for Wordsworth'. This is the key to his distinctive reading, for those heroic figures suggest to Johnston that Wordsworth's unease is related to 'his imagination's betrayal' by the French Revolution. The dangers surrounding the explorers mirror the poet's uncertainty about his own imaginative restoration. Mary Jacobus pursues a different line in *Romanticism, Writing and Sexual Difference: Essays on The Prelude* (see pp. 186–96). Taking her lead from De Man, she argues

---

[74] *Wordsworth's Second Nature* (Chicago, 1984) (hereafter Chandler), pp. 93–119, repr. as 'Wordsworth, Rousseau, and the Politics of Education', in *Romanticism: A Critical Reader*, 57–83.

[75] Book IV, ll. 372–452.

[76] Chandler, 112.

[77] Ibid., p. 113.

that the explorers – particularly Park and Dampier – 'become the sign of a continued life in writing and even beyond – surviving to travel on past the vividly anticipated endings to their stories'. Alan Liu's *Wordsworth: The Sense of History* extends many of the preoccupations of Chandler, in an effort to show how 'Wordsworth's logos is ideologically determined in the full historical sense'.[78] He uses the *Five-Book Prelude* in part of a discussion aimed at demonstrating how 'Wordsworth hated Napoleon in a special way that had everything to do with how he chose to close his poem'.[79]

In 1991 the most detailed survey of the manuscripts to date was provided by Mark L. Reed in his magisterial Cornell Wordsworth Series edition of *The Thirteen-Book Prelude*, which contains transcriptions of MSS W and WW with photographs of the relevant pages.[80] And, through a meticulous review of the circumstances of composition and a thorough survey of textual sources, Reed offers numerous insights and speculations as to the poem's possible content.[81] Its editors will be enduringly grateful for this exemplary labour of scholarship – in the light of which it is surprising to find the poem still unavailable at the time of writing. It is to be hoped that the present edition will serve as a stimulus to further debate, and that in due course the work will join its disjecta, the celebrated analogy passage, in the critical canon.

Editorial Procedure

The principal text in this edition is a reading text of the *Five-Book Prelude* as reconstructed from the two surviving manuscripts used to draft and assemble the poem, and extant notebooks relating to other versions of it. Textual sources are listed in Appendix II, where a schedule is also supplied, integrated with notes on the reconstructed work. With these materials it should be possible for anyone interested to retrace my steps using Mark L. Reed's photographs and transcriptions of the relevant

---

[78] *Wordsworth: The Sense of History* (Stanford, Calif., 1989), p. 394.

[79] Ibid., p. 401.

[80] Cornell *13-Book Prelude*, i. 329–430, ii. 237–313. The infra-red photographs of MS WW supplied to Reed by Robert Woof are easier to read than the folia themselves.

[81] Ibid., i. 11–39.

drafts in Cornell *13-Book Prelude*. For the convenience of those wishing to compare the present text with the thirteen-Book version, line numbers of parallel passages in the later work are provided, enclosed within square brackets, for Books IV and V, keyed to the text in *Romanticism*, 284–474.

Manuscripts   The aim of these procedures is to present each draft as it stood when it had reached completion. Deletions are accepted only when alternative readings are provided; where they are not, the original is retained. Alternative readings are accepted only when the original has been deleted; where they are not, the original is retained. Where the original reading is deleted but legible, and the alternative is either fragmentary, illegible, or inchoate, the original has been retained. Where, in the rush of composition, words are omitted from a draft, as is not infrequently the case in Wordsworth's manuscripts, they are supplied from adjacent drafts or manuscripts. As a rule, I have silently corrected all scribal errors. Ampersands are expanded to 'and' throughout.

Spelling   Spelling is modernized throughout, with the exception of place-names, 'sate' and 'spake'.

Punctuation   Punctuation is editorial, though based on that of the manuscript. Ellipses have been filled in – 'thro'' is thus rendered as 'through' – except where to do so would be significantly to affect the pronunciation or the metre; on this basis 'giv'st' and 'suffer'st' have been allowed to stand, as is 'th'' (for 'the'). Paragraph breaks are also supplied by the editor, although most of those in manuscript sources have been preserved. Italics are Wordsworth's unless otherwise stated.

Annotations   The notes aim to gloss difficult or archaic words and constructions, and to inform readers of echoes, allusions and verbal borrowings from other works. References to poems by Wordsworth are in all cases to texts in the Cornell Wordsworth Series.

Further Reading

Bloom, Harold (ed.), *William Wordsworth's The Prelude* (New York, 1986).

Byatt, A. S., *Unruly Times: Wordsworth and Coleridge in their Time* (London, 1989).

Chandler, James K., *Wordsworth's Second Nature: A Study of the Poetry and Politics* (Chicago, 1984).

Finch, John Alban, 'Wordsworth, Coleridge, and *The Recluse*, 1798–1814' (thesis, Cornell University, 1964).

Gill, Stephen, *William Wordsworth: A Life* (Oxford, 1989).

——, *Wordsworth: The Prelude* (Cambridge, 1991).

——, 'Wordsworth's Poems: The Question of Text', in *Romantic Revisions*, ed. Robert Brinkley and Keith Hanley (Cambridge, 1992), pp. 43–63.

Hartman, Geoffrey, *Wordsworth's Poetry 1787–1814* (New Haven, 1964).

Harvey, W. J., and Gravil, Richard (eds), *Wordsworth: The Prelude* (London, 1972).

Jarvis, Robin, 'The Five-Book *Prelude*: A Reconsideration', *JEGP* 80 (1981), 528–51.

Johnston, Kenneth R., *Wordsworth and The Recluse* (New Haven, 1984).

Lindenberger, Herbert, *On Wordsworth's Prelude* (Princeton, 1963).

Lindop, Grevel, *A Literary Guide to the Lake District* (London, 1993).

Liu, Alan, *Wordsworth: The Sense of History* (Stanford, Calif., 1989).

Newlyn, Lucy, *Coleridge, Wordsworth, and the Language of Allusion* (Oxford, 1986).

Nuttall, A. D., 'The Prelude', in *Openings: Narrative Beginnings from the Epic to the Novel* (Oxford, 1992).

Onorato, Richard J., *The Character of the Poet: Wordsworth in The Pre-lude* (Princeton, 1971).

Reed, Mark L., *Wordsworth: The Chronology of the Early Years, 1770–1799* (Cambridge, Mass., 1967).

——, *Wordsworth: The Chronology of the Middle Years, 1800–1815* (Cambridge, Mass., 1975).

Roe, Nicholas, *Wordsworth and Coleridge: The Radical Years* (Oxford, 1988).

Schneider, Ben Ross, Jr., *Wordsworth's Cambridge Education* (Cambridge, 1957).

Thompson, T. W., *Wordsworth's Hawkshead*, ed. Robert Woof (Oxford, 1970).

Trott, Nicola, 'Wordsworth's Revisionary Reading' (thesis, University of Oxford, 1990).

——, 'Wordsworth and the Picturesque: A Strong Infection of the Age', *WC* 18 (1987), 114–21.

Woof, Robert, 'Presentation of the Self in the Composition of *The Prel-ude*', in *Presenting Poetry: Composition, Publication, Reception*, ed. Howard Erskine-Hill and Richard A. McCabe (Cambridge, 1995), pp. 138–62.

——, 'The Literary Relations of Wordsworth and Coleridge, 1795–1803: Five Studies' (thesis, University of Toronto, 1959).

Wordsworth, Jonathan, *William Wordsworth: The Borders of Vision* (Oxford, 1982).

——, 'Revision as Making: *The Prelude* and its Peers', in *Romantic Revisions*, ed. Robert Brinkley and Keith Hanley (Cambridge, 1992), pp. 18–42.

——, 'Wordsworth and the Ideal of Nature in 1800', in *The Lake District: A Sort of National Property* (London, 1986).

Chronology

1770   *7 April* William Wordsworth born at Cockermouth, Cumberland, second son of John Wordsworth (1741–83), lawyer and agent to Sir James Lowther, later Earl of Lonsdale.

           16 August Mary Hutchinson born at Penrith, Cumberland, home of Wordsworth's grandparents (marries poet 1802, dies 1859).

1771   *25 December* Birth of Dorothy Wordsworth, only sister of poet (d. 1855).

1772   *21 October* Birth of Samuel Taylor Coleridge (d. 1834).

           4 December Birth of John Wordsworth, sailor brother of poet and Dorothy (drowned 5 February 1805).

1774   *9 June* Birth of Christopher, fifth and last child of John and Ann Wordsworth (later Master of Trinity, Cambridge; d. 1846).

1778   *c.8 March* Ann Wordsworth, poet's mother, dies aged 30, probably of pneumonia.

           June Dorothy sent to live with cousins in Halifax, on the grounds that she could not be properly brought up in an all-male household.

1779   *c.15 May* Wordsworth sent to Hawkshead Grammar School, where he lives (at one point with all three brothers) in lodgings with Ann Tyson.

1783   *30 December* Unexpected death of poet's father, John Wordsworth, aged 42 (Book V, ll. 364–89).

1785   *May–June* Composition of earliest extant poem, *Lines*

Written as a School Exercise, to commemorate the foundation of Hawkshead Grammar School 200 years before.

1786   *12 June*   Death, aged 32, of the Revd William Taylor, Fellow of Emmanuel College, Cambridge, headmaster of Hawkshead Grammar School since 1781.

1787   *March*   Appearance in *European Magazine* of first published poem, *Sonnet, On Seeing Miss Helen Maria Williams Weep at a Tale of Distress*.

Spring–summer   Composition of 1,000-line, partly autobiographical *Vale of Esthwaite*.

Early summer   Reunion at Penrith of Wordsworth and Dorothy (living with relatives at Halifax for previous nine years) coincides with 'blessed time of early love' for Mary Hutchinson (see Book V, ll. 319–29, below).

30 October   Takes up residence at St John's College, Cambridge (Book III, ll. 1ff.).

1788   Unsuccessful suit against Lord Lonsdale for repayment of £4,625 owed to John Wordsworth at his death (repaid to the family by Lonsdale's heir, 1803).

Spring–summer   Composition of translations from Virgil's *Georgics*.

Summer   Wordsworth spends nine weeks of Cambridge long vacation at Hawkshead (Book IV), giving rise to accounts of Dedication Scene (ll. 143–7) and Discharged Soldier (ll. 180–321).

1789   Composition of *An Evening Walk* (published 1793); height of Wordsworth's interest, which had been brewing since at least 1787, in the picturesque theories of William Gilpin; see Book V, ll. 213–30 (*WR* i. 116).

14 July   Fall of Bastille.

1790   *10 July–mid-October*   Walking tour with Robert Jones (Cambridge student from north Wales) through France and the 'gorgeous Alps', and back down the Rhine (mentioned Book V, ll. 267–8).

1791   *21 January*   Wordsworth awarded BA without honours, having dropped mathematics (the only subject in which the University of Cambridge held examinations); moves to London.

May–August   Stays with Jones in Wales; climbs Snowdon (Book V, ll. 1–65).

26 November   Crosses to France, visits National Assembly in Paris before leaving for Orleans on 5 December.

1792   *Spring*   Meets Annette Vallon; moves to Blois, and is converted by French army officer Michel Beaupuy to the Revolutionary cause.

10 August   Louis XVI deposed.

29 October   Wordsworth in Paris *en route* for London, presumably intending to raise money and return to marry Annette; leaves France end of November.

15 December   Anne-Caroline Wordsworth, poet's daughter by Annette Vallon, baptized in Orleans Cathedral.

1793   *21 January*   Execution of Louis XVI.

29 January   *An Evening Walk* and *Descriptive Sketches* published.

1 February   France declares war on England; England follows suit on 11 February, separating Wordsworth from Annette and Caroline till 1802 (Peace of Amiens).

1795   *c.9 January*   Wordsworth receives legacy of £900 at the death from tuberculosis of Raisley Calvert (younger brother of a Hawkshead schoolfriend), designed to enable him to write instead of taking a job.

20 August   Coleridge composes *The Eolian Harp* (*Romanticism*, 505–7).

Late August–September   Wordsworth, on visit to Bristol, meets Southey and Coleridge.

26 September   Wordsworth and Dorothy go to live at Racedown, a substantial house lent them by the Pinneys near Bridport in Dorset, taking with them the child Basil Montagu (aged two-and-a-half), who has been entrusted to their care.

4 October   Coleridge marries Sara Fricker.

1797   *May–June*   First version of *The Ruined Cottage* written.

c.5 June Coleridge arrives on a visit to Racedown, taking the Wordsworths back with him to Nether Stowey on 4 July, where on 7 July they lease Alfoxden House.

c.5 November   Coleridge writes *Kubla Khan;* half-length

version of *The Ancient Mariner* complete by 20 November.

1798   *February*   *Discharged Soldier* (Book IV, ll. 180–321) written as independent fragment; Coleridge's *Frost at Midnight* composed (*Romanticism*, 516–18), and Wordsworth's *Pedlar* is written into *The Ruined Cottage*, which has now become part of *The Recluse*.

6 March   Scheme for *The Recluse* announced in letter.

c.Early March–July   Composition of *Lyrical Ballads* (*Romanticism*, 166–244).

14 May   Birth of Berkeley Coleridge, Coleridge's son.

16–19 September   Coleridge and the Wordsworths journey to Hamburg, he going on to Ratzeburg (30 September), they to Goslar (6 October).

18 September   Writing to his wife from Germany, Coleridge recommends her to read Richard Lovell and Maria Edgeworth's *Practical Education*, published earlier that year, no doubt one of the handbooks on child-rearing that Wordsworth has in mind at Book IV, ll. 452ff. (*WR* i, A9).

October   Wordsworth begins work on what comes to be *The Prelude*: he composes parts of Book I, including the boat-stealing episode (Book I, ll. 370–425), *Nutting*, and version of *There Was A Boy* (Book IV, ll. 471–504) as first-person narrative.

November–December   Composition (among other poetry) of first four Lucy poems (see *Romanticism*, 244–6) and skating episode (Book I, ll. 450–87).

1799   *January–early February*   Spots of time sequence (Book IV, ll. 531–54, Book V, ll. 280–389) composed; *Two-Part Prelude*, Part I, complete before the Wordsworths leave Goslar on 23 February.

February–June   Sir James Mackintosh, famous for *Vindiciae Gallicae* (his apology for the French Revolution – see *Romanticism*, 157–8), gives a series of lectures renouncing his radical sympathies (see Book II, ll. 448–53).

10 February   Death of Berkeley Coleridge, at less than nine months old.

6 April   Having heard about Berkeley's death, Coleridge writes to Poole (*Romanticism*, 526).

13 May Wordsworths at Sockburn-on-Tees, home of the Hutchinson family, where they stay till the end of the year.

Autumn 1799 *Two-Part Prelude*, Part II, composed, and Part I revised.

25–6 October Coleridge, in England since mid-July, arrives at Sockburn; accompanies Wordsworth and his brother John (back from two-year voyage) on Lake District walking tour, ending *c*.20 November.

18–19 November Wordsworth composes glad preamble (Book I, ll. 1–54) on two-day walk from Ullswater to Grasmere to rent Dove Cottage. Coleridge returns to Sockburn, falls lastingly in love with Mary Hutchinson's younger sister Sara, and goes south to be a journalist in London.

20 December Having walked across the country from Sockburn via Wensleydale, Wordsworth and Dorothy take possession of Dove Cottage, their home till 1808.

1800   *January–early March* Composition of Prospectus to *The Recluse* (*Romanticism*, 246–8) and bulk of *Home at Grasmere* (intended as first Book of *The Recluse*).

Late September Wordsworth writing Preface to *Lyrical Ballads* (*Romanticism*, 250–66).

November and December Wordsworths at Dove Cottage visited by John Stoddart as he researches his *Remarks on Local Manners and Scenery in Scotland* (1801) (*WR* ii. 375).

1801   *c.25 January* Publication in London of *Lyrical Ballads* (1800).

28 December Wordsworth working on *Prelude*, Book III.

1802   *9 July–6 October* Wordsworth and Dorothy leave Grasmere on a journey that takes them to London, Dover and Calais, where they spend a month with Annette Vallon and Anne-Caroline Wordsworth; thence, with a week spent in London, to Yorkshire, where Wordsworth and Mary are married on 4 October, and finally, with Mary, to Grasmere. The journey produces some of Wordsworth's greatest sonnets, including *The World is Too Much With Us*, *To Toussaint L'Ouverture*, *1 September 1802*, *Composed Upon Westminster Bridge*, and *London 1802* (*Romanticism*, 274–6).

September   Lamb shows the Wordsworths Bartholomew Fair and Tipu's Tiger (Book IV, l. 171).

4 October   Coleridge's *Dejection: An Ode* published in the *Morning Post*, as a sort of wedding-present for Wordsworth (*Romanticism*, 560–4).

1803   *18 June*   Birth of poet's eldest son, John (d. 1875).

15 August   Wordsworth, Coleridge and Dorothy set out on Scottish tour. Tour includes visits to Burns's house and grave, and a meeting with Walter Scott.

1804   *4 January*   Wordsworth reads Coleridge 'the second part of his divine self-biography' (*Two-Part Prelude*, Part II). At around this time Wordsworth composes most of the last seven stanzas of the *Intimations Ode*.

14 January   Coleridge leaves Grasmere for a visit to Liverpool, London, the west country, and travel to and residence in Malta and Italy; his primary motive is the search for improved health.

Late January   Wordsworth begins *Five-Book Prelude*, composing rapidly for the next six weeks.

20–4 February   Composition of *Five-Book Prelude* probably halts when Dorothy falls ill.

29 February   Wordsworth completes *Five-Book Prelude*, Book III.

6 March   Books III and IV are complete; Wordsworth ready to begin on Book V; reads *Hamlet*.

c.10 March   At around this time the *Five-Book Prelude* is either completed or comes very close to it.

12 March   Wordsworth decides to reorganize his material and work towards a longer version of *The Prelude*. He probably did not at this stage realize that the next version would consist of thirteen Books, only that it would be longer than the *Five-Book Prelude*, and that it would include some account of the 1790 walking tour.

18 March   By this date Coleridge has been sent *The Thirteen-Book Prelude*, Books I–V, in almost their final shape.

9 April   Coleridge sails for Malta on the *Speedwell*; Wordsworth at work on *Thirteen-Book Prelude*, Book VI.

1805   *5 February*   John Wordsworth drowned when *Earl of*

Abergavenny sinks off Portland; news reaches Dove Cottage on 11 February, halting composition of *Thirteen-Book Prelude*.

c.20 May *Thirteen-Book Prelude* completed.

26 December Two-thirds of *Prelude* transcribed; Wordsworth, 'very anxious to get forward with *The Recluse*', is 'reading for the nourishment of his mind preparatory to beginning'.

1806   *Early January* *The Waggoner* written.

1807   *Early January* Wordsworth reads *The Thirteen-Book Prelude* to Coleridge (to whom it is addressed), inspiring Coleridge to write *To William Wordsworth* (*Romanticism*, 567–9).

1809   *28 December* Version of *Five-Book Prelude*, Book I, ll. 426–87 ('Wisdom and spirit of the universe' up to skating episode) published in Coleridge's *The Friend*.

1813   *26 April* Through patronage of Lord Lonsdale, Wordsworth becomes Distributor of Stamps (civil servant with responsibility for stamp duties) for Westmorland and part of Cumberland.

12 May Household moves to Rydal Mount.

1814   *Early August* Publication of *The Excursion*.

1815   *Early April* Publication of *Poems* (1815), first collected edition of Wordsworth's poetry.

30 May Coleridge writes to Wordsworth explaining disappointment with *The Excursion* (*Romanticism*, 572–4).

1817   *July* Coleridge publishes *Biographia Literaria* (*Romanticism*, 574–7).

28 December 'Immortal Dinner' takes place in Haydon's studio, with Wordsworth, Keats and Lamb (*Romanticism*, 706–8).

1834   *25 July* Death of Coleridge.

27 December Death of Lamb.

1835   *21 November* Death of James Hogg, following upon those of Scott, Coleridge, Lamb, Crabbe and Hemans, prompts Wordsworth to write *Extempore Effusion* (*Romanticism*, 479–80).

1842–3   *Winter* 'Fenwick Notes', on the circumstances of individual poems, dictated to Isabella Fenwick (*Romanticism* 480–2).

1843   *21 March*   Death of Southey; succeeded as Poet Laureate by Wordsworth in April.

1850   *23 April*   Wordsworth dies, aged 80.

       July   Publication of *The Prelude*, much revised, in fourteen Books (title chosen by Mary).

1855   *25 January*   Death of Dorothy Wordsworth.

1859   *17 January*   Death of Mary Wordsworth.

THE FIVE-BOOK
PRELUDE

Book One

Oh there is blessing in this gentle breeze[1]
That blows from the green fields, and from the clouds,
And from the sky: it beats against my cheek,
And seems half-conscious of the joy it gives.
Oh welcome messenger, oh welcome friend!   5
A captive greets thee, coming from a house
Of bondage, from yon city's walls set free,
A prison where he hath been long immured.[2]
Now I am free, enfranchised and at large,
May fix my habitation where I will.   10
What dwelling shall receive me? In what vale
Shall be my harbour? Underneath what grove
Shall I take up my home, and what sweet stream
Shall with its murmur lull me to my rest?
The earth is all before me:[3] with a heart   15
Joyous, nor scared at its own liberty,

---

[1] Ll. 1–54 comprise the glad preamble, probably composed 18–19 November 1799, but not inserted in *The Prelude* until work began on the present version in late January 1804. They record the exuberance and optimism as Wordsworth walked from Ullswater to Grasmere to arrange the renting of Dove Cottage, which he and Dorothy would occupy until 1808.

[2] *immured*   confined, walled up. The city from which Wordsworth has been released is probably a mixture of Goslar in Germany (where he spent the cold winter of 1798–9) and London.

[3] *The earth is all before me*   an allusion to the conclusion of *Paradise Lost*, as Adam and Eve are driven out of Eden:

I look about, and should the guide I choose
Be nothing better than a wandering cloud,[4]
I cannot miss my way. I breathe again;
Trances of thought and mountings of the mind   20
Come fast upon me. It is shaken off,
As by miraculous gift 'tis shaken off,
The heavy weight of many a weary day
Not mine, and such as were not made for me.
Long months of peace (if such bold word accord   25
With any promises of human life),
Long months of ease and undisturbed delight
Are mine in prospect – whither shall I turn?
By road or pathway, or through open field,
Or shall a twig or any floating thing   30
Upon the river, point me out my course?
    Enough that I am free, embrace today
An uncontrolled enfranchisement; for months
To come may live a life of chosen tasks,
May quit the tiresome sea and dwell on shore –   35
If not a settler on the soil, at least
To drink wild waters, and to pluck green herbs,
And gather fruits fresh from their native tree.
Nay more: if I may trust myself, this hour
Hath brought a gift that consecrates my joy,   40
For I, methought, while the sweet breath of heaven
Was blowing on my body, felt within
A corresponding mild creative breeze,[5]

Some natural tears they dropped, but wiped them soon;
The world was all before them, where to choose
Their place of rest, and Providence their guide.
They hand in hand, with wandering steps and slow,
Through Eden took their solitary way.

Wordsworth's poem begins where Milton leaves off. He too is making a new start, but does so in a spirit of profound optimism.

[4] Providence guided Adam and Eve out of Eden (see preceding note).

[5] *A corresponding mild creative breeze* the subject of much comment among recent critics; see, most notably, M. H. Abrams's title essay in *The Correspondent Breeze: Essays on English Romanticism* (New York and London, 1984).

A vital breeze which travelled gently on
O'er things which it had made, and is become 45
A tempest, a redundant[6] energy
Vexing its own creation. 'Tis a power
That does not come unrecognized, a storm
Which, breaking up a long-continued frost,
Brings with it vernal promises, the hope 50
Of active days, of dignity and thought,
Of prowess in an honourable field,[7]
Pure passion, virtue, knowledge, and delight,
The holy life of music and of verse.

    Thus far, oh friend,[8] did I, not used to make 55
A present joy the matter of my song,
Pour out that day my soul in measured strains,[9]
Even in the very words which I have here
Recorded. To the open fields I told
A prophecy; poetic numbers came 60
Spontaneously,[10] and clothed in priestly robes
My spirit, thus singled out, as it might seem,
For holy services – great hopes were mine!
My own voice cheered me, and, far more, the mind's
Internal echo of the imperfect sound; 65
To both I listened, drawing from them both
A cheerful confidence in things to come.

    Whereat, being not unwilling now to give
A respite to this passion, I paced on
Gently, with careless steps, and came erelong 70
To a green shady place where down I sat

---

  [6] *redundant* overflowing, exuberant.

  [7] *prowess in an honourable field* a reference to the composition of *The Recluse*; see Introduction.

  [8] *friend* Coleridge; see Introduction above.

  [9] *measured strains* verse.

  [10] In the Preface to *Lyrical Ballads* Wordsworth had described poetry as 'the spontaneous overflow of powerful feelings. But though this be true, poems to which any value can be attached were never produced on any variety of subjects but by a man who, being possessed of more than usual organic sensibility, had also thought long and deeply' (*Romanticism*, 253).

Beneath a tree,[11] slackening my thoughts by choice
And settling into gentler happiness.
'Twas autumn, and a calm and placid day
With warmth as much as needed from a sun   75
Two hours declined towards the west, a day
With silver clouds and sunshine on the grass,
And, in the sheltered grove where I was couched,
A perfect stillness. On the ground I lay
Passing through many thoughts, yet mainly such   80
As to myself pertained. I made a choice
Of one sweet vale whither my steps should turn,
And saw, methought, the very house[12] and fields
Present before my eyes. Nor did I fail
To add meanwhile assurance of some work   85
Of glory, there forthwith to be begun –
Perhaps too there performed.[13] Thus long I lay
Cheered by the genial pillow of the earth
Beneath my head, soothed by a sense of touch
From the warm ground, that balanced me (else lost   90
Entirely), seeing nought, nought hearing, save
When here and there, about the grove of oaks
Where was my bed, an acorn from the trees
Fell audibly, and with a startling sound.[14]
    Thus occupied in mind, I lingered here   95
Contented, nor rose up until the sun
Had almost touched the horizon; bidding then

[11] Owen notes the echo of *Paradise Lost*, viii. 286–7: 'On a green shady bank profuse of flowers / Pensive I sat me down'. Adam, like Wordsworth, then dreams of paradise.

[12] *the very house*   Dove Cottage in Grasmere, into which the Wordsworths moved on 20 December 1799.

[13] *some work / Of glory . . . performed*   Although Wordsworth had composed a good deal of blank verse for *The Recluse* by early 1804, when these lines were written (including *Home at Grasmere*, dating from March 1800, and regarded at the time as Book I of *The Recluse*), the philosophical epic that Coleridge had proposed in 1797 would never be completed.

[14] Wordsworth was aware that he had such an intense imaginative existence that he was in danger of losing touch with physical reality; he later remarked: 'Many times while going to school have I grasped at a wall or tree to recall myself from this abyss of idealism to the reality' (*Romanticism*, 481).

A farewell to the city left behind,
Even with the chance equipment of that hour
I journeyed toward the vale which I had chosen.   100
It was a splendid evening, and my soul
Did once again make trial of the strength
Restored to her afresh – nor did she want
Aeolian visitations.[15] But the harp
Was soon defrauded, and the banded host   105
Of harmony dispersed in straggling sounds;
And lastly, utter silence. 'Be it so,
It is an injury', said I, 'to this day
To think of anything but present joy.'
So, like a peasant, I pursued my road   110
Beneath the evening sun, nor had one wish
Again to bend the sabbath of that time
To a servile yoke. What need of many words?
A pleasant loitering journey, through two days
Continued, brought me to my hermitage.[16]   115
    I spare to speak, my friend, of what ensued:
The admiration and the love, the life
In common things, the endless store of things
Rare (or at least so seeming) every day
Found all about me in one neighbourhood,   120
The self-congratulation,[17] the complete
Composure, and the happiness entire.
But speedily a longing in me rose
To brace myself to some determined aim,[18]
Reading or thinking, either to lay up   125
New stores, or animate the old convened

---

[15] *Aeolian visitations* moments of poetic inspiration. The eighteenth-century equiva-lent of wind-chimes, the Aeolian harp was left in front of an open window, or hung on a tree, where its strings would be 'played' by the wind (Aeolus is the Greek god of storms and winds); cf. Coleridge, *The Eolian Harp* (1795).

[16] *hermitage* Dove Cottage. Wordsworth spent the night of 17 November 1799 at the foot of Ullswater, just over 20 miles' walk from Grasmere.

[17] *self-congratulation* rejoicing; used with none of the connotations of smugness now associated with the word.

[18] *aim* i.e., to write an epic poem, namely *The Recluse*.

Unto some common purpose. I had hopes
Still higher: that I might give a life to shapes
And phantoms which I long had marshalled forth,[19]
And to these beings temperately deal out   130
The many feelings that oppressed my heart.
But I have been discouraged; gleams of light
Flash often from the east, then disappear,
And mock me with a sky that ripens not
Into a steady morning. If my mind,   135
Remembering the sweet promise of the past,
Would gladly grapple with some noble theme,
Vain is her wish; where'er she turns she finds
Impediments from day to day renewed.

    And now it would content me to yield up   140
Those lofty hopes awhile, for present gifts
Of humbler industry.[20] But oh dear friend,
The poet, gentle creature as he is,
Hath, like the lover,[21] his unruly times,
His fits when he is neither sick nor well,   145
Though no distress be near him but his own
Unmanageable thoughts. The mind itself,
The meditative mind (best pleased perhaps
While she, as duteous as the mother dove,
Sits brooding[22]), lives not always to that end,   150
But hath less quiet instincts, goadings-on
That drive her as in trouble through the groves.
With me is now such passion, which I blame

[19] Ll. 128–9 are different in this early draft from the better-known reading in the *Thirteen-Book Prelude*; here, the shapes and phantoms are 'marshalled' by the poet, who seems to have greater control over them than in the later version, where they are described as 'floating loose about so long'.

[20] *gifts / Of humbler industry*   shorter poems. Coleridge's view was that Wordsworth's shorter works were a good deal humbler than the more important project of *The Recluse*; see, for instance, the letter to Thomas Poole of 14 October 1803 (*Romanticism*, 566).

[21] In tone Wordsworth is close to *A Midsummer Night's Dream*, V. i. 7–8: 'The lunatic, the lover, and the poet / Are of imagination all compact.'

[22] *mother dove / Sits brooding*   In *Paradise Lost* the Holy Spirit 'Dove-like sat'st brooding' over Chaos, 'And madest it pregnant' (i. 21–2). The mind is engaged in a similarly creative act.

No otherwise than as it lasts too long.
    When, as becomes a man who would prepare   155
For such a glorious work, I through myself
Make rigorous inquisition, the report
Is often friendly, for I neither seem
To lack that first great gift – the vital soul,
Nor general truths which are themselves a sort   160
Of elements and agents, under-powers,
Subordinate helpers of the living mind.
Nor am I naked in external things –
Forms, images[23] – nor numerous other aids
Of less regard, though won perhaps with toil   165
And needful to build up a poet's praise.
Time, place, and manners,[24] these I seek, and these
I find in plenteous growth, but nowhere such
As I can single out with steady choice –
No little band of yet remembered names   170
Whom I, in perfect confidence, might hope
To summon back from lonesome banishment
And make them inmates in the hearts of men
Now living, or to live in times to come.
    Sometimes, mistaking vainly (as I fear)   175
Proud spring-tide swellings for a regular sea,
I settle on some British theme, some old
Romantic tale by Milton left unsung;[25]
More often, resting at some gentler place
Within the groves of chivalry, I pipe   180
Among the shepherds, with reposing knights
Sit by a fountain-side and hear their tales.[26]
Sometimes, more sternly moved, I would relate
How vanquished Mithridates northward passed

---

[23] Wordsworth carries with him in his imagination recollected (and enhanced) visions of the natural world; cf. *Tintern Abbey*, 23–5: 'Though absent long, / These forms of beauty have not been to me / As is a landscape to a blind man's eye.'

[24] *manners* customs, ways of life.

[25] *Romantic tale . . . unsung* Before writing *Paradise Lost*, Milton had planned an epic on the life of King Arthur; see *Paradise Lost*, ix. 29–41.

[26] Wordsworth has in mind the work of Spenser.

And, hidden in the cloud of years, became   185
That Odin,[27] father of a race by whom
Perished the Roman Empire; how the friends
And followers of Sertorius, out of Spain
Flying, found shelter in the Fortunate Isles,
And left their usages, their arts and laws,   190
To disappear by a slow gradual death,
To dwindle and to perish one by one,
Starved in those narrow bounds – but not the soul
Of liberty, which fifteen hundred years
Survived and, when the European came   195
With skill and power that could not be withstood,
Did, like the pestilence, maintain its hold
And wasted down by glorious death that race
Of natural heroes.[28] Or I would record
How in tyrannic times some unknown man,   200
Unheard of in the chronicles of kings,
Suffered in silence for the love of truth;
How that one Spaniard,[29] through continued force
Of meditation on the inhuman deeds
Of the first conquerors of the Indian Isles,   205
Went single in his ministry across
The ocean – not to comfort the oppressed,

[27] *How vanquished Mithridates . . . became / That Odin*   Gibbon associates Mithridates the Great, King of Pontus (131–61 BC), with Odin, in his *Decline and Fall of the Roman Empire*: 'This wonderful expedition of Odin . . . might supply the noble groundwork of an epic poem [but] cannot be received as authentic history.' Other sources must include Joseph Cottle's *Alfred* and Paul-Henri Mallet's *Northern Antiquities*, see WR ii. 64(ii), 167 and A10.

[28] Sertorius, a Roman general (*c.*112–72 BC), was the subject of one of Plutarch's *Lives* and an ally of Mithridates. He gained control of most of Spain before being assassinated; according to legend, his followers fled to the Canary Islands, where their descendants thrived until the Spanish arrived at the end of the fifteenth century. The image of 'liberty' invading the Canaries like a 'pestilence' derives from the fact that the invading Spaniards brought disease with them. Wordsworth learnt all this from George Glas's *History of the Discovery and Conquest of the Canary Islands* (1764).

[29] *Spaniard*   an error, corrected in all later drafts of this passage; Wordsworth is about to tell the story of a Frenchman, Dominique de Gourges, who in 1568 avenged the massacre of the French by the Spaniards in Florida. Wordsworth's source in this case was a travel-book, Hakluyt's *Voyages* (1582); see WR ii. 195.

But, like a thirsty wind, to roam about,
Withering the oppressor; how Gustavus found
Help at his need in Dalecarlia's mines;[30]   210
How Wallace fought for Scotland, left the name
Of Wallace to be found like a wild-flower
All over his dear country, left the deeds
Of Wallace, like a family of ghosts,
To people the steep rocks and river banks,   215
Their natural sanctuaries, with a local soul
Of independence and stern liberty.[31]
Sometimes it soothes me better to shape out
Some tale from my own heart, more near akin
To my own passions and habitual thoughts,   220
Some variegated story, in the main
Lofty, with interchange of gentler things;
But deadening admonitions will succeed,
And the whole beauteous fabric seems to lack
Foundation, and withal appears throughout   225
Shadowy and unsubstantial.[32]
              Then, last wish,
My last and favourite aspiration – then
I yearn towards some philosophic song
Of truth that cherishes our daily life;
With meditations passionate from deep   230
Recesses in man's heart, immortal verse

---

[30] Gustavus I of Sweden (1496–1560) raised support among the miners of Dalecarlia, and in 1521–3 freed the country from Danish rule. Wordsworth read a play dramatizing these events, Henry Brooke's *Gustavus Vasa, the Deliverer of his Country* (1739), in 1797–8; see *WR* i. 36(ii).

[31] William Wallace (*c*.1272–1305), Scottish general and patriot, was captured and executed by Edward I. The Wordsworths had visited Wallace's haunts and heard about his exploits while touring Scotland in 1803; in her journal Dorothy had recorded a visit to two of Wallace's caves: 'There is scarce a noted glen in Scotland that has not a cave for Wallace or some other hero' (*DWJ* i. 228). Reed suggests that Wordsworth's immediate source is literary – John Stoddart's *Local Manners and Scenery in Scotland* (1801): 'The name of Wallace is attached to every spot, with which there is a bare possibility of historically connecting it'. The Wordsworths knew Stoddart, who had lodged with them in 1800; see *WR* ii. 375(i).

[32] Wordsworth has in mind Prospero's speech, *Tempest*, IV. i. 148–63.

Thoughtfully fitted to the Orphean lyre.[33]
But from this awful burden I full soon
Take refuge, and beguile myself with trust
That mellower years will bring a riper mind   235
And clearer insight. Thus from day to day
I live, a mockery of the brotherhood
Of vice and virtue, with no skill to part
Vague longing that is bred by want of power
From paramount impulse not to be withstood;   240
A timorous capacity from prudence;
From circumspection, infinite delay.[34]
Humility and modest awe themselves
Betray me, serving often for a cloak
To a more subtle selfishness, that now   245
Doth lock my functions up[35] in blank reserve,
Now dupes me by an over-anxious eye
That with a false activity beats off
Simplicity and self-presented truth.
Ah! better far than this to stray about   250
Voluptuously through fields and rural walks
And ask no record of the hours given up
To vacant musing, unreproved neglect
Of all things, and deliberate holiday;
Far better never to have heard the name   255
Of zeal and just ambition, than to live
Thus baffled by a mind that every hour
Turns recreant to her task, takes heart again,

[33] Within two months of postponing the 'awful burden' of getting on with *The Recluse*, Wordsworth was writing to Coleridge, who was believed to be dying, for instructions on how to proceed. 'I cannot say', Wordsworth wrote on 29 March, 'what a load it would be to me, should I survive you and you die without this memorial left behind' (*EY* 464). Orpheus was traditionally represented as a philosopher as well as a poet-musician; cf. *Paradise Lost*, iii. 17.

[34] Wordsworth means simply that he feels so indecisive as to be incapable of choosing between vice or virtue, between vague longings to write *The Recluse* and a strong desire to do so.

[35] *Doth lock my functions up* a recollection of Pope, *Imitations of Horace*, Epistle I. i. 39–40: 'So slow th' unprofitable Moments roll, / That lock up all the Functions of my soul.'

Then feels immediately some hollow thought
Hang like an interdict[36] upon her hopes.   260
This is my lot; for either still I find
Some imperfection in the chosen theme,
Or see of absolute accomplishment
Much wanting – so much wanting in myself
That I recoil and droop, and seek repose   265
In indolence from vain perplexity,
Unprofitably travelling towards the grave
Like a false steward who hath much received
And renders nothing back.[37]
                 Was it for this
That one, the fairest of all rivers, loved   270
To blend his murmurs with my nurse's song,
And from his alder shades and rocky falls,
And from his fords and shallows, sent a voice
That flowed along my dreams?[38] For this didst thou,
Oh Derwent, travelling over the green plains   275
Near my 'sweet birthplace',[39] didst thou, beauteous stream,
Make ceaseless music through the night and day
Which with its steady cadence tempering
Our human waywardness, composed my thoughts
To more than infant softness, giving me   280
Among the fretful dwellings of mankind
A knowledge, a dim earnest,[40] of the calm
Which Nature breathes among the fields and groves?

[36] *interdict* prohibition – pronounced 'interdite'.

[37] Christ told the parable of how the servant is rebuked for burying, rather than invest-ing, his 'talent' of silver. Making silent use of the pun (the modern word actually derives from the parable), Wordsworth convicts himself of failure to make use of God-given poetic talents. See Matthew 25:14–30.

[38] This question marks the opening of the *Two-Part Prelude*, expressing disappoint-ment at being unable to compose *The Recluse* (see Introduction). The River Derwent, as present-day visitors can see, flows along the far side of the garden wall of the Wordsworths' house in Cockermouth.

[39] The quotation marks, which appear in the manuscript, refer the reader to Coleridge's *Frost at Midnight*, 33; it is particularly appropriate that the *Prelude*, which is addressed to Coleridge, should allude to his work.

[40] *earnest* foretaste, pledge.

When, having left his mountains, to the towers
Of Cockermouth[41] that beauteous river came,   285
Behind my father's house he passed, close by,
Chafing his waves against our terrace-walk –
He was a playmate whom we dearly loved.
Oh many a time have I, a five years' child,
A naked boy, in one delightful rill,   290
A little mill-race severed from his stream,
Made one long bathing of a summer's day,
Basked in the sun, and plunged and basked again
Alternate all a summer's day, or coursed[42]
Over the sandy fields, leaping through groves   295
Of yellow grunsel;[43] or, when crag and hill,
The woods, and distant Skiddaw's lofty height,[44]
Were bronzed with a deep radiance, stood alone
Beneath the sky, as if I had been born
On Indian plains and from my mother's hut   300
Had run abroad in wantonness to sport,[45]
A naked infant[46] in the thunder shower.
　　Fair seed-time had my soul, and I grew up
Fostered alike by beauty and by fear,
Much favoured in my birthplace, and no less   305
In that beloved vale to which erelong
I was transplanted.[47] Well I call to mind
('Twas at an early age, ere I had seen

---

[41] *the towers / Of Cockermouth*　De Selincourt notes the reference to Cockermouth Castle, ruined by Wordsworth's day: 'At the end of the garden of my Father's house at Cockermouth was a high terrace that commanded a fine view of the River Derwent and Cockermouth Castle. This was our favourite play-ground' (*FN* 8).

[42] *coursed*　run.

[43] *grunsel*　ragwort.

[44] Skiddaw is the fourth highest peak in the Lake District at 3,053 feet.

[45] Wordsworth's reference is to the American Indian, which he knew about from a travel-book, Jonathan Carver's *Travels through North America* (1768); see *WR* ii. 84.

[46] *infant*　The reading in the *Two-Part Prelude*, 'savage', was temporarily altered in this draft; it was reinstated in subsequent ones.

[47] Wordsworth went to live in Hawkshead in the vale of Esthwaite, where he attended the Grammar School.

Nine summers[48]) when upon the mountain-slope
The frost and breath of frosty wind had snapped   310
The last autumnal crocus, 'twas my joy
To wander half the night among the cliffs,
And the smooth hollows where the woodcocks ran
Along the open turf. In thought and wish
That time, my shoulder all with springes[49] hung,   315
I was a fell destroyer. On the heights,
Scudding away from snare to snare, I plied
My anxious visitation – hurrying on,
Still hurrying, hurrying onward; moon and stars
Were shining o'er my head; I was alone,   320
And seemed to be a trouble to the peace
That was among them. Sometimes it befell
In these night-wanderings, that a strong desire
O'erpowered my better reason, and the bird
Which was the captive of another's toils[50]   325
Became my prey; and when the deed was done
I heard among the solitary hills
Low breathings coming after me, and sounds
Of undistinguishable motion, steps
Almost as silent as the turf they trod.[51]   330
   Nor less in springtime, when on southern banks
The shining sun had from her knot of leaves
Decoyed the primrose flower, and when the vales
And woods were warm, was I a plunderer then
In the high places, on the lonesome peaks   335

---

[48] Wordsworth probably entered Hawkshead Grammar School in May 1779, when, although nine years old, he had seen ten summers; the events he recalls here therefore date from autumn 1779.

[49] *springes*   traps; Wordsworth is thinking of *Hamlet*, I. iii. 115: 'Ay, springes to catch woodcocks.'

[50] *toils*   a pun, meaning both 'trap' and 'labours'.

[51] Wordsworth's guilt might be explained partly by the fact that woodcock were a delicacy and fetched a good price for those who could catch them – 16 or 20 pence a couple on the spot before being sent to London on the Kendal stage-coach. They were trapped by snares set at the ends of narrowing avenues of stones which the birds would not jump over.

Where'er among the mountains and the winds
The mother-bird had built her lodge.[52] Though mean
My object and inglorious, yet the end
Was not ignoble.[53] Oh, when I have hung
Above the raven's nest, by knots of grass   340
And half-inch fissures in the slippery rock
But ill sustained, and almost (as it seemed)
Suspended by the blast which blew amain,[54]
Shouldering the naked crag[55] – oh, at that time
While on the perilous ridge I hung alone,[56]   345
With what strange utterance did the loud dry wind
Blow through my ears! The sky seemed not a sky
Of earth, and with what motion moved the clouds!
    The mind of man is framed even like the breath
And harmony of music; there is a dark   350
Invisible workmanship that reconciles
Discordant elements, and makes them move
In one society. Ah me! that all
The terrors, all the early miseries,
Regrets, vexations, lassitudes, that all   355
The thoughts and feelings which have been infused
Into my mind, should ever have made up
The calm existence that is mine when I
Am worthy of myself. Praise to the end –
Thanks likewise for the means! But I believe   360
That Nature, oftentimes, when she would frame
A favoured being, from his earliest dawn
Of infancy doth open out the clouds
As at the touch of lightning, seeking him

[52] *lodge* nest.
[53] Ravens preyed on lambs, and those who destroyed their eggs were rewarded by the parish. The 'end' (result) was not, in Wordsworth's case, monetary. A recollection of a raven's-nesting expedition of 1783 involving Wordsworth is given by Thompson, 211–14.
[54] *amain* strongly.
[55] *Shouldering the naked crag* the slightly inflated diction suggests that Wordsworth is recalling Atlas, the Titan of myth, who bore the world on his shoulders.
[56] *I hung alone* see Wordsworth's comments in the 1815 Preface, in *Romanticism*, 476–7.

With gentle visitation; not the less, 365
Though haply aiming at the self-same end,
Doth it delight her sometimes to employ
Severer interventions, ministry[57]
More palpable – and so she dealt with me.

One evening (surely I was led by her) 370
I went alone into a shepherd's boat,
A skiff that to a willow-tree was tied
Within a rocky cave, its usual home.
'Twas by the shores of Patterdale,[58] a vale
Wherein I was a stranger, thither come 375
A schoolboy-traveller at the holidays.
Forth rambled from the village inn alone
No sooner had I sight of this small skiff,
Discovered thus by unexpected chance,
Than I unloosed her tether and embarked. 380
The moon was up, the lake was shining clear
Among the hoary mountains; from the shore
I pushed, and struck the oars, and struck again
In cadence, and my little boat moved on
Even as a man who walks with stately step 385
Though bent on speed.[59] It was an act of stealth
And troubled pleasure; nor without the voice
Of mountain-echoes did my boat move on,
Leaving behind her still on either side
Small circles glittering idly to the moon 390
Until they melted all into one track
Of sparkling light.[60] A rocky steep uprose
Above the cavern of the willow-tree,
And now, as suited one who proudly rowed
With his best skill, I fixed a steady view 395
Upon the top of that same craggy ridge,

---

[57] *ministry* guidance.
[58] *Patterdale* on the western side of Ullswater in the north-east Lake District.
[59] Wordsworth recalls the description of Michael from *Paradise Lost*, xii. 1–2: 'As one who in his journey bates at noon, / Though bent on speed.'
[60] *sparkling light* probably a recollection of the 'tracks of shining white' made by the water-snakes in Coleridge's *Ancient Mariner* (1798), 266.

The bound of the horizon, for behind
Was nothing but the stars and the grey sky.
She was an elfin pinnace;[61] lustily
I dipped my oars into the silent lake,   400
And as I rose upon the stroke my boat
Went heaving through the water like a swan –
When, from behind that craggy steep (till then
The bound of the horizon), a huge cliff,[62]
As if with voluntary power instinct,[63]   405
Upreared its head. I struck and struck again,
And growing still in stature, the huge cliff
Rose up between me and the stars, and still,
With measured motion, like a living thing
Strode after me. With trembling hands I turned   410
And through the silent water stole my way
Back to the cavern of the willow-tree.
There in her mooring-place I left my bark,
And through the meadows homeward went with grave
And serious thoughts; and after I had seen   415
That spectacle, for many days my brain
Worked with a dim and undetermined sense
Of unknown modes of being.[64] In my thoughts
There was a darkness – call it solitude
Or blank desertion; no familiar shapes   420
Of hourly objects,[65] images of trees,
Of sea or sky, no colours of green fields,
But huge and mighty forms that do not live
Like living men moved slowly through my mind

---

[61] *elfin pinnace*   The language embodies the child's imaginative absorption; the boat
seems to be enchanted.

[62] *a huge cliff*   Glenridding Dodd, the stepped-back summit of which causes its peak
to make a sudden, delayed appearance above the 'craggy steep' of Stybarrow Crag as one
rows out from the shores of Patterdale (see Grevel Lindop, *A Literary Guide to the Lake
District* (London, 1993), pp. 317–18).

[63] *instinct*   imbued, filled.

[64] *unknown modes of being*   forms of life beyond human experience. The vagueness
and imprecision are meant to evoke the child's fear.

[65] *hourly objects*   objects that can be depended on to be the same from one hour to the
next.

By day, and were the trouble of my dreams.[66]   425
   Wisdom and spirit of the universe![67]
Thou soul that art the eternity of thought,
That giv'st to forms and images a breath
And everlasting motion, not in vain,
By day or star-light thus from my first dawn   430
Of childhood didst thou intertwine for me
The passions that build up our human soul,
Not with the mean and vulgar works of man,
But with high objects, with eternal things,
With life and Nature, purifying thus   435
The elements of feeling and of thought,
And sanctifying by such discipline
Both pain and fear, until we recognize
A grandeur in the beatings of the heart.[68]
   Nor was this fellowship vouchsafed to me   440
With stinted kindness.[69] In November days
When vapours rolling down the valleys made
A lonely scene more lonesome, among woods
At noon, and mid the calm of summer nights
When by the margin of the trembling lake   445
Beneath the gloomy hills I homeward went
In solitude, such intercourse[70] was mine –
'Twas mine along the fields both day and night,
And by the waters all the summer long.

---

[66] As the alien mountain forms take hold of his imagination, the boy is 'deserted' by the reassuring memories of ordinary things.

[67] A version of ll. 426–87 comprises only one of five extracts from *The Prelude* published during the poet's lifetime. It was printed by Coleridge in *The Friend*, 28 December 1809, as *Growth of Genius from the Influences of Natural Objects on the Imagination in Boyhood and Early Youth*. Wordsworth included it in collections of his poetry from 1815 onwards.

[68] The feelings and thoughts of Wordsworth's childhood were purer for having been associated not with man-made things (as in a town), but with the enduring forms of Nature. This natural education has sanctified – that is to say, has given value to – the otherwise unpleasant sensations of pain and fear; thus, when his heart beat with terror, he recognized the 'grandeur' of the experience.

[69] This special relationship with Nature ('fellowship') was not given grudgingly.

[70] *intercourse* companionship (with Nature).

And in the frosty season, when the sun   450
Was set, and visible for many a mile,
The cottage windows through the twilight blazed,
I heeded not the summons;[71] happy time
It was indeed for all of us – to me
It was a time of rapture. Clear and loud   455
The village clock tolled six; I wheeled about,
Proud and exulting like an untired horse
That cares not for his home. All shod with steel
We hissed along the polished ice[72] in games
Confederate,[73] imitative of the chase   460
And woodland pleasures – the resounding horn,
The pack loud bellowing, and the hunted hare.
So through the darkness and the cold we flew,
And not a voice was idle. With the din,
Meanwhile, the precipices rang aloud,   465
The leafless trees and every icy crag
Tinkled like iron, while the distant hills
Into the tumult sent an alien sound
Of melancholy, not unnoticed – while the stars
Eastward were sparkling clear, and in the west   470
The orange sky of evening died away.
    Not seldom from the uproar I retired
Into a silent bay, or sportively
Glanced sideway, leaving the tumultuous throng,
To cut across the image[74] of a star   475
That gleamed upon the ice. And oftentimes,
When we had given our bodies to the wind,
And all the shadowy banks on either side
Came sweeping through the darkness, spinning still
The rapid line of motion – then at once   480
Have I, reclining back upon my heels,
Stopped short: yet still the solitary cliffs

[71] The lights through the cottage windows tell the boy that it is time to go home.

[72] Wordsworth's phrasing recalls Erasmus Darwin's *Botanic Garden*: 'Hang o'er the sliding steel, and hiss along the ice' (*Economy of Vegetation*, iii. 570).

[73] *Confederate*   collective; games played in groups.

[74] *image*   reflection; altered to 'reflex' for *Fourteen-Book Prelude* i 450.

Wheeled by me, even as if the earth had rolled
With visible motion her diurnal[75] round;
Behind me did they stretch in solemn train[76]   485
Feebler and feebler, and I stood and watched
Till all was tranquil as a dreamless sleep.
  Ye presences of Nature, in the sky
Or on the earth! Ye visions of the hills!
Ye souls of lonely places![77] Can I think   490
A vulgar hope was yours when ye employed
Such ministry[78] – when ye through many a year
Haunting me thus among my boyish sports,
On caves and trees, upon the woods and hills,
Impressed[79] upon all forms the characters[80]   495
Of danger or desire, and thus did make
The surface of the universal earth
With triumph and delight, and hope and fear,
Work like a sea?[81]
                    Not uselessly employed,
I might pursue this theme through every change   500
Of exercise and play to which the year
Did summon us in its delightful round.
We were a noisy crew; the sun in heaven
Beheld not vales more beautiful than ours,
Nor saw a race in happiness and joy   505
More worthy of the fields where they were sown.
I would record with no reluctant voice
The woods of autumn and their hidden[82] bowers

[75] *diurnal*   daily, as in *A slumber did my spirit seal*, in which Lucy is 'Rolled round in earth's diurnal course / With rocks and stones and trees' (ll. 7–8).

[76] *train*   sequence, succession.

[77] Wordsworth is recalling *Tempest*, V. i. 33: 'Ye elves of hills, brooks, standing lakes, and groves'.

[78] *ministry*   guidance.

[79] *Impressed*   stamped, printed.

[80] *characters*   signs, marks.

[81] See Cowper, *Task*, vi. 737–8: 'this tempestuous state of human things, / Is merely as the working of a sea'. Its association with 'boyish sports' has given the impression of movement to the poet's recollection of the landscape in which he grew up.

[82] *hidden*   'hazel' is the reading in subsequent drafts.

With milk-white clusters hung, the rod and line
(True symbol of the foolishness of hope)   510
Which with its strong enchantment led us on
By rocks and pools shut out from every star
All the green summer, to forlorn cascades
Among the windings of the mountain brooks.
Unfading recollections! – even now   515
The heart is almost mine with which I felt
From some hill-top on sunny afternoons
The kite high up among the fleecy clouds
Pull at its chain[83] like an impatient courser,
Or, from the meadows launched on gusty days,   520
Beheld her breast the wind, then suddenly
Dashed headlong, and rejected by the storm.
    Ye lowly cottages in which we dwelt,
A ministration of your own was yours,
A sanctity, a presence, and a love.   525
Can I forget you, being as ye were
So beautiful among the pleasant fields
In which ye stood? Or can I here forget
The plain and seemly countenance with which
Ye dealt out your plain comforts? Yet had ye   530
Delights and exultations of your own:
Eager and never weary we pursued
Our home amusements by the warm peat-fire
At evening, when with pencil and with slate
(In square divisions parcelled out, and all   535
With crosses and with cyphers scribbled o'er[84])
We schemed and puzzled, head opposed to head,
In strife too humble to be named in verse;
Or round the naked table, snow-white deal,
Cherry or maple, sate in close array,   540
And to the combat, loo or whist,[85] led on

---

[83] *chain*   the alternative reading in later manuscripts is 'rein'.

[84] Noughts and crosses (tick-tack-toe); the line echoes *Paradise Lost*, viii. 83, where man is ridiculed for attempting to map the heavens: 'With centric and eccentric scribbled o'er'.

[85] *loo or whist*   The description of these eighteenth-century card-games recalls the game of ombre in Pope's *Rape of the Lock*, iii.

A thick-ribbed army[86] – not (as in the world)
Neglected and ungratefully thrown by
Even for the very service they had wrought,
But husbanded through many a long campaign.   545
It was a motley host, of which no few
Had changed their functions – some, plebeian cards[87]
Which fate, beyond the promise of their birth,
Had glorified, and called to represent
The persons of departed potentates.   550
Oh with what echoes on the board they fell!
Ironic diamonds – clubs, hearts, spades alike,
All furnished out in chimney-sweeper garb;[88]
Cheap matter did they give to boyish wit,
Those sooty knaves, precipitated down   555
With scoffs and taunts, like Vulcan out of heaven;[89]
The paramount ace, a moon in her eclipse;
Queens gleaming through their splendour's last decay,
And monarchs surly with the wrongs sustained
By royal visages. Meanwhile abroad   560
The heavy rain was falling, or the frost
Raged bitterly with keen and silent tooth,[90]
And, interrupting the impassioned game,
From Esthwaite's neighbouring lake the splitting ice,
While it sank down towards the water, sent   565
Among the meadows and the hills its long
And dismal yellings, like the noise of wolves
When they are howling round the Bothnic main.[91]

[86] The cards' edges have thickened through use.

[87] *plebeian cards* This allusion to Pope is in keeping with the mock-heroic tone of this passage; cf. *Rape of the Lock*, iii. 54: 'Gain'd but one Trump and one Plebeian Card'.

[88] Once again, Wordsworth's point is that frequent use has blackened the cards; this line appears only in this version of the poem; ll. 552–3 seem to recall Cowper, *Task*, iv. 214–19.

[89] Vulcan was thrown out of Olympus by Zeus; his fall took nine days.

[90] *keen and silent tooth* 'Thy tooth is not so keen', Amiens tells the winter wind in *As You Like It*, II. vii. 177. But as Owen *WC* 107 points out, ll. 560–2 are based on Cowper's *Winter Evening*: 'how the frost / Raging abroad, and the rough wind, endear / The silence and the warmth enjoyed within' (*Task*, iv. 308–10; *Romanticism*, 10).

[91] *Bothnic main* the northern Baltic.

Nor, sedulous[92] as I have been to trace
How Nature by extrinsic passion[93] first   570
Peopled my mind with beauteous forms or grand
And made me love them, may I well forget
How other pleasures have been mine, and joys
Of subtler origin – how I have felt,
Not seldom, even in that tempestuous time,   575
Those hallowed and pure motions of the sense
Which seem in their simplicity to own
An intellectual[94] charm, that calm delight
Which (if I err not) surely must belong
To those first-born affinities[95] that fit   580
Our new existence to existing things,
And in our dawn of being constitute
The bond of union betwixt life and joy.
    Yes, I remember when the changeful earth
And twice five seasons on my mind had stamped   585
The faces of the moving year; even then,
A child, I held unconscious intercourse
With the eternal beauty, drinking in
A pure organic[96] pleasure from the lines
Of curling mist, or from the level plain   590
Of waters coloured by the steady clouds.
    The sands of Westmoreland, the creeks and bays
Of Cumbria's rocky limits,[97] they can tell
How when the sea threw off his evening shade
And to the shepherd's hut beneath the crags   595
Did send sweet notice to the rising moon,
How I have stood, to fancies such as these
(Engrafted in the tenderness of thought)

---

[92] *sedulous* careful, anxious.

[93] *extrinsic passion* emotions not directly related to the natural scenes that were to 'educate' the poet. Nature operated on the boy without his being aware of it.

[94] *intellectual* spiritual – the sense in which Wordsworth often uses the word.

[95] *first-born affinities* affinities with which the child is born.

[96] *organic* sensuous, bodily.

[97] Westmorland and Cumberland no longer exist; thanks to subsequent redrawing of country boundaries they make up parts of present-day Cumbria.

A stranger, linking with the spectacle
No conscious memory of a kindred sight,   600
And bringing with me no peculiar sense
Of quietness or peace[98] – yet I have stood,
Even while mine eye has moved o'er three long leagues[99]
Of shining water, gathering, as it seemed,
Through every hair-breadth of that field of light   605
New pleasure like a bee among the flowers.
     Thus often in those fits of vulgar[100] joy
Which through all seasons on a child's pursuits
Are prompt attendants, mid that giddy bliss
Which like a tempest works along the blood   610
And is forgotten – even then I felt
Gleams like the flashing of a shield. The earth
And common face of Nature spake to me
Rememberable things – sometimes, 'tis true,
By chance collisions and quaint accidents   615
(Like those ill-sorted unions, work supposed
Of evil-minded fairies[101]), yet not vain
Nor profitless, if haply they impressed
Collateral objects and appearances,
Albeit lifeless then and doomed to sleep   620
Until maturer seasons called them forth
To impregnate and to elevate the mind.
     And if the vulgar joy by its own weight
Wearied itself out of the memory,
The scenes which were a witness of that joy   625
Remained in their substantial lineaments
Depicted on the brain,[102] and to the eye

[98] At the time which he is remembering, Wordsworth appreciated natural scenes in and for themselves, without associating them with similar sights and feelings.

[99] *three long leagues* at least nine miles (a league is a varying measure of about three miles).

[100] *vulgar* ordinary, unremarkable.

[101] Wordsworth has in mind the sort of mischief portrayed in *A Midsummer Night's Dream*.

[102] *in their substantial lineaments ... brain* The storing up of visual images is described in similar terms at *Pedlar*, 32–4: 'on his mind / They lay like substances, and almost seemed / To haunt the bodily sense'.

Were visible, a daily sight. And thus,
By the impressive discipline of fear,[103]
By pleasure, and repeated happiness   630
(So frequently repeated), and by force
Of obscure feelings representative
Of joys that were forgotten, these same scenes
So beauteous and majestic in themselves,
Though yet the day was distant, did at length   635
Become habitually dear, and all
Their hues and forms were by invisible links
Allied to the affections.[104]
              I began
My story early, feeling (as I fear)
The weakness of a human love for days   640
Disowned by memory, ere the birth of spring
Planting my snowdrops among winter snow.
Nor will it seem to thee, my friend, so prompt
In sympathy, that I have lengthened out
With fond and feeble tongue a tedious tale.   645
Meanwhile my hope has been that I might fetch
Invigorating thoughts from former years,
Might fix the wavering balance of my mind,
And haply meet reproaches too whose power
May spur me on, in manhood now mature,   650
To honourable toil.[105] Yet should these hopes
Be vain, and should I neither thus be taught
To understand myself, nor thou to know
With better knowledge how the heart was framed
Of him thou lovest, need I dread from thee   655
Harsh judgements if I am so loath to quit

---

[103] *the impressive discipline of fear*   fear's ability to stamp 'impressions' on the memory.

[104] *invisible links / Allied to the affections*   associative connections capable of reviving past emotions ('affections'). Wordsworth draws on the theory of the mind's association of ideas derived from sense-experience, as expounded by David Hartley (1705–57) in his *Observations of Man* (1749) – a strong influence on Coleridge.

[105] When he composed these lines in February 1799, Wordsworth expected to go on with *The Recluse*.

Those recollected hours that have the charm
Of visionary things,[106] and lovely forms
And sweet sensations that throw back our life
And almost make our infancy itself   660
A visible scene on which the sun is shining?
   One end hereby at least hath been attained:
My mind hath been revived; and if this mood
Desert me not, I will forthwith bring down
Through later years the story of my life.   665
The road lies plain before me; 'tis a theme
Single and of determined bounds, and hence
I choose it rather at this time, than work
Of ampler or more varied argument
Where I might be discomfited and lost;[107]   670
And certain hopes are with me, that to thee
This labour will be welcome, honoured friend!

[106] *visionary things*   things seen imaginatively.
[107] These comments reveal how anxious Wordsworth had become by January 1804 about *The Recluse*.

Book Two

Thus far, my friend, have we, though leaving much
Unvisited, retraced my life in part
Through its first years, and also measured back
The way I travelled when I first began
To love the woods and fields. The passion yet   5
Was in its birth, sustained (as might befall)
By nourishment that came unsought;[1] for still
From week to week, from month to month, we lived
A round of tumult. Duly were our games
Prolonged in summer till the daylight failed.   10
No chair remained before the doors; the bench
And threshold steps were empty; fast asleep
The labourer, and the old man who had sat
A later lingerer – yet the revelry
Continued, and the loud uproar! At last,   15
When all the ground was dark, and the huge clouds
Were edged with twinkling stars, to bed we went,
With weary joints and with a beating mind.[2]
      Ah! is there one who ever has been young
And needs a monitory voice to tame   20
The pride of virtue and of intellect?[3]

---

[1] *nourishment that came unsought* Where in Book I Wordsworth discussed his unconscious reponse to the influence of nature, he aims to show in Book II how nature in adolescence was 'sought / For her own sake'.

[2] Cf. *The Tempest*, IV. i. 162–3: 'A turn or two I'll walk, / To still my beating mind'.

[3] 'How can anyone who remembers what it was like to be young need a warning ("monitory voice") not to overrate the achievements of maturity?'

And is there one, the wisest and the best
Of all mankind, who does not sometimes wish
For things which cannot be, who would not give,
If so he might, to duty and to truth   25
The eagerness of infantine desire?
A tranquillizing spirit presses now
On my corporeal frame,[4] so wide appears
The vacancy between me and those days
Which yet have such self-presence[5] in my heart   30
That sometimes, when I think of them I seem
Two consciousnesses – conscious of myself
And of some other being.
                              A grey stone
Of native rock, left midway in the square
Of our small market-village, was the home   35
And centre of these joys; and when, returned
After long absence, thither I repaired,
I found that it was split, and gone to build
A smart assembly-room that perked and flared
With wash and rough-cast,[6] elbowing the ground   40
Which had been ours. But let the fiddle scream
And be ye happy! Yet, my friends,[7] I know
That more than one of you will think with me
Of those soft starry nights, and that old dame
From whom the stone was named, who there had sat   45
And watched her table with its huckster's wares,
Assiduous for the length of sixty years.[8]
    We ran a boisterous race: the year span round
With giddy motion. But the time approached

---

[4] *corporeal frame*   body; the effect is similar to that described in *Tintern Abbey*, 44–6.
[5] *self-presence*   presence to himself – actuality, immediacy.
[6] Hawkshead Town Hall, built 1790, covered with gravel stucco ('rough-cast') and whitewash. Wordsworth didn't like white buildings because of the way they stuck out in the landscape.
[7] An address to Coleridge and John Wordsworth (the poet's brother), with whom the poet visited Hawkshead on 2 November 1799.
[8] Thompson tells the story of Ann Holme, who set out her wares – cakes, pies and sweets – on the large stone at the end of the market square in Hawkshead (Thompson, 253–6).

That brought with it a regular desire   50
For calmer pleasures, when the beauteous forms
Of Nature were collaterally attached
To every scheme of holiday delight
And every boyish sport – less grateful[9] else,
And languidly pursued.[10] When summer came   55
It was the pastime of our afternoons
To beat along the plain[11] of Windermere
With rival oars, and the selected bourn[12]
Was now an island musical with birds
That sang for ever; now a sister isle   60
Beneath the oak's umbrageous[13] covert, sown
With lilies-of-the-valley, like a field;
And now a third small island where remained
An old stone table and a mouldered cave –
A hermit's history.[14] In such a race,   65
So ended, disappointment could be none,
Uneasiness, or pain, or jealousy;
We rested in the shade, all pleased alike,
Conquered and conqueror. Thus the pride of strength
And the vainglory of superior skill   70
Were interfused[15] with objects which subdued
And tempered them, and gradually produced
A quiet independence of the heart.
And to my friend who knows me, I may add,
Unapprehensive of reproof, that hence   75
Ensued a diffidence and modesty,
And I was taught to feel (perhaps too much)
The self-sufficing power of solitude.

---

[9] *grateful*   pleasing.

[10] Natural beauty is still only an additional ('collateral') pleasure, though it is beginning to be valued.

[11] *plain*   flat surface of the lake.

[12] *bourn*   aim, destination.

[13] *umbrageous*   shady.

[14] The 'third small island' is Lady Holm, where there was once a chapel to the Virgin Mary. The 'hermit' is borrowed from St Herbert's isle on Derwentwater.

[15] *interfused*   mingled; cf. *Tintern Abbey*, 97.

No delicate viands[16] sapped our bodily strength:
More than we wished we knew the blessing then   80
Of vigorous hunger, for our daily meals
Were frugal, Sabine fare;[17] and then, exclude
A little weekly stipend, and we lived
Through three divisions of the quartered year
In penniless poverty.[18] But now, to school   85
Returned from the half-yearly holidays,
We came with purses more profusely filled,[19]
Allowance which abundantly sufficed
To gratify the palate with repasts
More costly than the dame of whom I spake,   90
That ancient woman,[20] and her board, supplied.
Hence inroads into distant vales, and long
Excursions far away among the hills,
Hence rustic dinners on the cool green ground,
Or in the woods, or near a riverside,   95
Or by some shady fountain[21] – while soft airs[22]
Among the leaves were stirring, and the sun
Unfelt shone sweetly round us in our joy.
     Nor is my aim neglected if I tell
How twice in the long length of those half-years   100
We from our funds perhaps with bolder hand
Drew largely – anxious for one day, at least,
To feel the motion of the galloping steed.
And with the good old innkeeper,[23] in truth,
I needs must say that sometimes we have used   105

[16] *delicate viands*   decorative delicacies of no nutritional value.

[17] The Roman poet Horace had a Sabine farm and recommended a frugal diet, although Thompson says that Ann Tyson, Wordsworth's landlady, fed the poet pasties, cakes, dumplings, eggs and porridge (Thompson, 100–3).

[18] In 1787, the year he left Hawkshead, Wordsworth received sixpence a week.

[19] When Wordsworth returned to school in January 1787, after the half-yearly holiday, he had an extra guinea (worth 42 'weekly stipends').

[20] *That ancient woman*   Ann Tyson was 73 in January 1787.

[21] *fountain*   spring or stream.

[22] Wordsworth has in mind *The Tempest*, III. ii. 135–6, where the isle is 'full of noises, / Sounds, and sweet airs, that give delight and hurt not'.

[23] *innkeeper*   who hired out the horses.

Sly subterfuge, for the intended bound
Of the day's journey was too distant far
For any cautious man: a structure famed
Beyond its neighbourhood – the antique walls
Of a large Abbey with its fractured arch,   110
Belfry, and images, and living trees,
A holy scene![24] Along the smooth green turf
Our horses grazed. In more than inland peace
Left by the winds that pass high overhead
In that sequestered valley, trees and towers,   115
Both silent and both motionless alike,
Hear all day long the murmuring sea that beats
Incessantly upon a craggy shore.
    Our steeds remounted and the summons given,
With whip and spur we by the chantry[25] flew   120
In uncouth race, and left the cross-legged knight,
And the stone abbot,[26] and that single wren
Which one day sang so sweetly in the nave
Of the old church that, though from recent showers
The earth was comfortless, and, touched by faint   125
Uncertain breezes – sobbings of the place
And inward breathings[27] – from the roofless walls
The shuddering ivy dripped large drops, yet still
So sweetly mid the gloom the invisible bird
Sang to itself that there I could have made   130
My dwelling-place, and lived forever there
To hear such music.[28] Through the walls we flew
And down the valley, and, a circuit made

---

[24] Furness Abbey is about 20 miles south of Hawkshead near Barrow-in-Furness. It was founded by Cistercian monks in 1127, and dissolved by Henry VIII in 1539. The fractured arch is still to be seen. Its roof-timbers, stripped of their valuable lead, had long since fallen by Wordsworth's day.

[25] *chantry* chapel where masses were once said for the dead.

[26] The stone figures of several cross-legged knights and an abbot may still be seen in the museum at Furness Abbey.

[27] *inward breathings* this reading occurs only in this version of the poem; 'respirations' is that of the *Thirteen-Book Prelude*.

[28] Cf. Shakespeare, Sonnet 73: 'Bare ruined choirs, where late the sweet birds sang'.

In wantonness of heart, through rough and smooth
We scampered homeward. Oh, ye rocks and streams, 135
And that still spirit of the evening air!
Even in this joyous time I sometimes felt
Your presence, when with slackened step we breathed[29]
Along the sides of the steep hills, or when,
Lighted by gleams of moonlight from the sea, 140
We beat with thundering hoofs the level sand.[30]
   Upon the eastern shore of Windermere
Above the crescent of a pleasant bay,
There was an inn[31] – no homely-featured shed,
Brother of the surrounding cottages, 145
But 'twas a splendid place, the door beset
With chaises, grooms, and liveries, and within
Decanters, glasses, and the blood-red wine.[32]
In ancient times, or ere the hall was built
On the large island,[33] had the dwelling been 150
More worthy of a poet's love, a hut
Proud of its one bright fire and sycamore shade.
But though the rhymes were gone which once inscribed
The threshold, and large golden characters
On the blue-frosted signboard had usurped 155

---

[29] *breathed* i.e., let the horses get their breath back.

[30] The return journey took them along Levens Sands from Rampside to Greenodd.

[31] *an inn* the White Lion at Bowness, now the Royal Hotel.

[32] *the blood-red wine* an echo of the anonymous ballad, *Sir Patrick Spence*: 'The king sits in Dunfermling toune, / Drinking the blude-reid wine' (ll. 1–2). Wordsworth knew it from Percy's *Reliques of Ancient English Poetry* (1765), a copy of which he purchased in Hamburg shortly before starting work on the *Two-Part Prelude*; see *WR* i. 196(iii).

[33] The first and finest of the neoclassical villas in the Lakes was the circular mansion on Belle Isle in Windermere, designed by John Plaw in 1774 for Thomas English, but not completed until the early 1780s, when John Christian Curwen had become its owner. Wordsworth follows the guide-book writers of the day – Hutchinson, West and Gilpin – in deploring the changes that had taken place, including the felling of many trees and the demolition of the old buildings (including, perhaps, the 'hut' mentioned by Wordsworth). Dorothy had harsh words for the circular mansion in June 1802: '. . . & that great house! Mercy upon us! If it *could* be concealed it would be well for all who are not pained to see the pleasantest of earthly spots deformed by man' (*Grasmere Journals*, 107; emphasis original).

The place of the old lion, in contempt
And mockery of the rustic painter's hand,
Yet to this hour the spot to me is dear
With all its foolish pomp. The garden lay
Upon a slope surmounted by the plain   160
Of a small bowling-green; beneath us stood
A grove, with gleams of water through the trees
And over the tree-tops – nor did we want
Refreshment, strawberries and mellow cream.
And there, through half an afternoon, we played   165
On the smooth platform, and the shouts we sent
Made all the mountains ring. But ere the fall
Of night, when in our pinnace we returned
Over the dusky lake, and to the beach
Of some small island steered our course, with one,[34] 170
The minstrel of our troop, and left him there,
And rowed off gently while he blew his flute
Alone upon the rock, oh then the calm
And dead still water lay upon my mind
Even with a weight of pleasure, and the sky,   175
Never before so beautiful, sank down
Into my heart, and held me like a dream.
      Thus daily were my sympathies enlarged,
And thus the common range of visible things
Grew dear to me. Already I began   180
To love the sun – a boy I loved the sun
Not as I since have loved him (as a pledge
And surety of our earthly life, a light
Which while we view we feel we are alive),
But for this cause: that I had seen him lay   185
His beauty on the morning hills, had seen
The western mountains touch his setting orb
In many a thoughtless hour, when from excess
Of happiness my blood appeared to flow
With its own pleasure, and I breathed with joy.   190

---

[34] Robert Greenwood, another of Ann Tyson's boarders, who was elected Fellow of
Trinity College, Cambridge, in 1792. Wordsworth remained in touch with him for many
years.

And from like feelings, humble though intense
(To patriotic and domestic love
Analogous[35]), the moon to me was dear:
For I would dream away my purposes,
Standing to look upon her while she hung   195
Midway between the hills, as if she knew
No other region, but belonged to thee –
Yea, appertained by a peculiar right
To thee and thy grey huts,[36] my darling vale!
    Those incidental charms which first attached   200
My heart to rural objects day by day
Grew weaker, and I hasten on to tell
How Nature – intervenient till this time,
And secondary[37] – now at length was sought
For her own sake. But who shall parcel out   205
His intellect by geometric rules,
Split like a province into round and square?
Who knows the individual hour in which
His habits were first sown, even as a seed?
Who that shall point as with a wand, and say,   210
'This portion of the river of my mind
Came from yon fountain'? Thou, my friend, art one
More deeply read in thy own thoughts; to thee
Science[38] appears but what in truth she is –
Not as our glory and our absolute boast,   215
But as a succedaneum[39] and a prop
To our infirmity. Thou art no slave
Of that false secondary power by which
In weakness we create distinctions, then
Deem that our puny boundaries are things   220
Which we perceive, and not which we have made.
To thee, unblinded by these outward shows,

---

[35] His love for the moon was like love of country and family ('domestic love') because it gave him pleasure in the region where he lived.

[36] *grey huts* cottages built of grey stone.

[37] Nature had been experienced in the midst of other distractions.

[38] *Science* knowledge, erudition.

[39] *succedaneum* remedy (an incorrect usage in this sense).

The unity of all has been revealed;[40]
And thou wilt pause with me, less aptly skilled
Than many are to class the cabinet   225
Of their sensations,[41] and in voluble phrase
Run through the history and birth of each
As of a single independent thing.
Hard task[42] to analyse a soul, in which
Not only general habits and desires,   230
But each most obvious and particular thought –
Not in a mystical and idle sense,
But in the words of reason deeply weighed –
Hath no beginning.
                    Blessed the infant babe[43]
(For with my best conjectures I would trace   235
The progress of our being[44]) – blessed the babe
Nursed in his mother's arms, the babe who sleeps
Upon his mother's breast, who when his soul
Claims manifest kindred with an earthly soul,
Doth gather passion from his mother's eye![45]   240
Such feelings pass into his torpid life
Like an awakening breeze, and hence his mind,
Even in the first trial of its powers,
Is prompt and watchful, eager to combine

[40] Coleridge was a Unitarian, and capable of writing: ''tis God / Diffused through all that doth make all one whole' (*Religious Musings*, 144–5).

[41] *to class . . . sensations*   classify sensations as if they were exhibits in a cabinet. Jonathan Wordsworth notes that the metaphor is borrowed from Locke's *Essay Concerning Human Understanding*: 'The senses at first let in particular ideas, and furnish the yet empty cabinet'.

[42] *Hard task*   a deliberate echo of Milton, who speaks of having to describe the war in heaven as 'Sad task and hard' (*Paradise Lost*, v. 564); describing the growth of the mind is just as worthy of epic treatment for Wordsworth.

[43] The Infant Babe passage was probably inspired partly by the death of Coleridge's baby son Berkeley, news of which reached Coleridge in Germany in April 1799, several months after it had taken place; for Coleridge's reaction see his letter to Poole of 6 April 1799 (*Romanticism*, 526).

[44] *The progress of our being*   Just as Milton charted progress from the Garden of Eden, Wordsworth will trace that of the growing mind.

[45] When his soul first forms a relationship with another, the baby learns to love by seeing its mother's love in her eyes.

In one appearance all the elements 245
And parts of the same object, else detached
And loath to coalesce.[46] Thus day by day,
Subjected to the discipline of love,
His organs and recipient faculties[47]
Are quickened,[48] are more vigorous; his mind spreads, 250
Tenacious of the forms which it receives.[49]
In one beloved presence – nay and more;
In that most apprehensive habitude[50]
And those sensations which have been derived
From this beloved presence, there exists 255
A virtue which irradiates and exalts
All objects through all intercourse of sense.[51]
No outcast he, bewildered and depressed:
Along his infant veins are interfused
The gravitation and the filial bond 260
Of Nature that connect him with the world.[52]
Emphatically such a being lives
An inmate of this *active* universe.[53]
From Nature largely he receives, nor so
Is satisfied, but largely gives again – 265
For feeling has to him imparted strength;
And, powerful in all sentiments of grief,
Of exultation, fear, and joy, his mind,

[46] *loath to coalesce*   reluctant to come together, making wholes. Inspired by its mother's love, the baby becomes able to form parts into wholes, ordering what it perceives; in other words, its mind is working imaginatively.

[47] *recipient faculties*   senses.

[48] *quickened*   enlivened.

[49] The mind retains visual images; cf. *Tintern Abbey*, 23–50.

[50] A relationship ('habitude') best suited to learning ('most apprehensive').

[51] The mother's love is a power ('virtue') that infuses all objects which the child perceives, exalting them; cf. *Tintern Abbey*, 101–2: 'A motion and a spirit that impels / All thinking things, all objects of all thought'.

[52] The child's loving relationship with his mother is what connects him to natural objects.

[53] *this* active *universe*   the emphasis is Wordsworth's; the tone is reminiscent of the blank verse fragment, composed at the same time as the *Two-Part Prelude*, possibly for *The Recluse*: 'There is an active principle alive in all things' (see Cornell *LB* 309–10).

Even as an agent of the one great mind,[54]
Creates, creator and receiver both,   270
Working but in alliance with the works
Which it beholds.[55] Such, verily, is the first
Poetic spirit of our human life,
By uniform control of after-years
In most abated and suppressed, in some   275
Through every change of growth or of decay
Pre-eminent till death.
                              From early days,
Beginning not long after that first time
In which, a babe, by intercourse of touch,
I held mute dialogues with my mother's heart,   280
I have endeavoured to display the means
Whereby this infant sensibility,
Great birthright of our being, was in me
Augmented and sustained. Yet is a path
More difficult before me, and I fear   285
That in its broken windings we shall need
The chamois'[56] sinews and the eagle's wing.
For now a trouble came into my mind
From unknown causes: I was left alone,
Seeking the visible world, nor knowing why.   290
The props of my affections were removed,
And yet the building stood, as if sustained
By its own spirit.[57] All that I beheld
Was dear to me, and from this cause it came:
That now to Nature's finer influxes[58]   295
My mind lay open – to that more exact
And intimate communion which our hearts

---

[54] *the one great mind*   God.

[55] The child's mind becomes creative as well as receptive; it is imaginative – working in harmony with Nature. In so doing, it acts as an agent of God.

[56] *chamois*   mountain antelope, which Wordsworth may have seen on his 1790 walking tour which took him through the Alps.

[57] The 'props' of his feelings were the boyish sports that encouraged his love of Nature in adolescence. Later, they are no longer required for that love to exist in its own right.

[58] *influxes*   influences.

Maintain with the minuter properties
Of objects which already are beloved,
And of those only.
                              Many are the joys   300
Of youth, but oh what happiness to live
When every hour brings palpable access
Of knowledge, when all knowledge is delight,
And sorrow is not there! The seasons came,
And every season did to notice bring   305
A store of transitory qualities
Which, but for this most watchful power of love,
Had been neglected – left a register
Of permanent relations, else unknown.[59]
Hence life, and change, and beauty, solitude   310
More active even than 'best society',[60]
Society made sweet as solitude
By silent unobtrusive sympathies,
And gentle agitations of the mind
From manifold distinctions (difference   315
Perceived in things where to the common eye
No difference is) – and hence, from the same source,
Sublimer joy.[61] For I would walk alone
In storm and tempest, or in starlight nights[62]
Beneath the quiet heavens, and at that time   320
Have felt whate'er there is of power in sound
To breathe an elevated mood, by form
Or image unprofaned. And I would stand

[59] *every season . . . else unknown* Because the poet has come to love Nature for itself, he notices the countless characteristics and details of each successive season. Consequently, the mind registers them as permanent impressions.

[60] *best society* Wordsworth alludes to *Paradise Lost*, ix. 249, where Adam in Eden says: 'For solitude sometimes is best society'.

[61] A series of things follow from the permanently impressed features of Nature on the poet's mind: change, beauty, solitude more active than society, society as sweet as solitude, and the 'gentle agitations' produced by noticing many distinctions not observable to the untrained eye. From this last feature is produced 'sublimer joy'.

[62] Ll. 319–38 were composed in January–February 1798, probably as part of a passage describing the narrator of *The Ruined Cottage*. While boarding with the Tysons at Colthouse, Wordsworth was prone to get up for walks at 1 a.m.

Beneath some rock, listening to sounds that are
The ghostly language of the ancient earth   325
Or make their dim abode in distant winds:
Thence did I drink the visionary power.
I deem not profitless these fleeting moods
Of shadowy exultation – not for this,
That they are kindred to our purer mind   330
And intellectual life, but that the soul,
Remembering how she felt, but what she felt
Remembering not, retains an obscure sense
Of possible sublimity, to which
With growing faculties she doth aspire,   335
With faculties still growing, feeling still
That whatsoever point they gain they still
Have something to pursue.
     And not alone
In grandeur and in tumult, but no less
In tranquil scenes, that universal power   340
And fitness in the latent qualities
And essences of things, by which the mind
Is moved with feelings of delight, to me
Came strengthened with a superadded soul,
A virtue not its own.[63] My morning walks   345
Were early; oft before the hours of school
I travelled round our little lake, five miles
Of pleasant wandering – happy time more dear
For this, that one was by my side, a friend
Then passionately loved.[64] With heart how full   350
Will he peruse these lines, this page (perhaps
A blank to other men), for many years
Have since flowed in between us, and, our minds

[63] The 'superadded soul' is presumably an element of the 'visionary power' of l. 327. It is additional to natural objects, and is not conferred on them by the perceiving mind: it comes from beyond.

[64] School began at 6 or 6.30 a.m. during the summer; the five-mile walk would have taken Wordsworth round Esthwaite Water – although that seems a generous estimate for a lake which is little more than a mile long. The friend was John Fleming, who went up to Cambridge in 1785.

Both silent to each other, at this time
We live as if those hours had never been.   355
Nor seldom did I lift our cottage latch
Far earlier, and before the vernal[65] thrush
Was audible, among the hills I sate
Alone upon some jutting eminence
At the first hour of morning, when the vale   360
Lay quiet in an utter solitude.
How shall I trace the history, where seek
The origin of what I then have felt?
Oft in those moments such a holy calm
Did overspread my soul, that I forgot   365
That I had bodily eyes, and what I saw
Appeared like something in myself – a dream,
A prospect[66] in my mind.[67]
                'Twere long to tell
What spring and autumn, what the winter snows,
And what the summer shade, what day and night,   370
The evening and the morning, what my dreams
And what my waking thoughts supplied to nurse
That spirit of religious love in which
I walked with Nature. But let this at least
Be not forgotten – that I still retained   375
My first creative sensibility,
That by the regular action of the world
My soul was unsubdued. A plastic[68] power
Abode with me, a 'forming hand',[69] at times

[65] *vernal* springtime.

[66] *prospect* landscape, view.

[67] *Oft in those moments . . . mind* While not identical, Wordsworth's recollections of the intensity of childhood vision are similar: 'I was often unable to think of external things as having external existence, and I communed with all that I saw as something not apart from, but inherent in, my own immaterial nature. Many times while going to school have I grasped at a wall or tree to recall myself from this abyss of idealism to the reality. At that time I was afraid of such processes' (*Romanticism*, 481).

[68] *plastic* shaping, forming.

[69] *'forming hand'* the quotation marks appear only in this early draft; they signal an allusion to the creation of Eve at *Paradise Lost*, viii. 470: 'Under his forming hands a creature grew'.

Rebellious, acting in a devious mood,   380
A local spirit of its own, at war
With general tendency, but for the most
Subservient strictly to the external things
With which it communed.[70] An auxiliar[71] light
Came from my mind, which on the setting sun   385
Bestowed new splendour; the melodious birds,
The gentle breezes, fountains that ran on
Murmuring so sweetly in themselves, obeyed
A like dominion, and the midnight storm
Grew darker in the presence of my eye.   390
Hence my obeisance, my devotion hence,
And *hence* my transport![72]
                                        Nor should this, perchance,
Pass unrecorded, that I still[73] had loved
The exercise and produce of a toil
Than analytic industry[74] to me   395
More pleasing, and whose character I deem
Is more poetic, as resembling more
Creative agency – I mean to speak
Of that interminable building[75] reared
By observation of affinities   400
In objects where no brotherhood exists
To common minds. My seventeenth year was come,
And, whether from this habit rooted now
So deeply in my mind, or from excess
Of the great social principle of life   405
Coercing all things into sympathy,
To unorganic natures I transferred

---

[70] The imagination sometimes behaves with a will of its own, but is usually subordinate to the natural world (i.e., prepared to enhance it).

[71] *auxiliar* enhancing.

[72] *transport* ecstasy. It is because the mind is believed to be 'lord and master' over what it perceives that the poet devotes himself to Nature.

[73] *still* always.

[74] *analytic industry* rational thought.

[75] *interminable building* vast mental construction.

My own enjoyments,[76] or, the power of truth
Coming in revelation, I conversed
With things that really are, I at this time   410
Saw blessings spread around me like a sea.[77]
Thus did my days pass on, and now at length
From Nature and her overflowing soul[78]
I had received so much that all my thoughts
Were steeped in feeling.
                 I was only then   415
Contented when with bliss ineffable
I felt the sentiment of being spread
O'er all that moves, and all that seemeth still,
O'er all that, lost beyond the reach of thought
And human knowledge, to the human eye   420
Invisible, yet liveth to the heart;
O'er all that leaps and runs, and shouts and sings,
Or beats the gladsome air; o'er all which glides
Beneath the wave, yea in the wave itself
And mighty depth of waters. Wonder not   425
If such my transports were, for in all things
I saw one life, and felt that it was joy.
One song they sang, and it was audible –
Most audible then when the fleshly ear,
O'ercome by grosser prelude of that strain,[79]   430

[76] *or, from excess ... own enjoyments* As Jonathan Wordsworth has suggested, Wordsworth has in mind Coleridge's lines in the 1798 text of *Frost at Midnight* (*Romanticism*, 516–18):

> But still the living spirit in our frame
> That loves not to behold a lifeless thing,
> Transfuses into all its own delights
> Its own volition . . . (ll. 21–4)

[77] The boy either projected his own happiness onto inanimate ('unorganic') Nature, through excess of fellow-feeling, or he truly perceived the shared life-force that runs through all living things.

[78] Ll. 413–31 were composed originally for Wordsworth's great pantheist poem *The Pedlar* in early 1798.

[79] *grosser prelude of that strain* sensual joy preceding the more refined pleasures of response to the pantheist one life.

Forgot its functions and slept undisturbed.
    If this be error,[80] and another faith
Find easier access to the pious mind,
Yet were I grossly destitute of all
Those human sentiments which make this earth   435
So dear, if I should fail with grateful voice
To speak of you, ye mountains and ye lakes
And sounding cataracts, ye mists and winds
That dwell among the hills where I was born.
If in my youth I have been pure in heart,   440
If, mingling with the world, I am content
With my own modest pleasures, and have lived
With God and Nature communing, removed
From little enmities and low desires,
The gift is yours; if in these times of fear,   445
This melancholy waste[81] of hopes o'erthrown,
If, mid indifference and apathy
And wicked exultation, when good men
On every side fall off,[82] we know not how,
To selfishness, disguised in gentle names   450
Of peace and quiet and domestic love,
Yet mingled not unwillingly with sneers
On visionary minds – if in this time

---

[80] *If this be error*   It is characteristic of Wordsworth sometimes to express doubt; cf. *Tintern Abbey*, 50ff.: 'If this / Be but a vain belief . . .'. The phrasing is in fact borrowed from Shakespeare, Sonnet 116, l. 13.

[81] *waste*   desert.

[82] Wordsworth is reacting to Coleridge's exhortation to incorporate in *The Recluse* an address to 'those, who, in consequence of the complete failure of the French Revolution, have thrown up all hopes of the amelioration of mankind, and are sinking into an almost epicurean selfishness, disguising the same under the soft titles of domestic attachment and contempt for visionary *philosophes*' (Griggs, i. 527). The most obvious example is Sir James Mackintosh, former apologist for the French Revolution, who, in a series of notorious lectures of February–June 1799, attacked the progressive causes he had once advocated. His apostasy drew comments in Hazlitt's essay on Mackintosh in *The Spirit of the Age* (1825), an uncharacteristically harsh epigram by Lamb (*Romanticism*, 616), and a notebook entry by Coleridge: 'Did Mackintosh change his opinions, with a cold clear predetermination, formed at one moment, to make £5000 a year by that change?' (*Notebooks*, i. 947).

Of dereliction and dismay I yet
Despair not of our nature, but retain 455
A more than Roman confidence,[83] a faith
That fails not, in all sorrow my support,
The blessing of my life, the gift is yours,
Ye winds and sounding cataracts! – is yours,[84]
Ye mountains! – thine, oh Nature! Thou hast fed 460
My lofty speculations, and in thee,
For this uneasy heart of ours, I find
A never-failing principle[85] of joy
And purest passion.

        Thou, my friend, wast reared
In the great city, mid far other scenes,[86] 465
But we by different roads at length have gained
The self-same bourn. And for this cause to thee
I speak unapprehensive of contempt,
The insinuated scoff of coward tongues,
And all that silent language which so oft 470
In conversation betwixt man and man
Blots from the human countenance all trace
Of beauty and of love. For thou hast sought
The truth in solitude, and thou art one,
The most intense of Nature's worshippers, 475
In many things my brother, chiefly here
In this my deep devotion.

        Fare thee well![87]
Health and the quiet of a healthful mind

---

[83] *more than Roman confidence* Although Maxwell adduced the example of the Roman general, Varro, commended after his defeat by Hannibal at Cannae (216 BC) for not despairing of the republic, Wordsworth may simply be recommending Stoicism. His admiration for Roman history and thought is analysed by Jane Worthington, *Wordsworth's Reading of Roman Prose* (New Haven, 1946).

[84] This line was removed from all subsequent versions of the poem.

[85] *principle* source.

[86] *Thou, my friend . . . other scenes* In *Frost at Midnight*, Coleridge had written: 'For I was reared / In the great city, pent mid cloisters dim' (ll. 56–7).

[87] When these lines were first composed for the *Two-Part Prelude*, the farewell had an immediate context: Coleridge in November 1799 was about to go south to become a journalist in London; the Wordsworths were about to move into Dove Cottage.

Attend thee, seeking oft the haunts of men,
And yet more often living with thyself,   480
And for thyself. So haply shall thy days
Be many, and a blessing to mankind.

Book Three

It was a dreary morning[1] when the chaise
Rolled over the flat plains of Huntingdon
And through the open windows first I saw
The long-backed chapel of King's College rear
His pinnacles above the dusky groves.   5
Soon afterwards, we espied upon the road
A student clothed in gown and tasselled cap;
He passed – nor was I master of my eyes
Till he was left a hundred yards behind.
The place, as we approached, seemed more and more   10
To have an eddy's force, and sucked us in
More eagerly at every step we took.
Onward we drove beneath the castle; down
By Magdalene Bridge we went and crossed the Cam,
And at the Hoop we landed – famous inn!   15
    My spirit was up, my thoughts were full of hope;
Some friends I had – acquaintances who there
Seemed friends – poor simple schoolboys, now hung round
With honour and importance.[2] In a world
Of welcome faces up and down I roved;   20

---

[1] *a dreary morning*   probably that of 30 October 1787, on which date Wordsworth took up residence at St John's College, Cambridge.

[2] Wordsworth had no less than nine former school-friends at Cambridge, all of whom had by late October taken up residence; they would have included John Fleming (see Book II, ll. 348–50).

Questions, directions, counsel and advice,
Flowed in upon me from all sides. Fresh day
Of pride and pleasure! – to myself I seemed
A man of business and expense, and went
From shop to shop about my own affairs,   25
To tutors or to tailors as befell.
    I was the dreamer, they the dream; I roamed
Delighted through the motley spectacle –
Gowns (grave or gaudy), doctors, students, streets,
Lamps, gateways, flocks of churches, courts and towers: 30
Strange transformation for a mountain youth,
A northern villager! As if by word
Of magic or some fairy's power, at once
Behold me rich in moneys, and attired
In splendid clothes, with hose of silk, and hair   35
Glittering like rimy trees when frost is keen[3]
(My lordly dressing-gown, I pass it by,
With other signs of manhood which supplied
The lack of beard). The weeks went roundly on
With invitations, suppers, wine and fruit,   40
Smooth housekeeping within, and all without
Liberal, and suiting gentleman's array!
    The Evangelist St John my patron was:[4]
Three gloomy courts are his, and in the first
Was my abiding-place, a nook obscure.   45
Right underneath, the College kitchens made
A humming sound, less tuneable than bees
But hardly less industrious, with shrill notes
Of sharp command and scolding intermixed.
Near me was Trinity's loquacious clock   50
Who never let the quarters, night or day,
Slip by him unproclaimed, and told the hours

---

[3] Wordsworth wore his hair powdered, as was the fashion. Visiting him in December 1788, Dorothy remarked: 'it looked so odd to see smart powdered heads with black caps like helmets' (*EY* 19).

[4] *The Evangelist . . . was* St John's, Cambridge, is dedicated to the Evangelist; St John's, Oxford, to the Baptist.

Twice over with a male and female voice.[5]
Her pealing organ[6] was my neighbour too,
And from my bedroom I in moonlight nights   55
Could see right opposite, a few yards off,
The antechapel where the statue stood
Of Newton with his prism and silent face.[7]
    Of College labours, of the lecturer's room
(All studded round, as thick as chairs could stand,   60
With loyal students faithful to their books,
Half-and-half idlers, hardy recusants,[8]
And honest dunces), of important days –
Examinations, when the man was weighed
As in the balance[9] – of excessive hopes,   65
Tremblings withal and commendable fears,
Small jealousies and triumphs good or bad,
I make short mention. Things they were which then
I did not love, nor do I love them now:
Such glory was but little sought by me   70
And little won. But it is right to say
That even so early, from the first crude days
Of settling-time in this my new abode,
Not seldom I had melancholy thoughts
From personal and family regards[10]   75

[5] The clock of Trinity College Chapel sounds the hours with first a low-pitched, then a high-pitched bell.

[6] *pealing organ*   Cf. Milton, *Il Penseroso* 161–2: 'let the pealing organ blow, / To the full-voiced choir below'. Milton was himself an enthusiastic organist.

[7] The *Fourteen-Book Prelude* adds two lines at this point: 'The marble index of a Mind for ever / Voyaging through strange seas of Thought, alone' (iii. 62–3). Roubiliac's famous statue of Sir Isaac Newton (1755) stands inside the entrance of Trinity College Chapel.

[8] *recusants*   those who defied pressure to work.

[9] Cf. Daniel 5:27: 'Thou art weighed in the balances, and art found wanting'. Maxwell points to a pun on *examen* (balance). Wordsworth's College examinations produced varying results; see *WR* i. 166–8.

[10] Wordsworth felt pressured by his family's hope that he would distinguish himself at Cambridge and gain a fellowship at St John's, like his uncle, William Cookson. Although he read widely, with occasional good results in College examinations, he dropped mathematics, and was not therefore eligible for a classified degree.

(Wishing to hope without a hope), some fears
About my future worldly maintenance,
And, more than all, a strangeness in my mind,
A feeling that I was not for that hour,
Nor for that place. But wherefore be cast down?   80
Why should I grieve? I was a chosen son.
For hither I had come with holy powers
And faculties (whether to work or feel)
To apprehend all passions and all moods
Which time and place and season do impress   85
Upon the visible universe, and work
Like changes there by force of my own mind.
I was a freeman – in the purest sense
Was free – and to majestic ends was strong.
I do not speak of knowledge, moral truth   90
Or understanding; 'twas enough for me
To know that I was otherwise endowed.
    When the first glitter of the show was passed,
And the first dazzling of the taper-light,
As if with a rebound my mind returned   95
Into its former self. Oft did I leave
My comrades, and the crowd, buildings and groves,
And walked along the fields, the level fields,
With heaven's blue concave reared above my head
And now it was that, from such change entire   100
And this first absence from those shapes sublime
Wherewith I had been conversant, my mind
Seemed busier in itself than heretofore –
At least I more directly recognized
My powers and habits. Let me dare to speak   105
A higher language, say that now I felt
The strength and consolation that were mine.
As if awakened, summoned, roused, constrained,
I looked for universal things, perused
The common countenance of earth and heaven,   110
And, turning the mind in upon itself,
Pored, watched, expected, listened, spread my thoughts
And spread them with a wider creeping – felt

Incumbences[11] more awful,[12] visitings
Of the upholder, of the tranquil soul   115
Which underneath all passion lives secure,
A steadfast life. But peace; it is enough
To notice that I was ascending now
To such community with highest truth.
　A track pursuing not untrod before,   120
From deep analogies by thought supplied
Or consciousnesses not to be subdued,
To every natural form – rock, fruit or flower,
Even the loose stones that cover the highway –
I gave a moral life; I saw them feel,   125
Or linked them to some feeling. The great mass
Lay bedded in a quickening soul,[13] and all
Which I beheld respired[14] with inward meaning.
Thus much for the one presence, and the life
Of the great whole; suffice it here to add   130
That whatsoe'er of terror or of love
Or beauty, Nature's daily face put on
From transitory passions, unto this
I was as wakeful even as waters are
To the sky's motion, in a kindred sense   135
Of passion was obedient as a lute
That waits upon the touches of the wind.
So was it with me in my solitude;
So, often among multitudes of men.
Unknown, unthought of, yet I was most rich,   140
I had a world about me – 'twas my own,
I made it; for it only lived to me
And to the God who looked into my mind.
　Such sympathies would sometimes show themselves
By outward gestures and by visible looks –   145
Some called it madness; such indeed it was,
If childlike fruitfulness in passing joy,

---

[11] *Incumbences* spiritual broodings.
[12] *awful* awe-inspiring.
[13] The poet's soul gives life to (quickens) the natural world.
[14] *respired* breathed.

If steady moods of thoughtfulness matured
To inspiration, sort with such a name;
If prophecy be madness; if things viewed   150
By poets of old time, and, higher up,[15]
By the first men, earth's first inhabitants,
May in those tutored days no more be seen
With undisordered sight. But leaving this,
It was no madness; for I had an eye   155
Which in my strongest workings evermore
Was looking for the shades of difference
As they lie hid in all exterior forms,
Near or remote, minute or vast – an eye
Which from a stone, a tree, a withered leaf,   160
To the broad ocean and the azure heaven
Spangled with kindred multitude of stars,
Could find no surface where its power[16] might sleep,
Which spake perpetual logic to my soul,
And by an unrelenting agency   165
Did bind my feelings even as in a chain.
    And here, my friend, have I retraced my life
Up to an eminence, and told a tale
Of matters which not falsely I may call
The glory of my youth. Of genius, power,   170
Creation and divinity itself
I have been speaking, for my theme has been
What passed within me. Not of outward things
Done visibly for other minds – words, signs,
Symbols or actions – but of my own heart   175
Have I been speaking, and my youthful mind.
Oh heavens! how awful is the might of souls,
And what they do within themselves while yet
The yoke of earth is new to them, the world
Nothing but a wild field where they were sown.   180
This is in truth heroic argument[17]

[15] *higher up*   even longer ago.

[16] *its power*   The imagination sees beneath 'exterior' forms, speaks 'logic' to the soul, and 'binds' the emotions together.

[17] *This is in truth heroic argument*   As elsewhere, Wordsworth has in mind the opening

And genuine prowess, which I wished to touch
With hand however weak, but in the main
It lies far hidden from the reach of words.
Points have we all of us within our souls   185
Where all stand single; this I feel, and make
Breathings for incommunicable powers.
Yet each man is a memory to himself,
And therefore, now that I must quit this theme,
I am not heartless,[18] for there's not a man   190
That lives who hath not had his godlike hours,
And knows not what majestic sway we have
As natural beings in the strength of Nature.
   Enough – for now into a populous plain
We must descend. A traveller I am,   195
And all my tale is of myself; even so,
So be it, if the pure in heart delight
To follow me, and thou, oh honoured friend,[19]
Who in my thoughts art ever at my side,
Uphold as heretofore my fainting steps.[20]   200
   It hath been told already how my sight
Was dazzled by the novel show, and how
Erelong I did into myself return:
So did it seem, and so in truth it was –
Yet this was but short-lived; thereafter came   205
A less devout observance, visits paid
Remissly, at chance seasons, to a friend
Unsettled in the heart by cozenage
Of new affections.[21] I had made a change
In climate, and my nature's outward coat   210
Changed also, slowly and insensibly.

---

of *Paradise Lost*, Book IX, where Milton had claimed to be writing about a subject 'Not less but more heroic than the wrath / Of stern Achilles' (ll. 14–15). Wordsworth in turn is claiming that his subject – the growth of the mind – is 'Not less but more heroic' than Milton's.

[18] *heartless* disheartened.
[19] Coleridge.
[20] Cf. Milton, *Samson Agonistes*, 666: 'And fainting spirits uphold'.
[21] The friend who had been deceived in love appears only in this version of the poem.

To the deep quiet and majestic thoughts
Of loneliness succeeded empty shows
And superficial pastime, now and then
Forced labour, and more frequently forced hopes;   215
And, worse than all, a treasonable growth
Of indecisive judgements that impaired
And shook the mind's simplicity. And yet
This was a gladsome time. Could I behold
(Who, less insensible than sodden clay   220
On a sea-river's bed at ebb of tide,
Could have beheld) with undelighted heart
So many happy youths, so wide and fair
A congregation in its budding time
Of health, and hope, and beauty, all at once   225
So many diverse samples of the growth
Of life's sweet season? – could have seen unmoved
That miscellaneous garland of wild-flowers
Upon the matron temples[22] of a place
So famous through the world? To me at least   230
It was a goodly prospect, for, through youth,
Though I had been trained up to stand unpropped,
And independent musings pleased me so
That spells seemed on me when I was alone,
Yet could I only cleave to solitude   235
In lonesome places. If a throng was near,
That way I leaned by nature, for my heart
Was social, and loved idleness and joy.
   Not seeking those who might participate[23]
My deeper pleasures (nay, I had not once,   240
Though not unused to mutter lonesome songs,
Even with myself divided[24] such delight,
Or looked that way for aught that might be clothed
In human language), easily I passed
From the remembrances of better things,   245

---

[22] *That miscellaneous garland ... temples* undergraduates are like flowers that Cambridge, Wordsworth's *alma mater*, displays on her brow.
[23] *participate* share.
[24] *divided* shared.

And slipped into the weekday works of youth,
Unburdened, unalarmed, and unprofaned.[25]
Caverns there were within my mind which sun
Could never penetrate, yet did there not
Want[26] store of leafy arbours where the light   250
Might enter in at will. Companionships,
Friendships, acquaintances, were welcome all;
The meanest found some leaf or withered bough
To shine upon, and aid the gladsome show;[27]
We sauntered, played, we rioted, we talked   255
Unprofitable talk at morning hours,
Drifted about along the streets and walks,
Read lazily in lazy books, went forth
To gallop through the country in blind zeal
Of senseless horsemanship, or on the breast   260
Of Cam sailed boisterously, and let the stars
Come out, perhaps without one quiet thought.
   Such was the tenor of the opening act
In this new life. And yet I could not print
Ground where the grass had yielded to the steps   265
Of generations of illustrious men
Unmoved. I could not always lightly pass
Through the same gateways, sleep where they had slept,
Wake where they waked, range that enclosure old,
That garden of great intellects, undisturbed.   270
Place also by the side of this dark sense
Of nobler feeling, that those spiritual men,
Even the great Newton's own ethereal self,
Seemed humbled in these precincts, thence to be
The more beloved – invested here in tasks   275
Of life's plain business, as a daily garb
(Dictators at the plough[28]), a change that left
All genuine admiration unimpaired.

---

[25] *Unburdened, unalarmed, and unprofaned* a Miltonic phrasing (cf. *Paradise Lost*, v. 899), although it had been used also by Spenser and Shakespeare.
[26] *Want* lack.
[27] Ll. 253–4 appear only in this draft of the poem.
[28] Cincinnatus was ploughing when summoned to become Roman dictator in 458 BC.

Beside the pleasant mills of Trompington
I laughed with Chaucer;[29] in the hawthorn-shade   280
Heard him, while birds were warbling, tell his tales
Of amorous passion. And that gentle bard
Chosen by the muses for their page of state,
Sweet Spenser, moving through his clouded heaven
With the moon's beauty, and the moon's soft pace: 285
I called him brother, Englishman, and friend![30]
Yea, our blind poet, who in his later days
Stood almost single, uttering odious truth –
Darkness before, and danger's voice behind:[31]
Soul awful (if the earth hath ever lodged   290
An awful soul), I seemed to see him here
Familiarly, and in his scholar's dress
Bounding before me, yet a stripling youth –
A boy, no better, with his rosy cheeks
Angelical, keen eye, courageous look,   295
And conscious step of purity and pride.[32]
    Among the band of my compeers was one,
My class-fellow at school,[33] whose chance it was
To lodge in the apartments which had been,
Time out of mind, honoured by Milton's name –   300
The very shell reputed of the abode

---

[29] *The Reeve's Tale* is set in Trumpington and involves two Cambridge students from 'Fer in the north, I can nat telle where' (l. 95).

[30] Spenser was at Pembroke Hall, Cambridge, 1569–76. J. C. Maxwell notes echoes at ll. 284–5 of *Paradise Lost*, iv. 606–7, and viii. 163–6; see 'Milton in Wordsworth's Praise of Spenser', *N&Q*, 213 (1968), 22–3.

[31] Wordsworth is recalling Milton's description of himself:

On evil days though fallen, and evil tongues;
In darkness, and with dangers compassed round,
And solitude . . . (*Paradise Lost*, vii. 25–7)

[32] Milton attended Christ's College, Cambridge, 1625–32. Wordsworth sees him as the republican who denounced the Restoration; cf. *London 1802* (*Romanticism*, 276). The description of him may derive from the painting now in the National Portrait Gallery.

[33] *My class-fellow at school* Edward Birkett from Hawkshead Grammar School entered Christ's College in April 1786.

Which he had tenanted. Oh temperate bard!
One afternoon, the first time I set foot
In this thy innocent nest and oratory,[34]
Seated with others in a festive ring 305
Of commonplace convention, I to thee
Poured out libations, to thy memory drank,
Within my private thoughts, till my brain reeled,
Never so clouded by the fumes of wine
Before that hour or since. Thence forth I ran 310
From that assembly, through a length of streets
Ran ostrich-like, to reach our chapel door
In not a desperate or opprobrious time,
Albeit long after the importunate bell
Had stopped, with wearisome Cassandra[35] voice 315
No longer haunting the dark winter night
(Call back, oh friend, a moment to thy mind,
The place itself and custom of the rites).
Upshouldering in a dislocated lump
My surplice,[36] gloried in and yet despised, 320
I clove in pride through the inferior throng
Of the plain burghers, who in audience stood
On the last skirts of their permitted ground,
Beneath the pealing organ. Empty thoughts!
I am ashamed of them; and that great bard, 325
And thou, oh friend, who in thy ample mind
Hast stationed me for reverence and love,
Ye will forgive the weakness of that hour,
In some of its unworthy vanities
Brother of many more.
              In this mixed sort 330
The months passed on, remissly, not given up
To wilful alienation from the right,
Or walks of open scandal, but in vague
And loose indifference, easy likings, aims

[34] *oratory* shrine.

[35] Cassandra prophesied the fall of Troy; Wordsworth identifies himself with those who would prefer not to listen to her.

[36] *surplice* a white linen robe that members of College wore in Chapel.

Of a low pitch – duty and zeal dismissed,   335
Yet Nature, or a happy course of things,
Not doing in their stead the needful work.
The memory languidly revolved, the inner pulse
Of contemplation almost failed to beat.
Rotted as by a charm, my life became   340
A floating island,[37] an amphibious thing,
Unsound, of spongy texture, yet withal
Not wanting a fair face of water-weeds
And pleasant flowers. The thirst of living praise,
A reverence for the glorious dead, the sight   345
Of those long vistas, catacombs in which
Perennial minds lie visibly entombed,
There oft have stirred the heart of youth, and bred
A love of unremitting discipline.
Alas! such high commotion touched not me.   350
No look was in these walls to put to shame
My easy spirits, and discountenance
Their light composure, far less to instil
A patient strength of mind, firmly addressed
To arduous efforts. Nor was this the blame   355
Of others, but my own; I should in truth,
As far as doth concern my single self,
Misdeem most widely, lodging it elsewhere.
For I, bred up in Nature's lap, was even
As a spoiled child, and (rambling like the wind,   360
As I had done in daily intercourse
With those delicious rivers, solemn heights
And mountains, ranging like a fowl of the air)
I was ill-tutored for captivity –
To quit my pleasure, and from month to month   365
Take up a station calmly on the perch
Of sedentary peace. Those lovely forms
Had also left less space within my mind,

[37] Editors usually cite the floating island of Derwentwater, although there was one on Esthwaite which Wordsworth probably saw on a daily basis while at school. It was later the subject of a poem by Dorothy (*Romanticism*, 501–2).

Which, wrought upon instinctively, had found
A freshness in those objects of its love, 370
A winning power beyond all other power.
Not that I slighted books[38] (that were to lack
All sense), but other passions had been mine
More fervent, making me less prompt perhaps
To indoor study than was wise or well 375
Or fitted to my age.
　　　　　　　Yet I could shape
The image of a place which, soothed and lulled
As I had been, trained up in paradise
Among sweet garlands and delightful sounds,
Accustomed in my loneliness to walk 380
With Nature magisterially[39] – yet I,
Methinks, could shape the image of a place
Which with its aspect should have bent me down
To instantaneous service, should at once
Have made me pay to science and to arts 385
And written lore (acknowledged my liege-lord)
A homage frankly offered up, like that
Which I had paid to Nature. Toil and pains
In this recess which I had bodied forth[40]
Should spread from heart to heart; and stately groves, 390
Majestic edifices, should not want
A corresponding dignity within.
The congregating temper[41] which pervades
Our unripe years, not wanting, should be made
To minister to works of high attempt, 395
Which the enthusiast would perform with love.
Youth should be awed, possessed, as with a sense

---

[38] *Not that I slighted books* In June 1791 Dorothy wrote that her brother 'reads Italian, Spanish, French, Greek and Latin, and English, but never opens a mathematical book' (*EY* 52). Wordsworth's Cambridge reading included works by Ariosto, Tasso, Virgil, Marino, Petrarch, Metastasio, Sophocles, Tacitus, Horace, Livy, Demosthenes and Juvenal.

[39] *With Nature magisterially* as a master of Nature.

[40] *bodied forth* an echo of *A Midsummer Night's Dream*, V. i. 14–15: 'as imagination bodies forth / The forms of things unknown'.

[41] *The congregating temper* love of meeting together.

Religious, of what holy joy there is
In knowledge, if it be sincerely sought
For its own sake – in glory, and in praise,   400
If but by labour won, and to endure.
The passing day[42] should learn to lay aside
Her trappings here; she should retire, abashed
Before antiquity, and steadfast truth,
And strong book-mindedness, and over all   405
Should be a healthy, sound simplicity,
A seemly plainness – name it as you will,
Republican, or pious.[43]
                              If these thoughts
Be a gratuitous emblazonry
That does but mock this recreant age, at least   410
To folly and false-seeming[44] we might say:
'Wear not the vizard[45] of the ancient time
Upon a modest face; fling to the ground
Thy monkish caul,[46] and run no more abroad,
A grey-beard masquerader, dizened out[47]   415
In Superstition's cast-off garb, and jingling
Thy holy toy thou carriest in thy hand,
A bell as noisy as a common crier's[48] –
Dull thoughtless mummery, that brings disgrace
On the plain steeples of our English church,   420
Whose altars mid remotest village trees
Suffer for this![49] Even science[50] too, at hand
In daily sight of such irreverence,

[42] *The passing day* the present.

[43] Wordsworth leaves it to the reader to associate the plainness he recommends with either the republicanism of Plato or the puritanism of Milton.

[44] *To folly and false-seeming* Wordsworth's target is showy church ritual, as practised in the universities, contrasted with the lack of inner dedication.

[45] *vizard* mask.

[46] *caul* cap.

[47] *dizened out* dressed up.

[48] Incense is still swung, and bells sounded, at certain points of High Church communion services today.

[49] Ll. 408–22 exist in this version only in this early manuscript; they were thoroughly revised in subsequent drafts to form a much more focused attack on compulsory student attendance at Chapel.

[50] *science* knowledge, erudition.

Is smitten thence with an unnatural taint,
Loses her just authority, falls beneath   425
Collateral suspicion else unknown.'
This homespun truth did not escape me then,
Unthinking as I was, and I confess
That, having in my native hills given loose
To a schoolboy's dreaming, I had raised a pile[51]   430
Upon the basis of the coming time,
Which now before me melted fast away –
Which could not live, scarcely had life enough
To mock the builder.

                Oh, what joy it were
To see a sanctuary for our country's youth   435
Staid, venerable, a wide virgin grove
Primeval in its purity and depth,
Where, though the shades were filled with cheerfulness,
Nor indigent of[52] songs warbled from crowds
In under-coverts, yet the countenance   440
Of the whole place should wear a stamp of awe –
A habitation sober and demure
For ruminating creatures,[53] a domain
For quiet things to wander in, a haunt
In which the heron might delight to feed   445
By the shy rivers, and the pelican
Upon the cypress-spire in lonely thought
Might sit and sun himself.[54] Alas, alas!
In vain for such solemnity we look.
Our eyes are crossed by butterflies, our ears   450
Hear chattering popinjays; the inner heart
Is trivial, and the impresses without

---

[51] *raised a pile*   of hopes and expectations.

[52] *indigent of*   lacking.

[53] *ruminating creatures*   animals that chew (as well as think – their 'habitation' being the metaphor for the ideal university).

[54] De Selincourt notes that the pelican, and the metaphor of the virgin grove itself, was inspired by a travel-book, William Bartram's *Travels in North and South Carolina* (1794): 'The deep forests and distant hills re-echoed the cheering social lowings of domestic herds . . . . Behold, on yon decayed, defoliated cypress tree, the solitary wood pelican, dejectly perched upon its utmost elevated spire; he there, like an ancient venerable sage, sets himself up as a mark of derision, for the safety of his kindred tribes'. See *WR* i. 19.

Are of a gaudy region.[55]
                    Different sight
Those venerable doctors saw of old,
When all who dwelt within these famous walls   455
Led in abstemiousness a studious life,
When, in forlorn and naked chambers cooped
And crowded, o'er their ponderous books they sate,
Like caterpillars eating out their way
In silence, or with keen devouring noise   460
Not to be tracked or fathered.[56] Princes then
At matins[57] froze, and couched at curfew-time,[58]
Trained up through piety and zeal to prize
Spare diet, patient labour, and plain weeds.[59]
Oh seat of arts, renowned throughout the world,   465
Far different service in those homely days
The nurslings of the muses underwent
From their first childhood – in that glorious time[60]
When learning, like a stranger come from far,
Sounding through Christian lands her trumpet, roused   470
The peasant and the king; when boys and youths,
The growth of ragged villages and huts,
Forsook their homes, and (errant in the quest
Of patron, famous school or friendly nook
Where, pensioned, they in shelter might sit down)   475
From town to town and through wide-scattered realms
Journeyed with their huge folios in their hands,
And often, starting from some covert place,
Saluted the chance-comer on the road
Crying, 'An obolus, a penny give   480
To a poor scholar';[61] when illustrious men –

[55] *the impresses . . . region*   external impressions are of gaudiness.
[56] *fathered*   traced to a source.
[57] *matins*   morning prayer.
[58] *curfew-time*   dusk; scholars stopped working after dark since they could not afford candles.
[59] *weeds*   clothes.
[60] *that glorious time*   the Renaissance.
[61] Apparently a reference to the mendicancy of the deposed Byzantine general, Belisarius, said to have been blinded, and to have begged with the words: 'Date obolum Belisario'. As Owen points out, Belisarius was not a poor scholar.

Bucer, Erasmus, or Melancthon[62] – read
Before the doors and windows of their cells
By moonshine, through mere lack of taper-light.
    But peace to vain regrets! We see but darkly[63]   485
Even when we look behind us, and best things
Are not so pure by nature that they needs
Must keep to all (as fondly all believe)
Their highest promise. If the mariner,
When at reluctant distance he hath passed   490
Some fair enticing island, did but know
What fate might have been his, could he have brought
His bark to land upon the wished-for spot,
Good cause full often would he have to bless
The belt of churlish surf that scared him thence,   495
Or haste of the inexorable wind.
For me, I grieve not; happy is the man
Who only misses what I missed, who falls
No lower than I fell.
               I did not love
(As hath been noticed heretofore) the guise   500
Of our scholastic studies, could have wished
The river to have had an ampler range
And freer pace. But this I tax[64] not; far,
Far more I grieved to see among the band
Of those who in the field of contest stood   505
As combatants, passions that did to me
Seem low and mean – from ignorance of mine,
In part, and want of just forbearance, yet
My wiser mind grieves now for what I saw.
Willingly did I part from these, and turn   510
Out of their track to travel with the shoal[65]
Of more unthinking natures, easy minds
And pillowy, and not wanting love that makes

---

[62] Martin Bucer (1491–1551); Desiderius Erasmus (?1466–1536); Philip Melancthon (1497–1560) – great Renaissance scholars.
[63] *darkly* unclearly; Wordsworth echoes 1 Corinthians 13:12: 'For now we see through a glass, darkly'.
[64] *tax* blame.
[65] *shoal* crowd.

The day pass lightly on[66] – when foresight sleeps,
And wisdom and the pledges interchanged   515
With our own inner being are forgot.
      To books, our daily fare prescribed,[67] I turned
With sickly appetite, and when I went
At other times in quest of my own food
I chased not steadily the manly deer,   520
But laid me down to any casual feast
Of wildwood honey, or, with truant eyes
Unruly, peeped about for vagrant fruit.[68]
And as for what pertains to human life,
The deeper passions working round me here   525
(Whether of envy, jealousy, pride, shame,
Ambition, emulation, fear, or hope,
Or those of dissolute pleasure[69]) were by me
Unshared – nay more, were scarcely even observed,
So little was their hold upon my being,   530
As outward things that might administer
To knowledge or instruction. Hushed, meanwhile,
Was the under-mind, locked up in such a calm
That not a leaf of the great Nature stirred.
      Yet was this deep vacation[70] not given up   535
To utter waste. Hitherto I had stood
In my own mind remote from human life –
At least from what we commonly so name –
Even as a shepherd on a promontory
Who, lacking occupation, looks far forth   540
Into the endless sea, and rather makes

---

[66] These 'easy minds' had the kind of superficial love that makes time pass easily.

[67] Wordsworth's prescribed College syllabus is listed at *WR* i. 167–8.

[68] Books which he read for pleasure at Cambridge included *Paradise Lost*, Daniel Webb's *Inquiry into the Beauties of Painting* (1761), and the poems of William Drummond, John Ogilvie and Charlotte Smith.

[69] Counselling the undergraduate De Quincey in March 1804, about a month after composing these lines, Wordsworth remembered that 'The manners of the young men were very frantic and dissolute. . . . I need not say to you that there is no true dignity but in virtue and temperance, and, let me add, chastity' (*EY* 454).

[70] *vacation* ironic; for Wordsworth, term-time was a holiday from serious thought.

Than finds[71] what he beholds. And sure it is
That this first transit from the smooth delights
And wild outlandish walks of simple youth
To something that resembled an approach   545
Towards mortal business (to a privileged world
Within a world, a midway residence
With all its intervenient imagery)
Did better suit my visionary mind
(Far better than to have been bolted forth,[72]   550
Thrust out abruptly into fortune's way
Among the conflicts of substantial life),
By a more just gradation did lead on
To higher things, more naturally matured
For permanent possession[73] – better fruits,   555
Whether of truth or virtue, to ensue.
   In playful zest of fancy did we note
(How could we less?) the manners and the ways
Of those who in the livery were arrayed
Of good or evil fame, of those with whom   560
By frame of academic discipline
Perforce we were connected, men whose sway
And whose authority of office served
To set our minds on edge, and did no more.
Nor wanted we rich pastime of this kind,   565
Found everywhere but chiefly in the ring
Of the grave elders – men unscoured, grotesque
In character, tricked out like aged trees
Which through the lapse of their infirmity
Give ready place to any random seed   570
That chooses to be reared upon their trunks.
   Here on my view, confronting as it were

---

[71] *and rather makes / Than finds* The shepherd's mind is working imaginatively.
Wordsworth is recalling the shepherd in Thomson's *Castle of Indolence* who 'Sees on the
naked Hill . . . A vast Assembly moving to and fro: / Then all at once in Air dissolves the
wondrous Show' (i. 267–70).

[72] *bolted forth* expelled and locked out, cast into the rough-and-tumble of the world.

[73] University life was a 'midway' point that led the poet gradually ('By a more just
gradation') from the 'outlandish walks' of youth to 'higher things'.

Those shepherd swains whom I had lately left,
Did flash a different image of old age
(How different!), yet both withal alike   575
A book of rudiments for the unpractised sight,
Objects embossed, and which with sedulous care
Nature holds up before the eye of youth
In her great school – with further view,[74] perhaps:
To enter early on her tender scheme   580
Of teaching comprehension with delight
And mingling playful with pathetic thoughts.
    The surfaces of artificial life
And manners smoothed and trimmed, the delicate race[75]
Of colours, lurking, gleaming up and down   585
Through that state arras woven with silk and gold,
This wily interchange of snaky hues,[76]
Willingly and unwillingly revealed –
I had not learned to watch; and at this time,
Perhaps, had such been in my daily sight   590
I might have been indifferent thereto
As hermits are to tales of distant things.
Hence for these rarities elaborate
Having no relish yet, I was content
With the more homely produce rudely piled   595
In this our coarser warehouse. At this day

---

[74] *further view*   another aim, besides holding up the book of rudiments.

[75] *race*   Owen suggests possible meanings, including 'family', 'collection', 'series', 'contest' and 'rapid movement'. I suspect that Wordsworth is simply using the word metaphorically, meaning that the different threads 'run' rapidly through the fabric.

[76] The image in ll. 586–7 is drawn from Spenser, who describes an arras, or tapestry, thus:

Woven with gold and silke so close and nere,
That the rich metall lurked privily,
As faining to be hid from envious eye;
Yet here, and there, and every where unwares
It shewd it selfe, and shone unwillingly;
Like a discolourd Snake, whose hidden snares
Through the greene gras his long bright burnisht backe declares.
(*Faerie Queene*, III. xi. 28)

I smile in many a mountain solitude
At passages and fragments in my mind
Of that inferior exhibition, played
By wooden images, a theatre   600
For wake or fair. And oftentimes do flit
Remembrances before me of old men,
Old humorists[77] who have been long in their graves,
And having almost in my mind put off
Their human names, have into phantoms passed   605
Of texture midway betwixt life and books.
　　I play the loiterer; 'tis enough to say
That here in dwarf proportions were expressed
The limbs of the great world – its goings-on
Collaterally portrayed as in mock fight,   610
A tournament of blows, some hardly[78] dealt
Though short of mortal combat – and whate'er
Might of this pageant be supposed to hit
A simple rustic's notice (this way less,
More that way) was not wasted upon me.   615
And yet this spectacle may well demand
A more substantial name, no mimic show –
Itself a living part of a live whole,
A creek of the vast sea. For short-lived praise
Here lived in state, and, fed with daily alms,   620
Retainers won away from solid good.
And here was Labour, his own bond-slave; Hope,
That never set the pains against the prize;
Idleness, halting with his weary clog,
And poor misguided Shame, and witless Fear,   625
And simple Pleasure, foraging for Death;[79]
Honour misplaced, and Dignity astray;
Feuds, factions, flatteries, enmity, and guile;
Murmuring Submission and bald Government

[77] *humorists* eccentrics.
[78] *hardly* forcefully, severely.
[79] *And simple Pleasure, foraging for Death* Pleasure seeks food on behalf of Death; Owen suggests that this might be a reference to 'patrons of prostitutes who acquired syphilis'.

(The idol weak as the idolator),   630
And Decency and Custom starving Truth,
And blind Authority beating with his staff
The child that might have led him;[80] Emptiness
Followed as a good omen, and meek Worth
Left to itself, unheard of and unknown.   635
   Of these and other kindred notices[81]
I cannot say what portion is in truth
The naked recollection of that time,
And what more recent coinage. But delight
That, in an easy temper lulled asleep,   640
Is still, with[82] innocence, its own reward –
This surely was not wanting. Carelessly
I gazed, roving as through a cabinet[83]
Or wide museum (thronged with fishes, gems,
Birds, crocodiles, shells) where little can be seen   645
Well understood, or naturally endeared,
Yet still does every step bring something forth
That quickens,[84] pleases, stings; and here and there
A casual rarity is singled out
And has its brief perusal, then gives way   650
To others, all supplanted in their turn.
Meanwhile amid this gaudy congress,[85] framed
Of things by Nature most unneighbourly,
The head turns round and cannot right itself,
And though an aching and a barren sense   655
Of gay confusion still be uppermost,
With few wise longings and but little love,
Yet something to the memory sticks at last
Whence profit may be drawn in times to come.
   Thus in unburdened[86] idleness, my friend,   660

---

[80] Cf. Isaiah 11:6: 'a little child shall lead them'.
[81] *notices* observations.
[82] *still, with* always, like.
[83] *cabinet* display-case.
[84] *quickens* stimulates.
[85] *congress* throng, assembly.
[86] *unburdened* changed in subsequent drafts to 'submissive'.

The labouring time of autumn, winter, spring,
Nine months, rolled pleasingly away; the tenth
Returned me to my native hills again.

Book Four

Those walks, well worthy to be prized and loved –   [IV, 121]
Regretted, that word too was on my tongue,
But they were richly laden with all good
And cannot be remembered but with thanks
And gratitude and perfect joy of heart –   5   [IV, 125]
Those walks did now like a returning spring
Come back on me again.[1] When first I made
Once more the circuit of our little lake,[2]
If ever happiness hath lodged with man
That day consummate[3] happiness was mine,   10   [IV, 130]
Wide-spreading, steady, calm, contemplative.
The sun was set, or setting, when I left
Our cottage-door, and evening soon brought on
A sober hour – not winning or serene
(For cold and raw the air was, and untuned),   15   [IV, 135]
But as a face we love is sweetest then
When sorrow damps it, or, whatever look
It chance to wear is sweetest if the heart
Have fullness in itself: even so with me

---

[1] *Came back on me again* Wordsworth returned to Hawkshead during the long vacations of 1788 and 1789, when he again boarded with Ann Tyson. His brothers Christopher and Richard were also staying with her at that time. It was during the vacation of 1789 that he purchased an umbrella – still, at the time, an unusual possession – which he presumably took out on the walks he is about to mention (Thompson, 144).

[2] *our little lake* Esthwaite Water.

[3] *consummate* total, complete.

It fared that evening. Gently did my soul   20   [IV, 140]
Put off her veil,[4] and self-transmuted stood
Naked as in the presence of her God.
As on I walked, a comfort seemed to touch
A heart that had not been disconsolate;
Strength came where weakness was not known to be, 25   [IV, 145]
At least not felt; and restoration came,
Like an intruder knocking at the door
Of unacknowledged weariness.
                             I took
The balance in my hand and weighed myself.
I saw but little, and thereat was pleased;   30   [IV, 150]
Little did I remember, and even this
Still pleased me more. But I had hopes and peace
And swellings of the spirits, was wrapped and soothed,
Conversed with promises, had glimmering views
How life pervades the undecaying mind;   35   [IV, 155]
How the immortal soul with godlike powers
Informs, creates, and thaws the deepest sleep
That time can lay upon her; how, on earth,
Man, if he do but live within the light
Of high endeavours, daily spreads abroad   40   [IV, 160]
His being with a strength that cannot fail.
Nor was there want of milder thoughts – of love,
Of innocence and holiday repose,
And more than pastoral quiet in the heart
Of amplest projects, and a peaceful end   45   [IV, 165]
At last, or glorious, by endurance won.
Thus musing, in a wood I sate me down
Alone, continuing there to muse; meanwhile
The mountain-heights were slowly overspread
With darkness, and before a rippling breeze   50   [IV, 170]
The long lake lengthened out its hoary line.[5]

---

[4] *Gently did my soul . . . veil*   Moses unveiled his shining face in the presence of Jehovah on Mount Sinai, but covered it when he descended to meet the people (Exodus 34:33–4).
[5] *before a rippling breeze . . . hoary line*   At the time of his return to Hawkshead, during the long vacation of 1789, Wordsworth was an enthusiastic reader of the works of William

And in the sheltered coppice[6] where I sate,
Around me from among the hazel leaves
(Now here, now there, stirred by the straggling wind)
Came intermittingly a breath-like sound,   55   [IV, 175]
A respiration short and quick, which oft –
Yea, might I say, again and yet again –
Mistaking for the panting of my dog,
The off-and-on companion of my walk,[7]
I turned my head to look if he were there.[8]   60   [IV, 180]
   Nor less do I remember to have felt   [IV, 222]
Distinctly manifested at this time
A dawning, even as of another sense:
A human-heartedness about my love   [IV, 225]
For objects – hitherto the gladsome air   65
Of my own private being and no more,
Which I had loved even as a blessed spirit
Or angel if he were to dwell on earth
Might love, in individual happiness.   [IV, 230]

Gilpin, the popular theorist of the picturesque and the sublime, and author of *Observations on the Lakes* (*WR* i. 116(i) and (ii)). One of the most important of the effects Gilpin described was when a lake is skimmed by a breeze which causes it to be '*tremblingly alive all over*': 'This tremulous shudder . . . will run in lengthened parallels, and separate the reflections upon the surface, which are lost on one side, and taken up on the other. This is perhaps the most picturesque form, which water assumes; as it affords the painter an opportunity of throwing in those lengthened lights and shades, which give the greatest variety and clearness to water.' (*Observations on the Lakes*, i. 100) Wordsworth 'painted' this effect in his Hawkshead poem, *The Vale of Esthwaite* (1787):

> While winds, faint-rippling, paint it white,
> The long lake lengthening stretches on the sight . . . (DC MS 3)

A similar effect occurs at the climax of *An Evening Walk* (ll. 339–44), on which Wordsworth was probably working during his 1789 visit to Hawkshead. The picturesque wind is a forerunner of the *Prelude*'s correspondent breeze.

  [6] *coppice* copse, small wood.

  [7] *The off-and-on companion of my walk* Cowper addressed the 'dear companion of my walks' (*Task*, i. 144).

  [8] Anyone who thinks Wordsworth is incapable of self-parody should take a close look at this sentence, in which the numinous breeze familiar from Book I, ll. 1ff., collapses into the panting of his canine friend. The dog, a Lakeland terrier, belonged to Ann Tyson.

But now there opened in me other thoughts   70
Of change, congratulation and regret –
A new-born feeling. It spread far and wide:
The trees, the mountains shared it, and the brooks,
The stars of heaven (now seen in their old haunts),   [IV, 235]
White Sirius glittering o'er the southern crags,   75
Orion with his belt, and those fair seven[9]
(Acquaintances of every little child),
And Jupiter, my own beloved star.[10]
Whatever shadings of mortality   [IV, 240]
Had fallen upon these objects heretofore   80
Were different in kind. Not tender; strong,
Deep, gloomy were they, and severe, the scatterings
Of childhood – and moreover had given way
In later youth to beauty, and to love   [IV, 245]
Enthusiastic, to delight and joy.[11]   85
     Auspicious was this onset, and the days
That followed marched in flattering symphony[12]
With such a fair presage; but 'twas not long
Ere fallings-off and indirect desires
Told of an inner weakness. Much I loved –   90   [IV, 270]
Loved deeply all that I had loved before,
More deeply even than ever – but a throng
Of heady thoughts jostling each other, gauds[13]
And feast and dance and public revelry,[14]

---

⁹ *those fair seven*   the Pleiades – the seven daughters of Atlas, who became a constellation after death.

¹⁰ Wordsworth was born under Jupiter, 7 April 1770.

¹¹ Once again, Wordsworth is thinking in Burkean terms. What he had once considered sublime, he now began to think of as beautiful. Owen makes comparison with Wordsworth's comments on the sublime and the beautiful in a discarded prose fragment for his *Guide to the Lakes*: 'as we advance in life, we can escape upon the invitation of our more placid & gentle nature from those obtrusive qualities in an object sublime in its general character; which qualities, at an earlier age, precluded imperiously the perception of beauty which that object if contemplated under another relation would have been capable of imparting' (*Prose Works*, ii. 349).

¹² *symphony*   harmony; an unusual figurative usage of this word.

¹³ *gauds*   gaieties, parties.

¹⁴ *And feast . . . and public revelry*   Cf. Milton, *L'Allegro*, 127: 'pomp and feast and revelry'.

And sports and games less pleasing in themselves   95   [IV, 275]
Than as they were a badge, glossy and fresh,
Of manhood and of freedom – these did now
Seduce me from the firm habitual quest
Of feeding pleasures from that eager zeal,
Those yearnings which had every day been mine   100   [IV, 280]
(A wild, unworldly-minded youth, given up
To Nature and to books, or at the most
From time to time by inclination shipped[15]
One among many in societies
That were, or seemed, as simple as myself).   105   [IV, 285]
   This flattering idleness, this giddy chase[16]   [IV, 304]
Of trivial pleasure, was a poor exchange
For books and Nature at that early age –
'Tis true, some casual knowledge might be gleaned[17]
Of character or life, but at that time   110
Of outside manners I took little note,
And all my deeper purposes lay elsewhere.   [IV, 310]
Far better had it been to exalt the mind
By solitary study, to uphold
Intense desire by thought and quietness –   115
And yet in chastisement of these regrets
The memory of one particular hour   [IV, 315]
Doth here rise up against me. In a throng,
A festal company of maids and youths,
Old men and matrons staid – promiscuous rout,[18]   120
A medley of all tempers[19] – I had passed
The night in dancing, gaiety and mirth,   [IV, 320]
With din of instruments and shuffling feet,
And glancing forms and tapers glittering,

---

[15] *shipped*   Owen is unable to gloss this word (see Owen *WC* 103). The usage appears to be metaphorical – the young Wordsworth sets out of his own accord ('by inclination shipped') to mix with people who seemed 'as simple as myself'.

[16] *This flattering idleness, this giddy chase*   The *Thirteen-Book Prelude* revises this to 'This vague heartless chase'.

[17] *some casual . . . gleaned*   The draft contains an alternative reading: 'some embryo knowledge might be gathered thus'.

[18] *promiscuous rout*   a varied party of people.

[19] *tempers*   temperaments.

And unaimed prattle flying up and down,   125
Bustle, and spirits strained, and here and there
Slight shocks of young love-liking interpersed   [IV, 325]
That mounted up like joy into the head
And tingled through the veins.
                              Ere we retired
The cock had crowed, the sky was bright with day;   130
Two miles I had to walk along the fields
Before I reached my home.[20] Magnificent   [IV, 330]
The morning was, a memorable pomp
More glorious than I ever had beheld.
The sea was laughing at a distance; all   135
The solid mountains were as bright as clouds,
Grain-tinctured,[21] drenched in empyrean[22] light;   [IV, 335]
And in the meadows and the lower grounds
Was all the sweetness of a common dawn –
Dews, vapours, and the melody of birds,[23]   140
And labourers going forth into the fields.
Ah, need I say, dear friend, that to the brim   [IV, 340]
My heart was full? I made no vows, but vows
Were then made for me – bond unknown to me
Was given, that I should be, else sinning greatly,   145
A dedicated spirit.[24] On I walked
In blessedness, which even yet remains.   [IV, 345]

---

[20] Thompson suggests that Wordsworth was returning to Ann Tyson's cottage at Colthouse over Claife Heights from Belle Grange on Windermere (Thompson, 126).

[21] *Grain-tinctured* Milton described Raphael's wings as 'Sky-tinctured grain' (*Paradise Lost*, v. 285); he meant blue, but Wordsworth means scarlet (grain being the scarlet dye of cochineal).

[22] *empyrean* the highest heaven, sphere of the pure element of fire.

[23] *Dews, vapours, and the melody of birds* Cf. *Paradise Lost*, viii. 527–8: 'fruits and flowers, / Walks, and the melody of birds'.

[24] *A dedicated spirit* The dedication is, presumably, to poetry and, ultimately, *The Recluse*. Owen *WC* 108 points out that it is based on the rite of baptism in the Book of Common Prayer, where the godparents pray that Christ 'release [the infant] of his sins' ('else sinning greatly'), and act as 'sureties' for his Christian conduct ('bond unknown to me / Was given'). As Owen comments, 'Wordsworth is baptized, no doubt with Nature as his sponsor, into the company of the blessed.' Wordsworth would have known the Book of Common Prayer by heart; it is worth noting that his son John was baptized 17 July 1803, less than a year before these lines were composed.

Thus deep enjoyments did not fail me then –
Even deeper sometimes, as they found a mind
Engrossed with other matter, and estranged –   150
Instructed it to value and to know
What it possessed, though slighted and misused,
For surely at that time a falling-off
Had taken place, not light and yet
A flagging of the season. It would ask   155   [IV, 286]
Some skill, and longer time than may be spared,
To unfold even to myself these vanities
And how they wrought – but sure it is that now
Contagious air did oft environ me,[25]   [IV, 290]
Unknown among these haunts in former days.   160
The very garments that I wore appeared
To prey upon my strength,[26] and stopped the course
And quiet stream of self-forgetfulness.
Something there was about me that perplexed   [IV, 295]
Th' authentic sight of reason, interfered   165
With that religious dignity of mind
Which is the very faculty of truth,
Which wanting – either, from the first
A function never lighted up, or else   [IV, 300]
Extinguished – man, a creature great and good,   170
Seems but a pageant plaything with vile claws,[27]
And this great frame of breathing elements
A senseless idol.[28]   [IV, 304]

[25] There is a general recollection of *Hamlet*, II. ii. 299–303: 'this most excellent canopy, the air, look you, this brave o'erhanging firmament . . . why, it appeareth nothing to me but a foul and pestilent congregation of vapors.'

[26] *strength* Wordsworth originally wrote 'self', deleted it, and entered the present reading. The classical reference is of course to the tunic of the centaur, Nessus. Tainted with venom, it burnt off Hercules' skin and some of his flesh when he put it on.

[27] *a pageant plaything with vile claws* Owen notes that Wordsworth refers to a life-sized model of a tiger attacking a white man, captured at Seringapatam in 1799 and probably shown to Wordsworth by Lamb at the East India Company in 1802; it is now at the Victoria and Albert Museum in London. See W. J. B. Owen, 'Tipu's Tiger', *N&Q* 115 (1970), 379–80.

[28] There is a general recollection of the tone and content of Hamlet's speech to Rosencrantz and Guildenstern: 'What a piece of work is a man, how noble in reason, how infinite in faculties . . . and yet to me what is this quintessence of dust?' (II. ii. 303–8).

                Nevertheless, my friend,
That summer was not seldom interspersed
With primitive hours,[29] when by these hindrances   175   [IV, 355]
Uncrossed, I realized within myself
Conformity as just as that of old
To the end and written spirit of God's works,
Whether held forth in Nature or in man.

    From many wanderings that have left   180   [IV, 360]
Remembrances not lifeless, I will here
Single out one, then pass to other themes.
A favourite pleasure hath it been with me,[30]
Even from the time of earliest youth, to walk
Along the public way, when, for the night   185   [IV, 365]
Deserted, in its silence it assumes
A character of deeper quietness
Than pathless solitudes. At such an hour
Once, ere these summer months were passed away,[31]
I slowly mounted up a steep ascent[32]   190   [IV, 370]
Where the road's watery surface, to the ridge
Of that sharp rising, glittered in the moon,
And seemed before my eyes another stream[33]
Stealing with silent lapse[34] to join the brook[35]
That murmured in the valley.

                          On I went   195   [IV, 375]
Tranquil, receiving in my own despite

---

   [29] *That summer ... hours* That summer, Wordsworth frequently engaged with Nature
as he had done in childhood.

   [30] Ll. 183–321 were first composed at Alfoxden in early February 1798 as an independent fragment, *The Discharged Soldier* (see Cornell *LB* 277–82). De Selincourt notes
that the encounter took place during Wordsworth's first long vacation from Cambridge in
summer 1788.

   [31] He had spent the day at a regatta on Windermere, and much of the night at a party
that followed it, probably at the Ferry Inn (see *Fourteen-Book Prelude*, iv. 370–8; Thompson,
134).

   [32] *a steep ascent* Briers Brow, above the ferry on the Hawkshead side of the lake.

   [33] *the road's watery surface ... stream* A few days before these lines were composed,
Dorothy had written in her journal: 'The road to the village of Holford glittered like
another stream' (*DWJ* i. 5).

   [34] *lapse* fall, flow; cf. *Paradise Lost*, viii. 263: 'And liquid lapse of murmuring streams'.

   [35] *brook* Sawrey Brook, Owen suggests.

Amusement, as I slowly passed along,
From such near objects as from time to time
Perforce intruded on the listless sense
Quiescent and disposed to sympathy,   200   [IV, 380]
With an exhausted mind worn out by toil
And all unworthy of the deeper joy
That waits on distant prospect – cliff or sea,
The dark blue vault and universe of stars.
Thus did I steal along that silent road,   205   [IV, 385]
My body from the stillness drinking in
A restoration like the calm of sleep,
But sweeter far. Above, before, behind,
Around me, all was peace and solitude:
I looked not round, nor did the solitude   210   [IV, 390]
Speak to my eye, but it was heard and felt.
Oh happy state, what beauteous pictures now
Rose in harmonious imagery! They rose
As from some distant region of my soul
And came along like dreams; yet such as left   215   [IV, 395]
Obscurely mingled with their passing forms
A consciousness of animal delight,
A self-possession felt in every pause
And every gentle movement of my frame.[36]
    While thus I wandered, step by step led on,[37]   220   [IV, 400]
It chanced a sudden turning in the road
Presented to my view an uncouth shape,[38]
So near that, slipping back into the shade
Of a thick hawthorn, I could mark him well,
Myself unseen. He was of stature tall,   225   [IV, 405]
A man more meagre, as it seemed to me,
Was never seen abroad by night or day.

[36] *self-possession . . . frame* awareness of physical well-being diffused through the body and its activity (Owen *WC* 103).

[37] *step by step led on* In *Paradise Regained* Christ wanders into the desert, 'Thought following thought, and step by step led on' (i. 192).

[38] *an uncouth shape* perhaps a reminiscence of *Paradise Lost*, ii. 666, which describes Death: 'The other shape, / If shape it might be called that shape had none'. Wordsworth would have known Burke's comments on the lines (see *Romanticism*, 3–4).

His arms were long, and bare his hands; his mouth
Looked ghastly in the moonlight; from behind,
A milestone propped him,[39] and his figure seemed   230
Half sitting and half standing. I could mark
That he was clad in military garb,
Though faded yet entire. He was alone,   [IV, 415]
Had no attendant, neither dog, nor staff,
Nor knapsack; in his very dress appeared   235
A desolation, a simplicity
That was akin to solitude. Long time
Did I peruse him with a mingled sense   [IV, 420]
Of fear and sorrow. From his lips meanwhile
There issued murmuring sounds, as if of pain   240
Or of uneasy thought; yet still his form
Kept the same steadiness, and at his feet
His shadow lay, and moved not. In a glen   [IV, 425]
Hard by, a village stood,[40] whose roofs and doors
Were visible among the scattered trees,   245
Scarce distant from the spot an arrow's flight.[41]
I wished to see him move, but he remained
Fixed to his place, and still from time to time   [IV, 430]
Sent forth a murmuring voice of dead complaint,
Groans scarcely audible.
              Without self-blame   250
I had not thus prolonged my watch; and now,
Subduing my heart's specious cowardice,[42]
I left the shady nook where I had stood   [IV, 435]
And hailed him. Slowly from his resting-place
He rose, and with a lean and wasted arm   255
In measured gesture lifted to his head
Returned my salutation, then resumed
His station as before. And when erelong   [IV, 440]
I asked his history, he in reply

---

[39] *A milestone propped him* Thompson (139) identified it as the third milestone from Hawkshead, just beyond Far Sawrey; the milestone has since disappeared from that spot.

[40] *a village stood* Far Sawrey.

[41] *an arrow's flight* 300 yards, according to Owen *WC* 101.

[42] *my heart's specious cowardice* he was motivated by fear rather than kindness.

Was neither slow nor eager, but unmoved   260
And with a quiet uncomplaining voice,
A stately air of mild indifference,
He told in simple fact a soldier's tale –   [IV, 445]
That in the tropic islands[43] he had served,
Whence he had landed scarcely ten days past;   265
That on his landing he had been dismissed,
And now was travelling to his native home.
At this I turned and looked towards the village,   [IV, 450]
But all were gone to rest, the fires all out,
And every silent window to the moon   270
Shone with a yellow glitter. 'No one there',
Said I, 'is waking; we must measure back
The way which we have come. Behind yon wood   [IV, 455]
A labourer dwells, and (take it on my word)
He will not murmur should we break his rest,   275
And with a ready heart will give you food
And lodging for the night.' At this he stooped
And from the ground took up an oaken staff   [IV, 460]
By me yet unobserved – a traveller's staff
Which I suppose from his slack hand had dropped, 280
And lain till now neglected in the grass.
   Towards the cottage without more delay
We shaped our course. As it appeared to me   [IV, 465]
He travelled without pain, and I beheld
With ill-suppressed astonishment his tall   285
And ghostly figure moving at my side;
Nor, while we thus were journeying, did I fail
To question him of what he had endured   [IV, 470]
From war, or battle, or the pestilence.
He all the while was in demeanour calm,   290
Concise in answer. Solemn and sublime
He might have seemed, but that in all he said
There was a strange half-absence, and a tone   [IV, 475]

---

[43] *tropic islands* West Indies. An anachronism: Wordsworth has in mind the campaigns
against the French that occurred in the mid-1790s, although the encounter took place
during the long vacation of 1788. Conditions were bad; 40,000 British troops had died of
yellow fever by 1796. Survivors were often diseased, and had no alternative but to beg in
the streets.

Of weakness and indifference, as of one
Remembering the importance of his theme 295
But feeling it no longer. We advanced
Slowly, and ere we to the wood were come
Discourse had ceased. Together on we passed [IV, 480]
In silence through the shades gloomy and dark;
Then, turning up along an open field, 300
We gained the cottage.⁴⁴ At the door I knocked,
Calling aloud, 'My friend, here is a man
By sickness overcome. Beneath your roof [IV, 485]
This night let him find rest, and give him food,
If food he need, for he is faint and tired.' 305
Assured that now my comrade would repose
In comfort, I entreated that henceforth
He would not linger in the public ways [IV, 490]
But ask for proper furtherance, and help
Such as his state required. At this reproof, 310
With the same ghastly mildness in his look,
He said, 'My trust is in the God of Heaven,
And in the eye of him that passes me.' [IV, 495]
   The cottage door was speedily unlocked,
And now the soldier touched his hat again 315
With his lean hand, and in a voice that seemed
To speak with a reviving interest [IV, 500]
Till then unfelt, he thanked me; I returned
The blessing of the poor unhappy man,
And so we parted. Back I cast a look, 320
And lingered near the door a little space,
Then sought with quiet heart my distant home.⁴⁵ [IV, 504]
   Enough of private sorrow – longest lived
Is transient, and severest doth not lack
A mitigation in th' assured trust 325
Of the grave's quiet comforts⁴⁶ – blessed home,⁴⁷

---

⁴⁴ The cottager apparently lived at Briers, where, Thompson (140) says, there were two principal houses and two cottages.

⁴⁵ Wordsworth had another three miles to walk before he would reach Colthouse.

⁴⁶ *severest . . . comforts* The prospect of death is enough to mitigate even the most severe.

⁴⁷ *home* the figurative use of 'home' as meaning the grave is fairly common; Wordsworth refers to the 'long long home' in *The Vale of Esthwaite* (1787).

Inheritance perhaps vouchsafed to man
Alone of all that suffer on the earth.
Yet even in the steadiest mood of reason, when[48]   [V, 1]
All sorrow for thy transient pains   330
Goes out, it grieves me for thy lot, oh man,
Thou paramount creature,[49] for thy race, while ye
Shall sojourn on this planet – not for what   [V, 5]
Thou suffer'st (that weight, albeit heavy,
I charm away[50]), but for thy powers, there   335
My sadness finds its fuel. Thou hast wrought,
By reason and by passion – which itself
Is highest reason in a soul sublime –
Great things well worthy of enduring life.
And yet we feel, we cannot help but feel,   340   [V, 20]
That these must perish. Trembling of the heart
It gives to think that the immortal spirit
No more should need such garments; and yet man
Might sorrow for the creative earth,
And man, as long as he is the child of earth,   345
Might almost weep to know what he may lose,[51]   [V, 25]
And yet not die themselves, but still survive,
Mother and son yet living as before –
Helpless, depressed, forlorn, disconsolate,
Abject, and all his glory passed away.[52]   350
A thought is sometimes with me, and I say:
'Should dislocation[53] on this star[54] of ours,

---

[48] Within only a few weeks of their composition, ll. 329–70 were revised to form *Thirteen-Book Prelude*, v. 1–48.

[49] *Thou paramount creature* Wordsworth is again recalling *Hamlet*: 'What a piece of work is man . . . how like an angel in comprehension, how like a god! the beauty of the world; the paragon of animals; and yet to me what is this quintessence of dust?' (II. ii. 303–8).

[50] *charm away* ignore.

[51] Shakespeare, Sonnet 64, ll. 13–14: 'This thought is as a death, which cannot choose / But weep to have that which it fears to lose'.

[52] Man goes on living, abject and disconsolate, knowing that works of art and other intellectual achievements ('Great things well worthy of enduring life') cannot endure.

[53] *dislocation* removal from its orbit.

[54] *star* earth, rather than the sun.

Seized, smitten, and wrenched to the heart;
Should fire be sent from far to wither all   [V, 30]
Her pleasant habitations, and dry up   355
Old Ocean in the bed, left singed and bare,[55]
Yet would the vital spirit of her frame
Subsist victoriously, and peace ensue,
And kindlings like the morning – presage   [V, 35]
(Though slow perhaps) of the returning day.   360
But all the meditation of man's mind,
The adamantine holds[56] of quiet thought
Or passionate (where bards and sages dwell,
Twin builders-up of consecrated truth),
Sensuous or intellectual, works of these   365
Exempt from all internal injury –
Where would they be? Oh why has not the mind   [V, 44]
Some element to stamp her image on
In Nature somewhat nearer to her own?[57]
Why, gifted with such powers to spread abroad   370
Her spirit, must it lodge in shrines so frail?'[58]   [V, 48]
    Rarely, and with reluctance, would I stoop   [V, 223]
To transitory themes,[59] yet I rejoice –
And, by these thoughts admonished, must speak out   [V, 225]
Thanksgivings from my heart – that I was reared   375

---

[55] Some of Wordsworth's ideas here may derive from Thomas Burnet's *Sacred Theory of the Earth*, Book III of which is entitled 'Concerning the Conflagration'; Wordsworth owned a copy of Burnet at Rydal Mount (Shaver, 42).

[56] *adamantine holds* indestructible fortresses.

[57] *own* Wordsworth heavily deleted a word at this point that Reed construes as '[?being]'. I cannot improve on this, but it is highly doubtful, and I have therefore substituted the reading of MS M. Wordsworth is lamenting the fact that works of imagination cannot be imprinted ('stamped') on a substance with the same indestructibility as quiet or passionate thought.

[58] The dream of the Arab with his stone and shell followed at this point in the preceding manuscript (*Thirteen-Book Prelude*, v. 49–165), and would do so in subsequent drafts. Given the arrangement of material in MS W, however, and in view of the various line-lengths involved, it seems unlikely to have been included in the *Five-Book Prelude*.

[59] Wordsworth rightly recognized the controversy over different ways of educating children to be of its time. However, the portrait of the infant prodigy was necessary as a foil to the Winander boy (ll. 472–505 below).

Safe from an evil which these days have laid
Upon the children of the land, a pest[60]
That might have dried me up, body and soul. 　　　　　　　　[V, 229]
Let few words paint it: 'tis a child – no child, 　　　　　　　[V, 294]
But a dwarf man – in knowledge, virtue, skill, 　　　380
In what he is not and in what he is,
The noontide shadow of a man complete;
A worshipper of worldly seemliness,
Not quarrelsome (for that were far beneath
His dignity), with gifts he bubbles o'er 　　　　　　　385　　[V, 300]
As generous as a fountain. Selfishness
May not come near him, gluttony or pride;
The wandering beggars propagate his name,
Dumb creatures find him tender as a nun.[61]
Yet deem him not for this a naked dish 　　　　　390　　[V, 305]
Of goodness merely, he is garnished out:
Arch are his notices,[62] and nice his sense
Of the ridiculous; deceit and guile
He can look through and through in pleasant spleen,[63]
At the broad follies of the licensed world;[64] 　　　395　　[V, 311]

---

[60] *pest* plague. Wordsworth's target is the tradition of educationalists who followed in the wake of Locke's *Some Thoughts Concerning Education* (1693). These include Rousseau's *Emile* (1762), which Wordsworth had read by 1796 (*WR* i. 214(iii)); Richard and Maria Edgeworth's *Practical Education* (1798) (read by Coleridge shortly after publication – see Griggs, i. 418) and Thomas Day's *Sandford and Merton* (1783–6). David V. Erdman, 'Coleridge, Wordsworth, and the Wedgwood Fund', *BNYPL* 60 (1956), 425–43, 487–507, suggests that Coleridge and Wordsworth were implicated in Tom Wedgwood's scheme to set up a school in which children would be removed from nature, locked up in bare rooms painted grey, and encouraged to become rationalists in fine Godwinian fashion. The infant prodigy passage is, he suggests, Wordsworth's response. See also OET *Prelude*, 542–3; Moorman i. 333–7; Gill, 130–1, and James Chandler, 'Wordsworth, Rousseau and the Politics of Education', in *Romanticism: A Critical Reader*, 57–83.

[61] De Selincourt notes that Thomas Day's hero, Harry Sandford, is 'brave, generous to beggars, kind to animals, even cockchafers, calm in the presence of an angry bull. Even the cattle were glad when he came back after an absence' (OET *Prelude*, 544). Jonathan Wordsworth is surely correct in noting that the literary model is Chaucer's portrait of the prioress (*General Prologue*, 118–62).

[62] *Arch are his notices* His observations are clever, crafty, even mischievous.

[63] *pleasant spleen* amusement, as at *Twelfth Night*, III. ii. 68–9: 'If you desire the spleen, and will laugh yourselves into stitches, follow me.'

[64] He is licensed to ignore deceit and guile, and other 'follies'.

Though shrewd, yet innocent himself withal,
And can read lectures upon innocence.[65]
  He is fenced round – nay armed, for aught we know,
In panoply complete;[66] and fear itself,   [V, 315]
Unless it leap upon him in a dream,   400
Touches him not.[67] In brief, the moral part
Is perfect; in learning and in books
He is a prodigy. His discourse moves slow,   [V, 320]
Massy and ponderous as a prison door,
Tremendously embossed with terms of art;[68]   405
With propositions are the younker's[69] brains
Filled to the brim; the path in which he treads
Is choked with grammars; cushion of divine   [V, 325]
Was never such a type of thought profound
As is the pillow where he rests his head.[70]   410
The ensigns of the empire which he holds,
The globe and sceptre of his royalties,
Are telescopes and crucibles and maps.[71]   [V, 330]
Ships he can guide across the pathless sea,[72]

---

  [65] Richly ironic. The child's sophistication belies his 'goodness'. He is in no position to speak learnedly on the subject of innocence.

  [66] *panoply complete* full armour; cf. Cowper's portrait of the clergyman (brought to mind, perhaps, by association with Chaucer's prioress), 'arm'd himself in panoply complete' (*Task*, ii. 345).

  [67] *fear itself . . . / Touches him not* Without fear, the infant prodigy is deprived of a principal formative influence; cf. Book I, l. 304, above.

  [68] *terms of art* technical jargon.

  [69] *younker's* youngster's – a rare use of this word by Wordsworth.

  [70] *cushion of divine . . . head* The prodigy's pillow is a better symbol ('type') of profound thought than the cushion on which the parson rests his Bible in front of a pulpit. The image is suggested by Cowper's 'plump convivial parson' who 'lays'

His rev'rence and his worship both to rest
On the same cushion of habitual sloth.
(*Task*, iv. 595–8)

  [71] *maps* Wordsworth first wrote 'prisms'; this he deleted and replaced with the present reading. The scientific instruments and maps indicate the prodigy's intellectual authority, just as flags ('ensigns'), orb and sceptre symbolize a king's sovereignty.

  [72] De Selincourt points out that Harry Sandford finds his way home by the pole-star when he is lost.

And tell you all their cunning;[73] he can read   415
The inside of the earth, and spell the stars;
He knows the policies of foreign lands,
Can string you names of districts, cities, towns   [V, 335]
The whole world over,[74] tight as beads of dew
Upon a gossamer thread! His teachers stare,   420
The country people pray for God's good grace
And shudder at his deep experiments.[75]   [V, 340]
He sifts, he weighs, takes nothing upon trust –
All things are put to question.[76] He must live
Knowing that he grows wiser every day   425
Or else not live at all[77] – and seeing too
Each little drop of wisdom as it falls
Into the dimpling cistern[78] of his heart.[79]   [V, 345]
Meanwhile old Grandam Earth is grieved to find

---

[73] *cunning*   secrets (of their operation).

[74] De Selincourt notes Locke, *Some Thoughts Concerning Education*: 'I now live in the house with a child . . . [who] knew the limits of the four parts of the world, could readily point, being asked, to any country upon the globe . . . and could find the longitude and latitude of any place, before he was six years old.'

[75] The country people, in their ignorance, fear the prodigy may be seeking forbidden knowledge.

[76] *he sifts . . . trust*   Cf. Coleridge's outrage at this tendency, in a letter to Poole, 16 October 1797: 'I have known some who have been *rationally* educated, as it is styled. They were marked by a microscopic acuteness; but when they looked at great things, all became a blank & they saw nothing – and denied (very illogically) that any thing could be seen . . . [they] called the want of imagination Judgment, & the never being moved to Rapture Philosophy!' (Griggs, i. 354–5).

[77] Wordsworth could get very indignant about the redundancy of facts: 'Lastly comes that class of objects which are interesting almost solely because they are known, and the knowledge may be displayed; and this unfortunately comprehends three fourths of what, according to the plan of modern education, children's heads are stuff'd with, that is, minute remote or trifling facts in geography, topography natural history chronology &c., or acquisitions in art, or accomplishments which the child makes by rote and which are quite beyond its age' (*MY* i. 287).

[78] The surface of the water in the barrel ('cistern') dimples with each drop that falls into it.

[79] It is worth comparing the manner in which the Wordsworths reared Basil Montagu during their residence at Alfoxden: 'You ask to be informed of our system respecting Basil; it is a very simple one, so simple that in this age of systems you will hardly be likely to follow it. We teach him nothing at present but what he learns from the evidence of his senses. He has an insatiable curiosity which we are always careful to satisfy to the best of our ability. It is directed to everything he sees, the sky, the fields, trees, shrubs, corn, the

The playthings which her love designed for him   430
Unthought of: in their woodland beds the flowers
Weep, and the riversides are all forlorn.
    Now this is hollow,[80] 'tis a life of lies   [V, 350]
From the beginning, and in lies must end.
Forth bring him to the air of common sense,   435
And, fresh and showy as it is, the corpse
Slips from us into powder. Vanity,
That is his soul, there lives he, and there moves –   [V, 355]
It is the soul of everything he seeks;
That gone, nothing is left which he can love.   440
Nay, if a thought of purer birth should rise
To carry him towards a better clime,
Some busy helper still is on the watch   [V, 360]
To drive him back, and pound[81] him like a stray
Within the pinfold[82] of his own conceit,   445
Which is his home, his natural dwelling-place.
Oh, give us once again the wishing-cap
Of Fortunatus, and the invisible coat   [V, 365]
Of Jack the giant-killer, Robin Hood,
And Sabra in the forest with St George![83]   450
The child[84] whose love is here at least does reap
One precious gain – that he forgets himself.[85]

---

making of tools, carts, &c &c &c. He knows his letters, but we have not attempted any further step in the path of *book learning*. Our grand study has been to make him *happy*' (*EY* 180; emphasis original).

[80] *Now this is hollow*   The phrasing is borrowed from Cowper, *Task*, ii. 455: 'Now this is fulsome. . . .'

[81] *pound*   impound.

[82] *pinfold*   enclosure for stray animals.

[83] Fortunatus's hat took him wherever he wanted; Jack's coat made him invisible while killing giants; St George married Sabra, daughter of the King of Egypt, after rescuing her from a dragon.

[84] *child*   'children' in the MS; the draft of ll. 450–1 is rough, and Wordsworth neglected to correct it.

[85] Wordsworth recommended that children be allowed to read 'faery tales, romances, the best biographies and histories, and such parts of natural history relating to the powers and appearances of the earth and elements, and the habits and structures of animals, as belong to it not as an art or science, but as a magazine of form and feeling' (*MY* i. 287). Coleridge testified: 'from my early reading of fairy tales and genii etc. etc., my mind had been habituated *to the Vast*' (*Romanticism*, 514).

These mighty workmen of our latter age[86]   [V, 370]
Who with a broad highway have overbridged[87]
The froward[88] chaos of futurity,[89]   455
Tamed to their bidding; they who have the art
To manage books, and things, and make them work
Gently on infant minds as does the sun   [V, 375]
Upon a flower – the tutors of our youth,
The guides, the wardens of our faculties   460
And stewards of our labour, watchful men
And skilful in the usury of time,
Sages who in their prescience would control   [V, 380]
All accidents, and to the very road which they
Have fashioned would confine us down   465
Like engines[90] – when will they be taught
That in the unreasoning progress of the world
A wiser spirit is at work for us,   [V, 385]
A better eye than theirs, most prodigal
Of blessings and most studious of our good,   470
Even in what seem our most unfruitful hours?
     There was a boy – ye knew him well,[91]
Ye cliffs and islands of Winander![92] Many a time   [V, 390]
At evening, when the stars had just begun

---

[86] Ll. 453–71 derive from a fragment probably composed in Goslar during the winter of 1798–9, intended as an introduction to 'There was a boy'; it is published as 'There are who tell us that in recent times', Cornell *LB* 314–16.

[87] The MS reads: 'Who with a broad high of overbridge'. The draft is unhelpfully, and ungrammatically, incomplete, and I have preferred in this instance the MS M reading.

[88] *froward* wayward, uncontrollable.

[89] *Who with a broad highway . . . futurity* Educationalists are compared to Milton's Sin and Death, who in *Paradise Lost* build a bridge over Chaos to their new empire on earth (x. 282–305).

[90] *engines* Educational theories are as imprisoning as manufacturing machines – machine-looms, for instance – which were just coming into use. For Wordsworth's views on industrialization, see Mary Wedd, 'Industrialization and the Moral Law in Books VIII and IX of *The Excursion*', *CLB*, n.s. 81 (1993), 5–25.

[91] Ll. 471–504 were published as a poem, 'There was a boy', in *Lyrical Ballads* (1800); see Cornell *LB* 139–41. The passage was originally composed in the first person, with all the experiences attributed to the poet.

[92] *Winander* Windermere.

To move along the edges of the hills, 475
Rising or setting, would he stand alone
Beneath the trees or by the glimmering lake,
And there, with fingers interwoven, both hands [V, 395]
Pressed closely palm to palm and to his mouth
Uplifted, he as through an instrument 480
Blew mimic hootings to the silent owls
That they might answer him. And they would shout
Across the watery vale, and shout again [V, 400]
Responsive to his call, with quivering peals
And long halloos, and screams, and echoes loud 485
Redoubled and redoubled – a concourse[93] wild
Of mirth and jocund din! And when it chanced
That pauses of deep silence mocked his skill, [V, 405]
Then sometimes in that silence while he hung
Listening, a gentle shock of mild surprise 490
Has carried far[94] into his heart the voice
Of mountain torrents; or the visible scene
Would enter unawares[95] into his mind [V, 410]
With all its solemn imagery, its rocks,
Its woods, and that uncertain heaven, received 495
Into the bosom of the steady lake.[96]
    This boy was taken from his mates, and died

---

[93] *concourse* intermingling, mixing together.

[94] 'The very expression, "far", by which space and its infinities are attributed to the human heart, and to its capacities of re-echoing the sublimities of nature, has always struck me as with a flash of sublime revelation', wrote De Quincey of this passage in 1839; see 'On Wordsworth's "There was a boy"', in *Romanticism*, 686–8.

[95] *unawares* unconsciously; it is important to Wordsworth and Coleridge that moments of vision occur spontaneously – cf. *The Ancient Mariner* (1798): 'A spring of love gusht from my heart / And I blessed them unaware!' (ll. 276–7).

[96] After reading 'There was a boy' in December 1798, Coleridge wrote of ll. 495–6: 'I should have recognised [them] any where; and had I met these lines running wild in the deserts of Arabia, I should have instantly screamed out "Wordsworth!"' (Griggs, i. 453). Wordsworth offered a gloss on ll. 492–6 in his 1815 Preface: 'The Boy, there introduced, is listening, with something of a feverish and restless anxiety, for the recurrence of the riotous sounds which he had previously excited; and, at the moment when the intenseness of his mind is beginning to remit, he is surprised into a perception of the solemn and tranquillizing images which the Poem describes' (*Prose Works*, iii. 35n.).

In childhood ere he was full ten years old.   [V, 415]
Fair are the woods, and beauteous is the spot,
The vale where he was born. The churchyard hangs   500
Upon a slope above the village school,
And there, along that bank, when I have passed
At evening, I believe that oftentimes   [V, 420]
A full half-hour together I have stood
Mute, looking at the grave in which he lies.[97]   505
   Even now, methinks, I have before my sight
That self-same village church; I see her sit[98]   [V, 424]
On her green hill, forgetful of this boy
Who slumbers at her feet – forgetful too
Of all her silent neighbourhood of graves,   510
And listening to the gladsome sounds
That, from the rural school ascending, play   [V, 430]
Beneath her and about her. May she long
Behold a race of young ones like to those
With whom I herded! (easily indeed   515
We might have fed upon a fatter soil
Of arts and letters, but be that forgiven[99]) –   [V, 435]
A race of real children, not too wise,
Too learned, or too good, but wanton, fresh,
And bandied up and down by love and hate;   520
Fierce, moody, patient, venturous, modest, shy,
Mad at their sports like withered leaves in winds;   [V, 440]
Though doing wrong and suffering, and full oft
Bending beneath our life's mysterious weight
Of pain and fear, yet still in happiness   525
Not yielding to the happiest upon earth.

---

[97] Although, as Wordsworth later recalled, the boy who hooted at the owls was a conflation of himself and a school-friend called William Raincock, the dead boy was in fact John Tyson, who died in 1782 at the age of 12.

[98] At this point in the *Thirteen-Book Prelude*, Wordsworth inserted a parenthesis: 'The throned lady spoken of erewhile', referring back to the description of Hawkshead Church at *Thirteen-Book Prelude*, iv. 13–15. It is omitted in the present text as the opening of Book IV had yet to be composed.

[99] Wordsworth was in fact remarkably well educated, fortunate in attending Hawkshead Grammar School under the tutelage of several excellent teachers; see *WR* i. 162–6.

Simplicity in habit, truth in speech,   [V, 445]
Be these the daily strengtheners of their minds;
May books and Nature be their early joy,[100]
And knowledge rightly honoured with that name –   530
Knowledge not purchased with the loss of power!
   Well do I call to mind the very week[101]   [V, 450]
When I was first entrusted to the care
Of that sweet valley[102] – when its paths, its shores
And brooks, were like a dream of novelty   535
To my half-infant thoughts; that very week,
While I was roving up and down alone   [V, 455]
Seeking I knew not what, I chanced to cross
One of those open fields which, shaped like ears,[103]
Make green peninsulas on Esthwaite's Lake.   540
Twilight was coming on, yet through the gloom
I saw distinctly on the opposite shore   [V, 460]
A heap of garments – left, as I supposed,
By one who there was bathing.[104] Long I watched,
But no one owned them; meanwhile the calm lake   545
Grew dark with all the shadows on its breast,
And now and then a fish up-leaping snapped   [V, 465]
The breathless stillness.[105] The succeeding day[106]
(Those unclaimed garments telling a plain tale)
Went there a company, and in their boat   550
Sounded with grappling-irons and long poles.
At length, the dead man, mid that beauteous scene   [V, 470]

---

[100] *May books and Nature be their early joy* echoed in a letter to De Quincey, shortly after this line was composed: 'love Nature and Books; seek these and you will be happy' (*EY* 454).

[101] Ll. 532–54 comprise the first of the spots of time from *Two-Part Prelude*, i. 258–79.

[102] Wordsworth was nine when he went to Hawkshead Grammar School in May 1779.

[103] *shaped like ears* There are three such peninsulas on the map; the one Wordsworth has in mind is Strickland Ees.

[104] John Jackson, village schoolmaster from Sawrey, was drowned while bathing, 18 June 1779.

[105] A deleted draft in the MS at this point reads: 'Soon as I reached home / I to our little household of this sight / Made casual mention'.

[106] A deleted draft of this line in the MS reads: 'The stillness with a startling sound. Next day'.

Of trees and hills and water, bolt upright
Rose with his ghastly face – a spectre-shape
Of terror even. And yet no vulgar fear,   555
Young as I was (a child of eight years old),
Possessed me, for my inner eye had seen   [V, 475]
Such sights before, among the shining streams
Of fairyland, and forests of romance.
Thence came a spirit hallowing what I saw   560
With decoration and ideal grace,
A dignity, a smoothness, like the works   [V, 480]
Of Grecian art and purest poesy.
    I had a precious treasure at that time,
A little yellow canvas-covered book,   565
A slender abstract[107] of the Arabian tales;[108]
And when I learned, as now I first did learn   [V, 485]
From my companions in this new abode,
That this dear prize of mine was but a block
Hewn from a mighty quarry – in a word,   570
That there were four large volumes,[109] laden all
With kindred matter – 'twas in truth to me   [V, 490]
A promise scarcely earthly. Instantly
I made a league, a covenant with a friend
Of my own age, that we should lay aside   575
The moneys we possessed, and hoard up more,
Till our joint savings had amassed enough   [V, 495]
To make this book our own. Through several months
Religiously[110] did we preserve that vow,
And spite of all temptation hoarded up   580
And hoarded up; but firmness failed at length,

---

[107] *abstract* selection.

[108] Coleridge told Poole that *The Arabian Nights* 'made so deep an impression on me
. . . that I was haunted by spectres, whenever I was in the dark – and I distinctly remember
the anxious & fearful eagerness, with which I used to watch the window, in which the
books lay – & whenever the Sun lay upon them, I would seize it, carry it by the wall, &
bask, & read –. My Father found out the effect, which these books had produced – and
burnt them' (Griggs, i. 347).

[109] Probably the Galland translation of 1777 (see *WR* i. 11).

[110] *Religiously* diligently.

Nor were we ever masters of our wish. [V, 500]
   And afterwards, when to my father's house
Returning at the holidays I found
That golden store of books[111] which I had left   585
Open to my enjoyment once again,
What joy was mine! Full often through the course [V, 505]
Of those glad respites in the summer hours,
When armed with rod and line we went abroad
For a whole day together, I have laid   590
Down by thy side, oh Derwent, murmuring stream,
On the hot stones and in the glaring sun, [V, 510]
And there have read, devouring as I read,
Defrauding the day's glory, desperate! –
Till, with a sudden bound of smart reproach   595
Such as an idler deals with in his shame,
I to my sport betook myself again. [V, 515]
   A gracious spirit o'er this earth presides,
And o'er the heart of man: invisibly
It comes, directing those to works of love   600
Who care not, know not, think not what they do.
The tales that charm away the wakeful night [V, 520]
In Araby, romances, legends penned
For solace by the light of monkish lamps;
Fictions for ladies, of their love, devised   605
By youthful squires; adventures endless, spun
By the dismantled warrior in old age [V, 525]
Out of the bowels of those very thoughts
In which his youth did first extravagate[112] –
These spread like day, and something in the shape   610
Of these will live till man shall be no more.
Dumb yearnings, hidden appetites, are ours, [V, 530]
And they must have their food. Our childhood sits,
Our simple childhood sits upon a throne

---

[111] *That golden store of books* Wordsworth's 'golden store' included copies of *Gil Blas*, *Don Quixote* and Goldsmith's *History of England*; see my article, 'The Wordsworth Family Library at Cockermouth: Towards a Reconstruction', *The Library* 14 (1992), 127–35.

[112] *extravagate* indulge, wander. The old warrior tells tales based on his youthful hopes and ambitions.

That hath more power than all the elements.[113]   615
I guess not what this tells of being past,[114]
Nor what it augurs of the life to come,   [V, 535]
But so it is. And in that dubious hour,
That twilight when we first begin to see
This dawning earth, to recognize, expect,   620
And, in the long probation that ensues
(The time of trial, ere we learn to live   [V, 540]
In reconcilement with our stinted[115] powers),
To endure this state of meagre vassalage,
Unwilling to forego, confess, submit,   625
Uneasy and unsettled – yoke-fellows[116]
To custom, mettlesome, and not yet tamed   [V, 545]
And humbled down – oh then we feel, we feel,
We know, when we have friends! Ye dreamers, then –
Forgers of lawless tales![117] – we bless you then   630
(Impostors, drivellers, dotards, as the ape
Philosophy[118] will call you), then we feel   [V, 550]
With what, and how great might ye are in league,
Who make our wish, our power, our thought a deed,
An empire, a possession; ye whom time   635
And seasons serve – all faculties – to whom
Earth crouches, th' elements are potter's clay,[119]   [V, 555]
Space like a heaven filled up with northern lights,
Here, nowhere, there, and everywhere at once.
    It might demand a more impassioned strain   640

---

[113] The imaginative responsiveness of the youthful mind is more powerful than the forces of nature ('elements').

[114] *being past*   life before we were born – pre-existence, as in the *Intimations Ode*.

[115] *stinted*   diminished – and diminishing.

[116] *yoke-fellows*   Untamed animals are yoked with more submissive ones in order to train them; Wordsworth looks back to a time when the mind is spirited and inspired ('mettlesome'), undulled by habit.

[117] *Forgers of lawless tales*   writers of fairy-tales.

[118] *the ape / Philosophy*   Locke, for instance, who would prefer the child's imagination to be suppressed.

[119] *th' elements are potter's clay*   Authors of romances and fairy-tales are all-powerful; even the elements of which matter is composed (fire, air, water, earth) obey them. Perhaps Wordsworth is recalling Jeremiah 18:6.

To tell of later pleasures linked to these,
A tract of the same isthmus[120] which we cross   [V, 560]
In progress from our native continent
To earth and human life. I mean to speak
Of that delightful time of growing youth   645
When cravings for the marvellous relent,
And we begin to love what we have seen;   [V, 565]
And sober truth, experience, sympathy
Take stronger hold of us, and words themselves
Move us with conscious pleasure.
                 I am sad   650
At thought of raptures now for ever flown;
Even unto tears I sometimes could be sad   [V, 570]
To think of, to read over, many a page,
Poems withal of name – which at that time
Did never fail to entrance me, and are now   655
Dead in my eyes as is a theatre
Fresh emptied of spectators. Thirteen years,   [V, 575]
Or haply less, I might have seen, when first
My ears began to open to the charm
Of words in tuneful order, found them sweet   660
For their own sakes – a passion and a power;
And phrases pleased me, chosen for delight,   [V, 580]
For pomp, or love.
                 Oft in the public roads,
Yet unfrequented, while the morning light
Was yellowing the hilltops, with that dear friend   665
(The same whom I have mentioned heretofore)[121]
I went abroad, and for the better part   [V, 585]
Of two delightful hours we strolled along
By the still borders of the misty lake
Repeating favourite verses[122] with one voice,   670

[120] *isthmus* The literary pleasures that followed Wordsworth's early reading were part of the isthmus connecting pre-existence with adulthood. There is a recollection of Pope's *Essay on Man*, which refers to humanity as 'this isthmus of a middle state' between divinity and the animal world (ii. 3).

[121] John Fleming, mentioned Book II, ll. 349–50.

[122] *favourite verses* those of Goldsmith and Gray, according to De Quincey (Masson, ii. 264–5; *WR* i. 120).

Or conning[123] more, as happy as the birds
That round us chaunted. Well might we rejoice,   [V, 590]
Lifted above the ground by airy fancies
More bright than madness or the dreams of wine.
And though full oft the objects of our love   675
Were false, and in their splendour overwrought,
Yet surely at such time no vulgar power   [V, 595]
Was working in us, nothing less in truth
Than that most noble attribute of man
(Though yet inordinate[124] and unmatured) –   680
That wish for something loftier, more adorned
Than is the common aspect, daily garb,   [V, 600]
Of human life. What wonder then if sounds
Of exultation echoed through the groves?
For images, and sentiments, and words,   685
And everything with which we had to do
In that delicious world of poesy,   [V, 605]
Kept holiday, a never-ending show
With music, incense, festival, and flowers!
     Here must I pause: this only will I add,   690
From heart-experience and in humblest sense
Of modesty, that he who in his youth,   [V, 610]
A wanderer among the woods and fields,
With living Nature hath been intimate,
Not only in that raw unpractised time   695
Is stirred to ecstasy (as others are)
By glittering verse, but he doth furthermore,   [V, 615]
In measure only dealt out to himself,
Receive enduring touches of deep joy
From the great Nature that exists in works   700
Of mighty poets.[125] Visionary power
Attends upon the motions of the winds   [V, 620]
Embodied in the mystery of words;

---

[123] *conning* memorizing. Learning by rote was a principal method by which children
were taught.

[124] *inordinate* 'unordered', as Maxwell notes.

[125] If the reader has known 'living Nature' from childhood, they will take pleasure from
'the great Nature' to be found in poetry.

There darkness makes abode, and all the host
Of shadowy things do work their changes there,　　705
As in a mansion kindred to their own.[126]
Even forms and substances are circumfused　　　　　　　[V, 625]
By that transparent veil with light divine,
And through the turnings intricate of verse
Present themselves as objects recognized　　710
In flashes, and with a glory scarce their own.[127]　　　[V, 629]
　　Thus far, by grateful retrospect at least
A scanty record is brought down, my friend
(And, as I fear, too fondly lengthened out),
Of what I owed to books in early life;　　715
Their later gifts do yet remain untold,
But as this meditative history
Was calling me to an ungracious task
Which must be undertaken now – I mean
To speak of an abasement in my mind[128]　　720
Not altogether wrought without the help
Of books ill chosen – I was loath to think
Of entering on this labour without first
Forth breathing these devout acknowledgements.

---

[126] *kindred to their own*　changed in subsequent version of the poem to 'like their proper home'.

[127] *Even forms and substances . . . scarce their own*　The reader of great poetry can enjoy the experience of recognizing everyday forms and substances, which have been bathed ('circumfused') in the divine light of the imagination.

[128] Presumably a reference to the tendencies discussed in Book V, 213ff., below.

Book Five

Once when a youth and with a youthful friend,[1]   [XIII, 2]
Travelling along the region of north Wales,[2]
We left Bethkellert's huts[3] at couching-time[4]
And westward took our way to see the sun
Rise from the top of Snowdon. Having reached   5   [XIII, 5]
The cottage at the mountain's foot, we roused
The shepherd up who is the stranger's guide,
And after short repose we sallied forth.

   It was a summer's night, close warm withal,   [XIII, 10]
White, dull and glaring,[5] with a dripping mist   10
Heavy, low-hung, that covered all the sky,

---

[1] Wordsworth climbed Snowdon with a College friend, Robert Jones, during the summer of 1791. Wordsworth was 21. This episode has a number of literary antecedents, including Wordsworth's earlier poem, *Descriptive Sketches* (1793), and Beattie's *The Minstrel*, for discussion of which readers should refer to *Borders of Vision*, 308ff. A good introduction to interpretive matters is provided by W. J. B. Owen, 'The Perfect Image of a Mighty Mind', *WC* 10 (1979), 3–16.

[2] Wordsworth originally wrote, 'Once (but I must premise that several years / Are overleaped to reach this incident)', and deleted it, replacing it with the present reading. For Jonathan Wordsworth, the deleted version is revealing: 'Wordsworth still regards himself as working within a chronological framework and is worried about skipping two years between the summers of 1789 and '91 – years memorable, of course, chiefly for the Long Vacation in France' (Wordsworth (1977), 16).

[3] *Bethkellert's huts* the cottages of Beddgelert, a village at the foot of Snowdon.

[4] *couching-time* bed-time.

[5] *glaring* Maxwell suggests that this word is used in the dialect sense of dull, rainy, sticky, clammy.

Half threatening storm and rain. But on we went
Unchecked, being young and blithe and having faith
In our tried pilot.[6] Little could we see,   [XIII, 15]
Edged round on every side with fog and damp, 15
And after ordinary travellers' chat
With the old shepherd, silently we sunk
Each into commerce with his private thoughts.
Thus did we breast the ascent, and by myself   [XIII, 20]
Was nothing either seen or heard the while 20
That took me from my musing, save that once
The shepherd's cur did to his own great joy
Unearth a hedgehog in the mountain crags
Round which he made a barking turbulent.[7]   [XIII, 25]
This small adventure (for even such it seemed 25
In that wild place and at the dead of night)
Being over and forgotten, on we went
In silence as before. With face towards   [XIII, 30]
The hill, as if in opposition set
Against an enemy, I panted up   30
With eager steps, and no less eager thoughts.
Thus did we wear an hour perhaps away,
Straggling at loose distance each from each,
And I, as chanced, the foremost of the band,   [XIII, 35]
When at my feet the ground in gentle sort 35
Brightened – at least, I fancied that it looked
More bright in that half-dream which wrapped me up.
Nor had I time to ask if it were so,
For instantly a light before my eyes
Fell like a flash. I looked about, and lo!   40 [XIII, 40]
The moon stood naked in the heavens at height
Immense above my head, and on the shore
I found myself of a huge sea of mist,
That meek and silent rested at my feet.
A hundred hills their dusky backs upheaved 45 [XIII, 45]

---

[6] *tried pilot* experienced guide.
[7] *barking turbulent* The Miltonic inversion of adjective and noun heightens the mock-heroic tone; dogs are fondly recalled in the *Prelude* – cf. Book IV, ll. 55–60.

All over this still ocean;[8] and beyond,
Far, far beyond, the vapours shot themselves
In headland, tongues, and promontory shapes,
Into the sea – the real sea, that seemed
To dwindle and give up its majesty,   50   [XIII, 50]
Usurped upon as far as sight could reach.[9]
Meanwhile, the moon looked down upon this show
In single glory, and we stood, the mist
Touching our very feet. And from the shore
At distance not the third part of a mile   55   [XIII, 55]
Was a blue chasm, a fracture in the mist,
A deep and gloomy breathing-place through which
Mounted the roar of waters, torrents, streams
Inseparable, roaring with one voice.[10]
The universal spectacle throughout   60   [XIII, 60]
Was shaped for admiration and delight,
Grand in itself alone, but in that breach
Through which the homeless voice of waters rose,
That dark deep thoroughfare, had Nature lodged
The soul, the imagination of the whole.[11]   65   [XIII, 65]
    To this one scene which I from Snowdon's breast
Beheld might more be added, to set forth
The manner in which ofttimes Nature works
Herself upon the outward face of things,   [XIII, 78]
As if with an imaginative power –   70

---

[8] *A hundred hills their dusky backs upheaved ... ocean* borrowed from Milton's
account of Creation, *Paradise Lost*, vii. 285–7:

> the mountains huge appear
> Emergent, and their broad backs upheave
> Into the clouds . . .

[9] *Far, far beyond ... could reach* The imagination confers on the mist the life and
functions of water, 'usurping' those of the real sea, the Irish Channel, beneath it.

[10] *A deep and gloomy breathing-place ... one voice* similar to the fountain of *Kubla
Khan*, 18: 'As if this earth in fast thick pants were breathing'.

[11] *The soul, the imagination of the whole* The revelation offered on Snowdon is of the
identity of soul and imagination. At this point in the manuscript Wordsworth continued
with the lines which have come to be known as the analogy passage, presented in Appendix I. However, it was abandoned before completion, and he began again at l. 66.

I mean so moulds, exalts, endues, combines,   [XIII, 79]
Impregnates,[12] separates, adds, takes away,
And makes one object sway another so,[13]   [XIII, 81]
By unhabitual influence or abrupt,[14]
That even the grossest minds must see and hear   75   [XIII, 83]
And cannot choose but feel.[15] The power which these
Are touched by, being so moved, which Nature thus   [XIII, 85]
Puts forth upon the senses (not to speak
Of finer operations), is in kind
A brother of the very faculty   80
Which higher minds bear with them as their own.   [XIII, 90]
These from their native selves can deal about
Like transformation, to one life impart   [XIII, 94]
The functions of another – interchange,
Trafficking in immeasurable thoughts.[16]   85
Such minds are truly from the Deity   [XIII, 104]

---

[12] *Impregnates*   Again, Wordsworth is recalling Milton's description of the Holy Spirit in *Paradise Lost*, i. 19–22:

> thou from the first
> Wast present, and with mighty wings outspread
> Dove-like sat'st brooding on the vast abyss
> And madest it pregnant.

[13] *I mean so moulds . . . another so*   Nature performs a function akin to the secondary imagination, analogous to the artist's act of creation. See the discussion of imagination in the 1815 Preface and Coleridge's definition of the primary and secondary imaginations in *Biographia Literaria* (*Romanticism*, 476–9, 574).

[14] *By unhabitual influence or abrupt*   using powers exerted rarely or suddenly. This line appears only in this version of the poem.

[15] *That even the grossest minds . . . choose but feel*   For Wordsworth and Coleridge it was necessary to the project of *The Recluse* that everyone, however untutored their sensibility, be susceptible to the redemptive power of the imagination.

[16] The favoured beings of whom Wordsworth writes are capable of transferring the qualities of one object to another, just as the mist 'usurps' the features of the sea. This process works in both directions, creating an 'interchange' of characteristics; though it should be noted that Wordsworth backs away from this notion in the *Thirteen-Book Prelude* (l. 86 occurs only in this version of the poem), and says, in an alternative draft in the manuscript:

For they are powers,[17] and hence the highest bliss
That can be known on earth – in truth, a soul
Growing, and still to grow, a consciousness
Of whom they are,[18] they habitually infused   90
Through every image and through every being,[19]   [XIII, 110]
And all impressions have religious faith
And endless occupation for the soul,
Whether discursive or intuitive.[20]   [XIII, 113]
Hither cheerfulness in every hour of life,   95   [XIII, 117]
Thus truth in moral knowledge and delight,
That fails not in the external universe.[21]
    Oh who is he that hath his whole life long   [XIII, 120]
Preserved, enlarged this freedom in himself? –
For this alone is genuine liberty.   100

> These from their native selves can deal about
> Like transformation, for themselves create
> Like imperatives of qualities,
> As by their own thoughts can build up greatest things
> From least suggestions, ever on the watch . . .

The equivalent passage in the longer work is *Thirteen-Book Prelude*, xiii. 93–9.

[17] *For they are powers* Wordsworth echoes – and through much of this passage catches the tones of – William Gilbert's praise of hurricanes in *The Hurricane* (1796) (see *WR* i. 114, ii. 177):

> For theirs are Nature's powers; Elemental strength
> Springs in their nerves . . .
> They hence are keenly sentient of all truth . . . (i. 75–9)

[18] *Of whom they are* The MS reads: 'In a [?]' The draft is unhelpful, and I have in this case preferred the reading of MS M. For Coleridge, the primary act of imagination was God's self-naming ('the infinite I AM'); here, the imagination confirms the identity of those who possess it.

[19] *they habitually infused . . . every being* At Book I, ll. 356–7, thoughts and feelings were 'infused' into the mind of the young Wordsworth; in maturity the imaginative mind infuses itself into everything it perceives ('every image').

[20] *Whether discursive or intuitive* This distinction is borrowed from *Paradise Lost*, where Raphael observes that 'discursive' reason belongs mainly to man and 'intuitive' reason to the angels (v. 486–90) – all of which was crucial to Coleridge's formulations concerning the imagination, which may already have been worked out and discussed with Wordsworth by the time these lines were written.

[21] *in the external universe* These words are absent from MS W; they are supplied from MS M.

Witness, thou solitude where I received
My earliest visitation, careless then
Of what was given me, and what now I saw –   [XIII, 125]
A meditative, oft a suffering, man,
And yet I trust with undiminished power[22] –   105
Witness if e'er I yielded
To low employments or to petty care;
Witness – whatever falls my better mind,
Revolving with the accidents of life,
May have sustained – that howsoe'er misled,   110   [XIII, 130]
I never, in the quest of right and wrong,
Did tamper with myself from private aims;[23]
Nor was in any of my hopes the dupe
Of selfish passions; nor did wilfully
Yield ever to mean cares and low pursuits,   115   [XIII, 135]
But rather did with jealousy[24] shrink back
From every combination that might aid
The tendency, too potent in itself,
Of habit to enslave the mind – I mean
Oppress it by the laws of vulgar sense   120   [XIII, 140]
And substitute a universe of death,[25]
The falsest of all worlds, in place of that

---

[22] *undiminished power*   Loss of imaginative power was a preoccupation of the moment; the *Intimations Ode* was recently completed, and within days he was to compose ll. 146ff., below.

[23] *never . . . from private aims*   clearer in the *Fourteen-Book Prelude*:

Never did I, in quest of right and wrong,
Tamper with conscience from a private aim . . .
(xiv. 150–1)

[24] *jealousy*   vigilance.

[25] *a universe of death*   When habit and unimaginative dependence on the senses govern the mind, everything that is perceived is dead. Wordsworth's phrasing echoes Milton's hell:

A universe of death . . .
Where all life dies, death lives, and nature breeds
Perverse, all monstrous, all prodigious things . . .
(*Paradise Lost*, ii. 622–5)

Which is divine and true.
　　　　　　　　To fear and love
(To love as first and chief, for there fear ends)
Be this ascribed, to early intercourse　　　　　125　[XIII, 145]
In presence of sublime and lovely forms
With the adverse principles of pain and joy –
Evil as one is rashly named by those
Who know not what they say.[26] From love (for here
Do we begin and end) all grandeur comes,　　　130　[XIII, 150]
All truth and beauty – from pervading love;
That gone, we are as dust. Behold the fields
In balmy springtime, full of rising flowers
And happiness! See the newborn lamb
And the lamb's mother, and their tender ways　　135　[XIII, 155]
Shall touch thee to the heart. Thou call'st this love,　　[XIII, 160]
And so it is – but there is higher love
Than this, a love that comes into the heart
With peace and a diffusive sentiment;
Thy love is human merely – this more near,　　　140
More from the pervading soul,[27] and is divine,　　　[XIII, 165]
Nor is't tinctured with any human flaw.
　　My present labour hath till lately béen[28]　　　[XI, 42]
A history of love, from stage to stage
Advancing hand in hand with power and joy.　　　145　[XI, 44]
The unremitting warfare from the first
Waged with this faculty, its various foes
Which for the most continue to increase.
With growing life and burdens which it brings[29]

---

[26] *To fear and love ... what they say* Wordsworth refers back to Book I, ll. 303–4, where he claimed to have been fostered by beauty and fear. Fear and pain are necessary adjuncts to the growth of the truly imaginative mind, and are not in themselves evil – once again, a swipe at the educationalists who recommended that children not be allowed to read ghost stories.

[27] *the pervading soul* presumably the Neoplatonic world soul of such fragments as 'There is an active principle in all things' (Cornell *LB* 309–10). Wordsworth backs away from this possibility and eliminates the reference in subsequent versions of the poem.

[28] *been* absent from this draft, but supplied from another on the same page of the MS.

[29] *The unremitting warfare ... brings* Wordsworth's syntax is confusing, but the sense is clear enough: 'the foes of love, which from the outset of life increase, waged with it an unremitting warfare ...'

Of petty duties and pressing cares,   150
Labour and penury, disease and grief,
Which to one object chain the impoverished mind
Enfeebled and defeated,[30] vexing strife
At home, and want of pleasure and repose,
And all that eats away the genial spirits,[31]   155
May be fit matter for another song;
Nor less the misery brought into the world
By the perversion of this power misplaced
And misemployed, whence emanates
Blinding cares, whence ambition, avarice,   160
And all the superstitions of this life –
A mournful catalogue. Gladly would I then,   [XI, 176]
Entering upon abstruser argument,[32]
Attempt to place in view the diverse means
Which Nature strenuously employs to uphold   165
This agency against the barren idleness
Of use and habit, and call the senses each   [XI, 180]
To counteract the other and themselves,
And makes even these, and the objects with which these
Are conversant, subservient in their turn   170
To the great ends of liberty and power.[33]   [XI, 184]
   'Tis true that earth with all her appanage   [XI, 108]
Of elements[34] and organs, storm and sunshine,
With her pure forms and colours, pomp of clouds,   [XI, 110]
Rivers and mountains, objects among which   175
It might be thought that no dislike or blame,
No sense of weakness or infirmity,
Or aught amiss could possibly have come,
Yea, even the universe was scanned   [XI, 115]

---

[30] *defeated*   The word which appears in the MS at this point is illegible. The present reading appears in an earlier draft of the same line, at MS W, 45v.

[31] *petty duties . . . genial spirits*   The Virgilian antecedent, and allusion to Coleridge, are discussed in the Introduction, pp. 10–11.

[32] *abstruser argument*   This 'abstruser' – more philosophical – line of thought would presumably be expounded in *The Recluse*.

[33] *liberty and power*   imaginative power, and the kind of liberty mentioned at l. 100.

[34] *appanage / Of elements*   natural attribute of elements.

With something of a kindred spirit,[35] fell   180
Beneath the domination of a taste[36]
Less elevated, which did in my mind
With its more noble influence interfere,
Its animation and its deeper sway.   [XI, 120]
There comes (if need be now to speak of this   185
After such long detail of our mistakes),
There comes a time when reason – not the grand
And simple reason,[37] but that humbler power
Which carries on its not inglorious work   [XI, 125]
By logic and minute analysis –   190
Is of all idols that which pleases most
The growing mind. A trifler would he be
Who on the obvious benefits should dwell
That rise out of this process; but to speak   [XI, 130]
Of all the narrow estimates of things   195
Which hence originate were a worthy theme
For philosophic verse.[38] Suffice it here
To hint that danger cannot but attend
Upon a function rather proud to be   [XI, 135]
The enemy of falsehood, than the friend   200
Of truth – to sit in judgement, than to feel.
    Oh soul of Nature, excellent and fair,
That did rejoice in me, with whom I too

---

[35] *a kindred spirit*   kindred, that is, to the 'various foes' which attempt to erode the imagination at ll. 144–62.

[36] *a taste*   for the picturesque theories of Gilpin and his followers; see Book IV, l. 51 and n. Wordsworth is clear about the meaning of the concept of 'taste' in his Essay, Supplementary (1815): 'It is a metaphor, taken from a *passive* sense of the human body, and transferred to things which are in their essence *not* passive, – to intellectual *acts* and *operations*' (*Prose Works*, iii. 81; emphasis original).

[37] *the grand / And simple reason*   Reason is a crucial element in imaginative thought; Wordsworth has described passion ('emotion') as 'highest reason in a soul sublime' (Book IV, l. 337, above), and in the *Thirteen-Book Prelude* will refer to imagination as 'reason in her most exalted mood' (xiii. 170). In both cases it corresponds to the 'intuitive' power mentioned at l. 94, above, and said by Raphael in *Paradise Lost* to pertain chiefly to angels. The analytical power mentioned at l. 190 is the 'discursive' faculty, which pleases the growing mind but should not be idolized.

[38] *philosophic verse*   i.e., *The Recluse*, rather than *The Prelude*.

Rejoiced, through early youth, before the winds [XI, 140]
And powerful waters, and in lights and shade 205
That marched and counter-marched about the hill
In glorious apparition[39] – now all eye
And now all ear, but ever with the heart
Employed, or the majestic intellect; [XI, 145]
Oh soul of Nature, that dost overflow 210
With passion and with life, what feeble men
Walk on this earth, how feeble have I been
When thou wert in thy strength! Nor this through stroke
Of human suffering such as justifies [XI, 150]
Remissness or irregularity of mind, 215
But through presumption[40] merely, and false wish
Of vain distinction – even when pleased
Not worthily, disliking here, and there
Liking, by rule transferred from mimic art
To things above all art.[41] And more – for this 220 [XI, 155]
Was never much my habit – giving way
To a comparison of scene with scene,
And hastening after idle novelties [XI, 160]
(Not cheered without a giddy keen delight),
Pampering myself with luxury 225
Of form and proportion, to the moods
Of Nature and the temper of the place
Insensible;[42] in short, an eye too oft [XI, 164]

[39] *glorious apparition* Wordsworth originally wrote 'visionary glory', before changing it to the present reading.

[40] *presumption* arrogance. Wordsworth wants to portray the impairment of his imagination as a prelude to its restoration in the 'spots of time' sequence (ll. 280ff., below). He accuses himself of three distinct forms of presumption that have made him insensitive to the 'soul of nature': 1. the picturesque (ll. 217–20); 2. aesthetic comparison (ll. 220–8); 3. soullessness (ll. 228–30).

[41] *even when pleased . . . things above all art* Wordsworth criticizes the technique of judging natural forms by the rules of the picturesque theorist, William Gilpin. It is worth pointing out that Wordsworth was an enthusiastic reader of Gilpin and a number of other picturesque writers for much of his life, and that his love of Nature was informed by them; see *WR* i. 116, ii 179; Trott, 'Wordsworth and the Picturesque'.

[42] *Insensible* insensitive. There is no evidence that Wordsworth was ever insensitive to Nature in the way he claims.

Without soul, a meagre untaught eye
And nothing more, yet without delight.   230
              I knew a maid[43]   [XI, 199]
Who, young as I was then, conversed with things
In higher style.[44] From appetites like these
She, gentle spirit, as well she might,
Was wholly free; her codes of critic   235
And barren intermeddling subtleties
Never perplexed,[45] but (wise as women are   [XI, 205]
When genial circumstance[46] hath favoured them)
She welcomed what was given, and craved no more.
Whatever scene was present to her eyes,   240
That was the best, to that she was attuned
Through her humility and lowliness,   [XI, 210]
And through a perfect happiness of soul,
Whose variegated feelings were in this
Sisters, that they were each some new delight.   245
For she was Nature's inmate:[47] her the birds
And every flower she met with, could they but   [XI, 215]
Have known her, would have loved. Methinks such sense
Of sweetness did her presence breathe around,
That all the trees, and all the silent hills,   250
And everything she looked on, would have
An intimation how she bore herself   [XI, 220]
Towards them and to all creatures; God delights
In such beings, for her common thoughts

---

[43] *a maid*   Mary Hutchinson. The line is incomplete in the manuscript.

[44] *higher style*   i.e., higher than the picturesque manner referred to in ll. 217–30.

[45] *her codes of critic . . . perplexed*   The word order is confusing: critical rules ('codes') and barren intermeddling subtleties never perplexed her. The subtleties and codes are presumably those of the picturesque.

[46] *genial circumstance*   happiness in life, good fortune.

[47] *For she was Nature's inmate*   she lived with Nature. The phrase derives from a fragment composed at the same time as the *Two-Part Prelude*, but there applied to Dorothy:

For she is Nature's inmate, and her heart
Is everywhere, even the unnoticed heath
That o'er the mountain spreads its prodigal bells
Lives in her love . . .
('I would not strike a flower', 25–8; Cornell *LB* 312–14)

Are piety, her life is blessedness.   255
    Even like this maid, before I was called forth
From this retirement of my native hills,[48]   [XI, 225]
I loved whate'er I saw – nor lightly loved,
But deeply – never dreamt of aught more grand,
More charmed, more fair, more exquisite,   260
Than those few nooks to which my happy feet
Were limited. And why? Upon myself   [XI, 230]
I was dependent, then else should I soon
Have languished and, familiar with the shape
And outside fabric of that little world,   265
Have undelighted looked on all delight.
And afterwards, when through the gorgeous Alps   [XI, 241]
I roamed,[49] I carried with me the same heart.
In truth, this malady of which I speak,[50]
Though aided by the times whose deeper sound   270
Without my knowledge sometimes might perchance
Make rural Nature's milder minstrelsies   [XI, 250]
Inaudible, did never take in me
Deep root or large action. I had received
Impressions[51] far too early and too strong   275
For this to last: I threw the habit off
Entirely and for ever, and again   [XI, 255]
In Nature's presence stood, as I do now,
A meditative and creative soul.
    There are in our existence spots of time   280
Which with distinct pre-eminence retain
A fructifying[52] virtue, whence, depressed   [XI, 260]
By trivial occupations and the round

---

[48] *before I was called . . . hills* Wordsworth's first long spell away from the Lakes came when he went up to Cambridge in October 1787 at the age of 17.

[49] *when through the gorgeous Alps / I roamed* Reed suggests that this allusion to the Continental walking tour of 1790, to be dealt with in the yet-unwritten *Thirteen-Book Prelude*, Book VI, indicates that by the time Wordsworth reached this point of the *Five-Book Prelude* he knew he had more to say (Cornell *13-Book Prelude*, i. 34).

[50] *this malady of which I speak* i.e., the tendencies described at ll. 217–30, above.

[51] *Impressions* Nature had stamped its images and forms, loaded with emotion, upon his mind; cf. Book I, l. 495, above.

[52] *fructifying* the power to make fruitful; this is the reading of the *Two-Part Prelude*.

Of ordinary intercourse, our minds
(Especially the imaginative power)   285
Are nourished and invisibly repaired.[53]   [XI, 265]
Such moments, worthy of all gratitude,   [XI, 274]
Are scattered everywhere, and take their date
In our first childhood – in our childhood even
Perhaps are most conspicuous.
                  At a time   290
While I was yet an urchin,[54] one who scarce   [XI, 280]
Could hold a bridle, with ambitious hopes
I mounted, and we rode towards the hills.
We were a pair of horsemen: honest James[55]
Was with me, my encourager and guide.   295
We had not travelled long ere some mischance   [XI, 285]
Disjoined me from my comrade, and, through fear
Dismounting, down the rough and stony moor
I led my horse, and, stumbling on, at length
Came to a bottom where in former times   300   [XI, 289]
A man, the murderer of his wife, was hung
In irons. Mouldered was the gibbet-mast,
The bones were gone, the iron and the wood,
Only a long green ridge of turf remained
Whose shape was like a grave.[56] I left the spot   305   [XI, 302]
And, reascending the bare slope, I saw

_____

What little evidence there is would suggest that Wordsworth had not yet revised this word to 'vivifying'. It appears in subsequent manuscripts of the *Thirteen-Book Prelude* as 'renovating' (xi. 260).

[53] The restorative effects of imaginative thought are mentioned in *Tintern Abbey*, 40–2.

[54] *an urchin*   Wordsworth was five at the time this incident took place. He was staying with his grandparents at Penrith.

[55] *honest James*   identified in the *Fourteen-Book Prelude* as being 'An ancient Servant of my Father's house' (xii. 229).

[56] *Mouldered was the gibbet-mast . . . like a grave*   The valley bottom was Cowdrake Quarry, east of Penrith, where Thomas Nicholson was hanged in 1767 for having murdered a butcher. However, *The Prelude* is not a record of fact, and it is worth noting that Nicholson's gibbet had not 'mouldered down' in 1775, and a five-year-old would not have ridden that far. Wordsworth may also have in mind a rotted gibbet in the watermeadows near Ann Tyson's cottage, the last remains of Thomas Lancaster, hanged in 1672 for poisoning his wife.

A naked pool that lay beneath the hills,
The beacon on the summit,[57] and, more near,   [XI, 305]
A girl who bore a pitcher on her head
And seemed with difficult steps to force her way   310
Against the blowing wind. It was in truth
An ordinary sight, but I should need
Colours and words that are unknown to man   [XI, 310]
To paint the visionary dreariness
Which, while I looked all round for my lost guide,   315
Did at that time invest the naked pool,
The beacon on the lonely eminence,
The woman and her garments vexed and tossed   [XI, 315]
By the strong wind.
               When, in a blessed time
With those two dear ones[58] – to my heart so dear –   320
When in the blessed time of early love
Long afterwards I roamed about
In daily presence of this very scene,   [XI, 320]
Upon the naked pool and dreary crags,
And on the melancholy beacon, fell   325
The spirit of pleasure and youth's golden dream –
And think ye not with radiance more divine
From these remembrances, and from the power   [XI, 325]
They left behind? So feeling comes in aid
Of feeling, and diversity of strength   330
Attends us if but once we have been strong.[59]
Oh mystery of man, from what a depth
Proceed thy honours! I am lost, but see   [XI, 330]
In simple childhood something of the base
On which thy greatness stands – but this I feel: 335
That from thyself it comes that thou must give,

---

[57] *The beacon on the summit*   built in 1719 to warn of invasion from Scotland, still standing.

[58] *When, in a blessed time . . . dear ones*   Wordsworth returned to Penrith to see Mary Hutchinson and Dorothy, in summer 1787, shortly before going up to Cambridge.

[59] *So feeling . . . been strong*   The early experience left a residue of imaginative power that revitalized the poet when he revisited Penrith in 1787 (he was, at the time, working on an ambitious 1,000-line poem, *The Vale of Esthwaite*).

Else never canst receive.[60] The days gone by
Come back upon me from the dawn almost   [XI, 335]
Of life; the hiding-places[61] of my powers
Seem open; I approach, and then they close.[62]   340   [XI, 337]
Yet have I singled out – not satisfied
With general feelings – here and there have culled
Some incidents that may explain whence come
My restorations, and with yet one more of these
Will I conclude.

               One Christmas-time,   345   [XI, 345]
The day before the holidays began,[63]
Feverish, and tired, and restless, I went forth
Into the fields, impatient for the sight
Of those three horses which should bear us home,
My brothers and myself.[64] There was a crag,   350   [XI, 350]
An eminence, which from the meeting-point
Of two highways ascending, overlooked
At least a long half-mile of those two roads,
By each of which the expected steeds might come,

---

[60] *That from thyself . . . canst receive*   Wordsworth quotes from 'Dejection: An Ode', addressed to him by Coleridge on 4 October 1802, as a sort of wedding-present: 'Oh Edmund, we receive but what we give' (l. 48).

[61] An earlier draft in the MS has 'the very fountains of my powers' (48v).

[62] MS Z has an extended, more pessimistic version of ll. 341–5, composed after the death of Wordsworth's brother John in February 1805:

> I see by glimpses now, when age comes on
> May scarcely see at all; and I would give
> While yet we may, as far as words can do,
> A substance and a life to what I feel,
> I would enshrine the spirit of the past
> For future restoration. Yet another
> Of these to me affecting incidents
> With which we will conclude.

The equivalent passage in the longer work is *Thirteen-Book Prelude*, xi. 338–45.

[63] *The day . . . began*   Probably 19 December 1783, when Wordsworth was 13.

[64] Wordsworth's brothers, Richard (1768–1816) and John (1772–1805), also attended Hawkshead Grammar School. The horses were to take them home to Cockermouth. They were in fact delayed; for the circumstances surrounding this see my article, 'Wordsworth's Poetry of Grief', *WC* 21 (1990), 114–17.

The choice uncertain. Thither I repaired   355   [XI, 355]
Up to the highest summit. 'Twas a day
Stormy, and rough, and wild, and on the grass
I sate, half-sheltered by a naked wall.
Upon my right hand was a single sheep,
A whistling hawthorn on my left, and there,   360   [XI, 360]
Those two companions at my side, I watched,
With eyes intensely straining, as the mist
Gave intermitting prospects of the wood
And plain beneath. Ere I to school returned
That dreary time, ere I had been ten days   365   [XI, 365]
A dweller in my father's house, he died,[65]
And I and my two brothers (orphans then)
Followed his body to the grave. The event,
With all the sorrow which it brought, appeared
A chastisement;[66] and when I called to mind   370   [XI, 370]
That day so lately past, when from the crag
I looked in such anxiety of hope,
With trite reflections of morality,
Yet with the deepest passion, I bowed low
To God, who thus corrected my desires.[67]   375   [XI, 375]
And afterwards the wind and sleety rain
And all the business of the elements,
The single sheep, and the one blasted tree,
And the bleak music of that old stone wall,
The noise of wood and water, and the mist   380   [XI, 380]
That on the line of each of those two roads
Advanced in such indisputable shapes[68] –
All these were spectacles and sounds to which

[65] *he died*   John Wordsworth Sr died on 30 December 1783 two weeks after spending a shelterless night during his return from the Seignory of Millom. His wife, Ann, had died five years previously, just before Wordsworth's eighth birthday.

[66] *chastisement*   punishment.

[67] *I bowed low to God . . . desires*   The child believes he has been punished for looking forward too eagerly to the Christmas holidays – in effect, he has killed his father.

[68] *indisputable shapes*   De Selincourt notes an interesting echo of Hamlet addressing his father's ghost: 'Thou com'st in such a questionable shape / That I will speak to thee' (I. iv. 43–4). The point at which two roads meet also, as Gordon Thomas has observed,

I often would repair, and thence would drink
As at a fountain.[69] And I do not doubt   385   [XI, 385]
That in this later time, when storm and rain
Beat on my roof at midnight, or by day
When I am in the woods, unknown to me
The workings of my spirit thence are brought.

---

echoes Oedipus (' "Orphans Then": Death in the *Two-Part Prelude*', *CLB* 96 (1996), 17–
34); Wordsworth read *Oedipus at Colonus* at Cambridge (*WR* i. 230).

   [69] *As at a fountain*   Owen notes the echo of Milton's description of the creation:

Hither as to their fountain other stars
Repairing, in their golden urns draw light . . .
(*Paradise Lost*, vii. 364–5)

Recent Critical
Commentary on
The Five-Book Prelude

The 'Analogy Passage' from Wordsworth's Five-Book *Prelude* (1981)

Joseph F. Kishel

Ernest de Selincourt's notes to Book XIII of Wordsworth's *Prelude* include a transcript of a lengthy passage from MS W.[1] What we may call the 'analogy passage' was written to follow the climbing of Snowdon lines, and it would have taken a central position in the last Book of the *Five-Book Prelude*, had Wordsworth completed that poem.

Wordsworth's letters of early 1804 plainly indicate his intention to write a five-Book *Prelude*, but upon or just prior to its completion, the project was expanded, and the eventual result was the 1805 poem in thirteen books. Although there is no extant text of the five-Book *Prelude*, MS W contains passages written for the poem, and on the evidence of these, J. R. MacGillivray made a tentative reconstruction.[2] The five-Book *Prelude* was to resemble the two-part *Prelude* of 1798–9, but with the addition of books similar to what we now know as Book III ('Residence at Cambridge'), Book V ('Books'), and a final book,

First published in *Studies in Romanticism*, 18 (1979), 273–85.

[1] OET *Prelude*, 623–8.

[2] J. R. MacGillivray, 'The Three Forms of *The Prelude*, 1798–1805', in *Essays in English Literature from the Renaissance to the Victorian Age, Presented to A. S. P. Woodhouse* (1964), pp. 229–44; repr. in W. J. Harvey and R. Gravil (eds), *Wordsworth: The Prelude* (London, 1972), pp. 99–115.

containing the climbing of Snowdon lines and the analogy passage.

In a more recent study of the five-Book *Prelude*,[3] Jonathan Wordsworth outlines the final book in greater detail and concludes that it was to have ended with the 'spots of time' passage now in Book XI. While MacGillivray found a 'clearly discernible formal structure' in the five-Book poem, Jonathan Wordsworth maintains almost defiantly that we should regard it as a finished work and the fifth Book forms an admirably powerful and appropriate coda to the whole. He leaves unexplained the peculiar role of the analogy passage in such a triumphant conclusion, saying only that it must have been dropped before the fifth Book reached final form.

Wordsworth's decision to expand his five-Book poem came suddenly. On 6 March 1804 he told both Coleridge and De Quincey that the five-Book poem was almost completed. Yet, less than two weeks later, the collection of poems sent to accompany Coleridge to the Mediterranean contained, not a finished five-Book poem, but the first five Books of a new, longer project. These five Books were a revised and expanded version of Books I–IV of the abandoned five-part poem. When the new *Prelude* was completed in thirteen Books in May 1805, the last Book – like the last Book of the abandoned five-part poem – still began with the climbing of Snowdon, but the analogy passage was gone.

Of course it might not seem unusual that in doubling the size of his poem Wordworth should decide to exclude a single passage of 114 lines. But, by showing that the lines were probably dropped even before the decision to expand the five-Book poem, Jonathan Wordsworth has helped to establish their significance. Wordsworth's composition of the passage, his rejection of it, his casting about for lines to take its place, and his sudden decision to write a longer poem, postponing the whole question of a final Book, all took place within a matter of several days. Even if Wordsworth regarded the five-Book poem as complete or virtually complete *circa* 10 March 1804,[4] it stood precariously between the composition and rejection of the analogy passage a few days earlier and the decision to expand the whole poem no more than a few days later. If a finished five-Book poem did exist, it lasted for less than a week. Given

---

[3] Wordsworth (1977).
[4] Ibid., p. 24.

that Wordsworth intended to use large blocks of previously composed material (the climbing of Snowdon and the 'spots of time' lines) for its introduction and conclusion, putting together the last book of the five-Book poem must have meant focusing on that central portion for which he wrote the analogy passage. Whether or not Book V was ever hammered into final shape, the attempt involved a significant struggle with the analogies. It should not be forgotten that the appearance of the passage in MS W suggests that it is the product of sustained attention. The passage occurs as an uninterrupted and quite legible block of verse; much of it has been copied a second time.[5]

It seems reasonable to theorize that the composition of the analogy passage played a significant role in Wordsworth's decision to rethink his entire poetic effort. Jonathan Wordsworth notes Wordsworth's anxiety at the prospect of finishing his autobiographical poem and returning to work on *The Recluse*, but he does not mention the effect that this anxiety must have had on the five-Book *Prelude* itself. A close look at the analogy passage supports something like the following speculation: As the five-Book poem neared completion in the first weeks of March 1804, Wordsworth began to think that it had not done its job. The thrust of the Snowdon episode – that *here* is a great mind prepared to write 'a work that should endure' – did not appear to be an earned conclusion, and the analogy passage followed.

The same letters that tell us that the five-Book poem is nearly complete are instructive in another way.

Early February 1804, to Francis Wrangham:

> . . . You do not know what a task it is to me, to write a Letter; I absolutely loath the sight of a Pen when I am to use it. . . . I have great things in meditation but as yet I have only been doing little ones. At present I am engaged in a Poem on my own earlier life which will take five parts or Books to complete, three of which are nearly finished. My other meditated works are a Philosophical Poem and a narrative one. These two will employ me some I ought to say several years, and I do not mean to appear before the world again as an Author till one of them at least be finished.

6 March 1804 to Thomas De Quincey:

---

[5] Microfilm of MS W in the Cornell Wordsworth Collection.

... I have a kind of derangement in my stomach and digestive organs which makes writing painful to me, and indeed almost prevents me from holding correspondence with any body: and this (I mean to say the unpleasant feelings which I have connected with the act of holding a Pen) has been the chief cause of my long silence.[6]

Apologies from tardy correspondents are not unusual, but Wordsworth's self-proclaimed letter phobia seems unusually severe. In both letters it crops up in close proximity to a discussion of the poem in progress or works planned. In addition, the apologies to Wrangham and De Quincey are related, chronologically and tonally, to the lines which follow the 'glad preamble' to the first Book of the 1805 *Prelude*. Significantly, these post-preamble lines appear for the first time in the collection of fair copies made for Coleridge in mid-March,[7] immediately following the period during which Wordsworth thought his five-Book poem was nearing completion – days which saw the composition of the analogy passage in MS W. The uneasy, self-deprecatory mood of the post-preamble centres on the poet's inability to write a great poem, one of the 'great things in meditation' mentioned in the letter to Wrangham:

> But from this awful burthen I full soon
> Take refuge, and beguile myself with trust
> That mellower years will bring a riper mind
> And clearer insight. Thus from day to day
> I live, a mockery of the brotherhood
> Of vice and virtue, with no skill to part
> Vague longing that is bred by want of power
> From paramount impulse not to be withstood,
> A timorous capacity from prudence;
> From circumspection, infinite delay.
> Humility and modest awe themselves
> Betray me, serving often for a cloak
> To a more subtle selfishness, that now
> Doth lock my functions up in blank reserve,
> Now dupes me by an over-anxious eye
> That with a false activity beats off

[6] *ET* 436, 453.
[7] MacGillivray, 'Three Forms', in Harvey and Gravil (eds), *Wordsworth*, p. 112.

Simplicity and self-presented truth.
– Ah! better far than this, to stray about
Voluptuously through fields and rural walks,
And ask no record of the hours.

(I. 235–54)

Wordsworth did not know whether or not he could bring himself to write his great 'Philosophical' and 'narrative' poems – awesome projects which must have loomed large as the five-Book *Prelude* neared completion in early March. The analogy passage appears to be an intuitive acting-out, in poetry, of the fears and self-doubts represented discursively in the post-preamble lines.

The analogy passage seems to have been generated by Wordsworth's fear that he might be incapable of producing a significant imaginative work. Geoffrey Hartman argues that Wordsworth's poems should be read as elaborate reactions to his deep-rooted fear of his own powerful 'apocalyptic imagination'.[8] But I would like to review Hartman's three-part reading of *The Prelude*, in order to establish that Wordsworth was less conscious of the dangerous growth of his autonomous imaginative powers than he was afraid that he might never achieve the mature self-possession necessary to great literary achievement. Hartman's ideas about Wordsworth's fear of imaginative power are hard to deny, but they can be seen in a different light by keeping in mind the poet's conscious fear of artistic failure.

According to Hartman, the first part of Book I (1805) shows Wordsworth's initial burst of self-confidence and imaginative autonomy challenged and subdued by a natural scene, the 'splendid evening' of Book I, line 101. Hartman asserts that the natural splendour of the evening 'teaches' the poet that 'the world demands' a more passive approach (p. 36). But in fact Wordsworth limits his description of the 'splendid evening' to those two words. It may well have been a very striking evening, but Wordsworth provides little justification for finding in it a powerful challenger to poetic effort. When the poet finds himself unable to compose – 'the harp / Was soon defrauded' – he turns to 'present joy' to escape from the 'utter silence' of his creative faculties (I. 104–9). He repeats the pattern later in the first Book, when the frustra-

---

[8] Geoffrey Hartman, *Wordsworth's Poetry 1787–1814* (New Haven, 1964), p. 61.

tions and 'false activity' of his poetic planning yield to a similar escapist impulse: 'better far than this, to stray about / Voluptuously through fields and rural walks' (I. 252–3).

The subject of Wordsworth's post-preamble is not so much metaphysical as moral. The poet is not struggling with an unresolved opposition between imagination and nature but with the much more straightforward, if no less difficult, question of his own recalcitrance. The post-preamble bears some resemblance to Samuel Johnson's essay on the same subject, *Rambler* 134.[9] Johnson explains why the man of 'more active faculties and more acute discernment' (not unlike Wordsworth's poet, in the 1800 Preface, with his 'greater promptness to think and feel without immediate external excitement') often finds it difficult to act:

> He to whom many objects of persuit arise at the same time, will frequently hesitate between different desires. . . . He who sees different ways to the same end, will, unless he watches carefully over his own conduct, lay out too much of his attention upon the comparison of probabilities.

Just as Wordsworth's escape to nature is interrupted: 'a longing in me rose / To brace myself to some determin'd aim' (I. 123–4), so Johnson recognizes that 'idleness can never secure tranquillity; the call of reason and conscience will pierce the closest pavilion of the sluggard, and, though it may not have force to drive him from his down, will be loud enough to hinder him from sleep'. Johnson counsels immediate engagement in some 'honest undertaking'; Wordsworth writes his autobiographical poem.

Hartman next focuses on the crossing the Alps passages in Book VI. He concludes that Wordsworth's realization of the independence of imagination from nature is so significant that it prompts the poet to interrupt his narrative of past events with the paean to 'Imagination' (VI. 525). The defiantly independent imagination – of young tourist and mature poet both – must be channeled back to nature via the 'narrow chasm' and the energetic reintegration of mind and nature that takes place there (pp. 43–8). What we might emphasize is the self-consciously literary context with which Wordsworth associates the crossing of the Alps. He and his 'brother Pilgrim' are representative young poets who dally deliberately with a literary melancholy:

---

[9] Repr. in *Selected Essays*, ed. W. J. Bate (New Haven, 1968), pp. 176–81.

> . . . dreams and fictions pensively compos'd,
> Dejection taken up for pleasure's sake,
>
> .   .   .   .
>
> . . . sober posies of funereal flowers,
> Cull'd from the gardens of Lady Sorrow,
> Did sweeten many a meditative hour.
>
> (VI. 481–7)

This conventional gloom is emphasized throughout Book VI:

> A melancholy from humours of the blood
> In part, and partly taken up, that lov'd
> A pensive sky, sad days, and piping winds,
> The twilight more than dawn, Autumn than Spring;
> A treasur'd and luxurious gloom . . . .
>
> (ll. 192–6)

> . . . a Poet's tender melancholy
> And fond conceit of sadness . . .
>
> (ll. 377–8)

Wordsworth tells the story of his experiences in the Simplon Pass to illustrate his passage from this vaguely poetic attitudinizing, through a 'dull and heavy slackening', and toward a profoundly renewed sense of imaginative activity. But his direct conclusion, drawn in the final lines of the tribute to the imagination, is that

> The mind beneath such banners militant
> Thinks not of spoils or trophies, nor of aught
> That may attest its prowess, blest in thoughts
> That are their own perfection and reward.
>
> (VI. 543–6)

Wordsworth's oddly martial language calls attention to the defiance in his assertion that the imagination is its own reward. The 'unripe' poet at least produced 'dreams and fictions', but the mature poet need produce nothing at all.

Hartman reads the climbing of Snowdon episode as Wordsworth's 'most astonishing avoidance of apocalypse' – his final and most successful attempt to evade self-conscious imaginative independence by insisting on the identity between the imagination and the powers of nature. For Hartman, the climbing of Snowdon is an ascent towards a shocking recognition of the human mind as a power radically separate from nature. The shock is overcome or 'elided' by a 'web of transfers' – the most important being Wordsworth's doubling of his central recognition: first light, then sound – which acts to blur and soften what might have proved to be a dangerous focus on imaginative power itself (pp. 63–6). Yet we should not overlook Wordsworth's announcement, as *The Prelude* comes to a close, of his intention and readiness to write the greater poems which were to follow. As though afraid that it might not be as clear as it should be, Wordsworth repeatedly and directly reminds himself and his reader that the growth of the poet's imagination has been his theme, that 'this faculty hath been the moving soul / Of our long labor' (XIII. 171–2), and

> we have reach'd
> The time (which was our object from the first)
> When we may, not presumptuously, I hope,
> Suppose my powers so far confirm'd, and such
> My knowledge, as to make me capable
> Of building up a work that should endure.
>
> (XIII. 273–8)

Wordsworth is asserting, not avoiding his imaginative autonomy, even though the assertion takes on an increasingly unconvincing note:

> Imagination, which, in truth,
> Is but another name for absolute strength
> And clearest insight, amplitude of mind,
> And reason in her most exalted mood.
>
> (XIII. 167–70)

As Jonathan Wordsworth observes, Wordsworth 'tries to impress by calling Imagination the most high-sounding names he can think of and fails because one is neither carried away nor intellectually convinced'.[10]

---

[10] Jonathan Wordsworth, 'The Climbing of Snowdon', in *Bicentenary Wordsworth Studies*, ed. Jonathan Wordsworth (Ithaca, NY, 1970), p. 467n.

Book XIII, as Jonathan Wordsworth puts it, begins with imaginative writing and trails off into writing about the imagination.[11] But during the composition of the five Book *Prelude,* Wordsworth's intention was to do more imaginative writing and less invincibly prosaic talking about it. The original gloss on the climbing of Snowdon was the analogy passage, and it shows Wordsworth unsure about his relationship to literary models, especially Milton, uneasy about the distance between suffering and tragic art, and humbled by natural powers so impressive that they defy artistic rendering.

The first two analogies – the rainbow and the statue horse – can be seen as relatively straightforward examples of nature working as an artist. The rainbow imposes order on chaos, or oneness on multiplicity, and the horse is an artefact, 'A living Statue or a statued Life' – a 'work of Nature's hand' that the poet and his companion contemplate with 'pleasure'. It is more difficult to understand the sense in which Wordsworth meant his series of four distressed voyagers to be representative of the 'analogy betwixt / The mind of man and nature'. De Selincourt's notes to the passage indicate the surprising number of phrases and whole lines which Wordsworth took directly from his travel-book sources.[12] This wholesale dependence on sources seems to indicate some flagging of the creative spirit, a sense of lost direction reflected in the powerlessness of the four adventurers themselves. There may even be some sense in which the passage anticipates the second half of the thirteen-Book *Prelude*. The faltering of Columbus's compass and Mungo Park's passage from despair to renewed hope bear a strong thematic resemblance to the upheaval of the French Revolution and Wordsworth's own spiritual crisis.

Overall, the four voyager analogies give an impression of the powerful ascendancy of nature over men tossing on the waves or lost in the desert. Nature is frighteningly energetic, thrusting her powers upon us, forcing us to notice her, as she calls man 'To give new grandeur to her ministry' (l. 53). But it is significant that the voyagers are available only to those 'who read the story at their ease' (l. 66). The awful powers of nature are distanced by the Books which relate them, just as in the 1815 Preface Virgil's imperilled goat becomes a much more affecting image

---

[11] Ibid., p. 473.
[12] OET *Prelude*, 625–7.

when we realize that a shepherd is watching it 'from the seclusion of the cavern in which he lies stretched at ease and in security'.[13] Even more interesting is Wordsworth's elaboration of artistic distance in the Sir Humphrey Gilbert analogy. We read Wordsworth, and he tells us that he has read the story of Gilbert's drowning. In the story, Gilbert's men watch him from the safety of the larger ship, while Gilbert himself sits calmly on the deck of his endangered pinnace, reading yet another book. This Chinese puzzle of distanced observers leaves us with a strong sense that Wordsworth is grappling with but not solving questions of con- scious artistic control. The lines on Gilbert's 'engulphment' are perhaps less moving than curious, but they leave the reader uneasy about the relationship between art and nature. Gilbert's calm is directly related to his reading, but it does him little apparent good.

A similar uneasiness about the power of art can be seen in the appear- ance of the rainbow over Coniston:

> A large unmutilated rainbow stood
> Immovable in heav'n, kept standing there
> With a colossal stride bridging the vale,
> The substance thin as dreams, lovelier than day, –
> Amid the deafening uproar stood unmov'd,
> Sustain'd itself through many minutes space;
> As if it were pinn'd down by adamant.

We begin to wonder whether the rainbow 'stood' or was 'kept stand- ing', whether it 'sustain'd itself' or was 'pinn'd down'. This deliberately sustained tension between actives and passives must be related to the peculiar energy of the word 'unmutilated', which implies the existence of a potent force bent on destroying and defiling. The 'substance thin as dreams' acquires the hardness and tangibility of adamant and 'stands' in an almost military posture of self-defence that recalls the 'bodies' of foam that 'took flight' a few lines earlier. The 'strange chance' by which the rainbow appears is hardly triumphant. Even while it lasts, the rain- bow is limited to the visual realm and has no effect on the 'deafening uproar' which remains unchecked.

The rainbow is not the central synthetic or ordering principle that it might at first seem to be. As an analogue for the mind of a poet who is

---

[13] *Prose Works*, iii. 33.

about to write the great works of his maturity it is hardly promising. Moreover, the passage owes a surprising debt to Milton. Wordsworth's 'ten thousand thousand waves' derive from the 'ten thousand thousand Saints' who accompany the triumphant Son of God during the war in heaven in *Paradise Lost* (vi. 767). The Son's (borrowed) chariot is decorated with all 'the colors of the show'ry Arch' (l. 759). The fallen angels have invented cannon, and the 'hollow engines long and round' (l. 484) reappear in Wordsworth's analogy passage when the wind over Coniston is 'compress'd as in a tunnel' (l. 10). Satan tries in vain to protect his 'ethereal substance' with a shield of 'tenfold adamant' (l. 255), and his legions wear armour only to have it 'crushed in and bruised, / Into their substance pent' (ll. 656–7). When Wordsworth wrote that the 'substance thin as dreams' of his rainbow looked as though it were 'pinn'd down by adamant', he must have had Milton's language in mind. When the battle in heaven escalates, both sides begin to throw entire mountains:

> They pluckt the seated Hills with all thir load,
> Rocks, Waters, Woods, and by the shaggy tops
> Uplifting bore them in thir hands. . . .
>
> .   .   .   .
>
> So Hills amid the Air encounter'd Hills
> Hurl'd to and fro with jaculation dire,
> That underground they fought in dismal shade:
> Infernal noise; War seem'd a civil Game
> To this uproar. . . .
>
> (VI. 644–6, 664–8)

In Wordsworth's passage, 'Green leaves were rent in handfuls from the trees' (l. 16), and when the rainbow appears, it displaces a suggestively latinate 'tumultuous' light (l. 15). Of course it might be said that Wordsworth is very little intimidated by the burden of the past if he is content to brave Milton in this way, but Wordsworth's rainbow has a much less significant effect on chaos than does Milton's Chariot of the Paternal Deity. Wordsworth returned to the same lines from Book VI of *Paradise Lost* when writing his 1815 Preface.[14] There the 'ten thousand

---

[14] *Prose Works*, iii. 35. It should be noted that the Wordsworthian coinages involving the word 'under', pointed out by de Selincourt (OET *Prelude*, 622), may derive from the odd jocularity of Milton's puns on '*under*standing' in Book VI of *Paradise Lost*.

thousand Saints' merged under Christ's leadership are cited as an example of the mind's ability to consolidate numbers into unity, a power
'proceeding from and governed by a sublime consciousness of the soul
in her mighty and almost divine powers'.

The much less confident poet of the analogy passage is not a creator
but an interpreter of artifacts provided by nature. He is dependent on
the chance appearance of objects like the rainbow and the statue horse –
objects which appear only momentarily and whose incommunicable significance he attempts to capture in verse. Wordsworth's carefully modulated repetitions serve to evoke rather than define the meaning of his
analogies; description moves toward patterned incantation:

> Bodies of foam took *flight*, and the whole vale
> Was wrought into commotion *high and low* –
> Mist *flying up and down*, bewilder'd showers,
>
> .   .   .   .
>
> Insensible and *still*, – *breath*, motion *gone*,
> Hairs, colour, all but shape and substance *gone*,
> Mane, ears, and tail, as *lifeless* as the trunk
> That had no stir of *breath*; . . .
>
> (ll. 11–13, 39–42; my italics)

Perhaps the most striking aspect of the analogies is the degree to which
they resemble the 'spots of time' – those 'moving episodes' which, tightly
clustered, made up most of the earliest *Prelude* in 1798. The analogies
amount almost to a catalogue of themes familiar from the 'spots'. The
storm over Coniston repeats the pattern of uproar followed by stasis
found in the skating scene (I. 460ff.) and the Winander boy lines (V.
389ff.). The statue horse, Mungo Park and Dampier analogies recall the
importance of the horizon in the 'spots' involving the stolen rowboat
(I. 372ff.), the dedication to poetry (IV. 316ff.), and the discharged
soldier (IV. 400ff). Several 'spots' centre around the appearance of a
ghostly figure on the horizon, and the statue horse – whatever 'pleasure' Wordsworth tells us it gave him – must be added to a list that
includes the discharged soldier, the drowned man (V. 450ff.), and the
'huge cliff' (I. 409) of the stolen rowboat episode. Even the self-consciously chivalric language with which so many of the 'spots' begin –
'She was an elfin Pinnace' (I. 401), 'We were a pair of horsemen; honest

James / Was with me . . .' (XI. 283) – turns up in the analogy passage as Dampier sees

> danger coming on, not in a shape
> Which in the heat and mettle of his blood
> He oft had welcomed . . . .
>
> (ll. 95–7)

The parallels between the analogies and the 'spots of time' seem to show that the impulse behind the analogies was autobiographical, but it appears that this impulse was complicated and obscured by Wordsworth's struggle to use the analogies to prove his artistic maturity. Perhaps the best way to explain the analogies is to see them as 'spots of time' on which Wordsworth has superimposed the concerns of a creative artist. We have seen the ways in which the analogies reveal Wordsworth's pre-occupation with Milton and his concern for artistic distance and control. The analogies even represent a brief catalogue of the arts of painting (the rainbow), sculpture (the statue horse), and dramatic 'spectacle' (the voyagers). But when Wordsworth tells us that he experienced a conventional neoclassical 'pleasure' at the sight of the statue horse, he gives perhaps the most obvious indication that the purpose of his analogies is not in tune with their effect. The horse, 'With all his functions silently sealed up', seems more likely to frighten than to please, and we glimpse Wordsworth trying to tailor an odd personal episode to fit at least one of the supposed demands of a more mature art. The same impulse led Wordsworth to the travel books in which he found dramatic, objectified versions of essentially personal events. The little boy in the stolen rowboat (I. 372ff.) becomes, in the analogy passage, Dampier in his Nicobar canoe. The difference between the two passages is that Dampier, unlike the little boy, is 'made calm, at length, by prayer and trust in God' (l. 101) – an anticipation of Wordsworth's own turn to the consolation of orthodox religion.

The analogy passage shows us Wordsworth at a particularly turbulent moment in his poetic career. About to finish *The Prelude* and facing the start of his great work, Wordsworth began to question his own imaginative strength. Ironically, the questions that haunt the analogies are vastly more interesting than the prosaic assertions that replaced them in 1805.

'Into a Populous Plain': The Five-Book *Prelude* (1982)

Jonathan Wordsworth

The two-Part *Prelude* of 1798–9 contains no version of the Fall. Though following closely on *Tintern Abbey*'s elegiac tones, and emerging from a moment of self-accusation and self-doubt, it is one of Wordsworth's most optimistic poems. The 'spots of time' of Part I successfully nourish adult creativity, and the babe of Part II, who is 'creator and receiver both', unlike the child of *Intimations*, who will convict the poet of his loss, is shown in his imaginative power to be a source of confidence:

> Such, verily, is the first
> Poetic spirit of our human life –
> By uniform control of after years
> In most abated or suppressed, in some
> Through every change of growth or of decay
> Preeminent till death.

> (*Two-Part Prelude*, ii 305–10)

The final implications of *1799* are that childhood and adolescence lead

Extracted from *William Wordsworth: The Borders of Vision* (Oxford, 1982), pp. 235–46.

forward to a period of fuller awareness; and this is still Wordsworth's position when in December 1801 he extends his poem into a third Part in order to take in the concluding lines of *The Pedlar*. 'I had an eye', he writes, adapting the third-person narrative of Alfoxden,

> Which from a stone, a tree, a withered leaf,
> To the broad ocean and the azure heavens
> Spangled with kindred multitudes of stars,
> Could find no surface where its power might sleep . . .
>   (Book III, ll. 160–3)[1]

As perhaps one would expect, the metaphor of lost paradise appears first at the beginning of 1804, when Wordsworth resumes work on Part III, intending now to create a *Prelude* in five Parts (or Books). Almost at once there are reminders that this is the period in which *Intimations* was completed –

> O Heavens, how awful is the might of souls,
> And what they do within themselves while yet
> The yoke of earth is new to them . . .
>   (Book III, ll. 177–9)

– but loss of vision was not merely a preoccupation of the moment, it had structural implications too. The first three Books of the five-Book *Prelude* are preserved as *1805*, I–III; Book IV was expanded to form *1805*, IV and V, and must have contained most of their important material; it was the last Book that gave the poem its unique and satisfying shape. Book V was to consist of the Climbing of Snowdon, followed by the 'spots of time' sequence that had been extracted from *1799*, Part I. The poem was thus to begin and end in childhood, the source of Wordsworth's adult power; and *en route* it was to portray and exemplify the loss and regaining of paradise. Imagination, nourished in childhood, sustained in adolescence, was to be impaired for a while by the poet's entry into adult life, yet shown once more in its full glory in the epiphany of Snowdon when he was 21.[2]

---

[1] Originally *Pedlar*, 350–3.
[2] For a detailed reconstruction of this intermediate *Prelude*, see Wordsworth (1977); a more general account of the content of Books IV and V is offered in note 6, below.

Wordsworth's immediate task in January 1804 was to take his poem on from the high point of 18-year-old communion, or creative perception, reached in the *Pedlar* insertions of 1801. By now he may well have felt that shades of the prison-house would have closed rather earlier round the growing boy, but in any event he lost no time in switching his story onto a downward course:

> And here, O friend, have I retraced my life
> Up to an eminence, and told a tale
> Of matters which not falsely I may call
> The glory of my youth . . . .
> Enough, for now into a populous plain
> We must descend.
>
> (Book III, ll. 167–95)

There is no lack of confidence as Wordsworth descends from his eminence. The glory of his youth is defined in claims that Blake could not have taken an inch further, and that are (as they would be in Blake) a deliberate affront to Milton:

> Of genius, power,
> Creation, and divinity itself,
> I have been speaking, for my theme has been
> What passed within me.
>
> (Book III, ll. 170–3)

And as if the implications might be missed, Wordsworth adds a defiant, almost truculent, allusion – '*This* is in truth heroic argument, / And genuine prowess' – which relegates Milton as firmly as Milton had once relegated Virgil and Homer, to a now outmoded past. It does not mean that he is any the less dependent on his predecessor, just that he can use him now for his own purposes. Wordsworth by this stage has clearly decided to include a version of the Fall that will demonstrate a need for restoration through the 'spots of time'. The populous plain of Cambridge turns out to have much in common with the 'spacious plain, whereon / Were tents of various hue' which is shown by Michael to Adam from the 'hill / Of Paradise the highest' (*Paradise Lost*, xi. 556–7 and 377–8). Wordsworth the freshman –

> I was a chosen son.
> For hither I had come with holy powers
> And faculties, whether to work or feel . . .
>
> (Book III, ll. 81–3)

– resembles the just men of Milton's poem, 'all their study bent / To worship God aright', who are seduced by the 'bevy of fair women richly gay' (*Paradise Lost*, xi. 577ff.) that represent false pleasures. And the test to which he is being submitted is surely implied in the terms of Michael's rebuke to Adam:

> Judge not what is best
> By pleasure, though to nature seeming meet,
> Created, as thou art, to nobler end
> Holy and pure, conformity divine.
> Those tents thou saw'st so pleasant, were the tents
> Of wickedness . . .
>
> (*Paradise Lost*, xi. 603–8)

The five-Book *Prelude* was to take Wordsworth's autobiography only to the age of 21, and he clearly started out with the intention of showing imagination impaired at, and by, Cambridge. In the event, however, he failed to portray a convincing deterioration in Book III, and had to make further attempts in IV and V. The problem was not that he didn't see the university as a temptation – his warnings to De Quincey six weeks later about Oxford were as moral as anyone could wish[3] – but that he couldn't feel that he himself had yielded. An odd see-saw movement is set up within the verse as the poet struggles to meet the demands of his chosen structure, yet is unable to bring himself to describe a fall from grace. 'It hath been told already how my sight / Was dazzled by the novel show', he writes of the early Cambridge days, but adds in haste, 'and how erelong / I did into myself return' (iii. 202–4). There was

---

[3] 'I am anxious to hear how far you are satisfied with yourself at Oxford; and, above all, that you have not been seduced into unworthy pleasures or pursuits.' He believes moral standards at both Universities to have improved very much since his day, when 'The manners of the young men were very frantic and dissolute', but goes on all the same, 'I need not say to you that there is no true dignity but in virtue and temperance, and, let me add, chastity' (*EY* 453–4).

> a treasonable growth
> Of indecisive judgements that impaired
> And shook the mind's simplicity. *And yet*
> This was a gladsome time . . .
>
> (Book III, ll. 216–19)

And so it goes on; or at least, the alternation goes on – the degree of blame attaching to the negative side of the balance gets progressively less and less. One moment of self-criticism does stand out –

> Yet could I only cleave to solitude
> In lonesome places – if a throng was near
> That way I leaned by nature, for my heart
> Was social and loved idleness and joy
>
> (Book III, ll. 235–8)

– but it is not easy at this stage in the poem to give the words full weight. The reader's final impression of Cambridge is contained in the typical statement *plus* retraction: 'Imagination slept, / And yet not utterly . . .'. Wordsworth it would seem was seldom deeply touched,[4] but one never feels that the sleeping imagination has truly been impaired, or that the activities of the day-to-day mind have power to cause it injury. They are a continuation, inappropriate perhaps but not harmful, of the boyhood pleasures of Book II:

> We sauntered, played, we rioted, we talked
> Unprofitable talk at morning hours,
> Drifted about along the streets and walks,
> Read lazily in lazy books, went forth
> To gallop through the country in blind zeal
> Of senseless horsemanship, or on the breast
> Of Cam sailed boisterously, and let the stars
> Come out perhaps without one quiet thought.
>
> (Book III, ll. 255–62)

Wordsworth makes one last attempt to show impairment at Cambridge in the bizarre simile of the floating island of Derwentwater:

---

[4] 'Caverns there were within my mind which sun / Could never penetrate' (iii. 248–9); 'Hushed meanwhile / Was the under-soul' (iii. 532–3).

> Rotted as by a charm, my life became
> A floating island, an amphibious thing,
> Unsound, of spungy texture, yet withal
> Not wanting a fair face of water-weeds
> And pleasant flowers
>
> (Book III, ll. 340–4)

The lines stand out both as eccentric poetry (a case in which vivid personal memory has not been successfully transmuted),[5] and because the implications of the image are felt to be too extreme. In the passage that follows, Wordsworth effusively takes on himself all blame for lack of academic commitment –

> I should in truth,
> As far as doth concern my single self,
> Misdeem most widely, lodging it elsewhere . . .
>
> (Book III, ll. 356–8)

– then slides into self-justification: as a spoilt child of Nature, used to rambling like the wind, he was 'ill-tutored for captivity' (iii. 363). Presumably he is unaware of meaning also that he was 'ill-tutored *in* captivity', but he goes on at once to

> The image of a place which – soothed shape and lulled
> As [he] had been, trained up in paradise
> Among sweet garlands and delightful sounds . . .
>
> (Book III, ll. 376–9)

should have 'bent [him] down / To instantaneous service' (iii. 383–4), drawn from him the homage that he had been used to give to Nature. Paradise it now seems has not been actively *lost* at all, merely left behind in childhood and the Lake District. When Wordsworth does for a moment return to his structural metaphor of the Fall, it is as if he has forgotten what it is there for:

---

[5] For Wordsworth's prose account of the floating island, see *Guide to the Lakes* (*Prose Works*, ii. 184). Catherine Drucker points out to me that a literary precedent for moralizing the island's instability is provided by Spenser's wandering islands of *Faerie Queene*, II. xii. 87ff.

> For me, I grieve not; happy is the man
> Who only misses what I missed, who falls
> No lower than I fell.
>
> (Book III, ll. 497–9)

Having failed to portray a Fall at Cambridge with any conviction, Wordsworth is left with the more difficult task of showing one on his return to the Lake District for the summer vacation of 1789. Book IV of the five-Book *Prelude* cannot be reconstructed in every detail;[6] but certainly present was the Hawkshead consecration scene, 'I made no vows, but vows / Were then made for me'. None of the great *Prelude* sequences is more lamely, more negatively, introduced:

> And yet, in chastisement of these regrets,
> The memory of one particular hour
> Doth here rise up against me.
>
> (Book IV, ll. 116–18)

Wordsworth the poet has been making another attempt to show 'an inner falling-off':

> sure it is that now
> Contagious air did oft environ me,
> Unknown among these haunts in former days.
> The very garments that I wore appeared
> To prey upon my strength, and stopped the course
> And quiet stream of self-forgetfulness.
>
> (Book IV, ll. 158–63)

To Wordsworth the student in this mood of Hamlet-like depression, man

---

[6] The original Book IV was completed at the end of February 1804 in 650 lines. It consisted of two clearly defined sections, the first concerned with the poet's experiences at Hawkshead in summer 1789, the second with education and the beneficial influence of books. *1805*, IV and V, were created in a matter of days when *c.*10 March Wordsworth decided to reorganize his poem, and it seems that all he had to do was divide his existing Book into its component halves, and work up an opening section for each from material at least partly written the previous month. The one major sequence of *1805*, IV and V, that was almost certainly not present in the five-Book poem (though it had been composed in February) is the Quixote dream.

> Seems but a pageant playing with vile claws,
> And this great frame of breathing elements
> A senseless idol.
>
> (Book IV, ll. 171–3)

The imagery is impressively vehement,[7] but as at Cambridge it is not clear what the falling-off amounts to, and as before the poet shies away from the implications of what he has said. A memory – no mere recollection, but a daemonic power within the self – on this occasion rises up against him like the mountain on Ullswater rather than let him tell us that imagination has been seriously impaired.

In Wordsworth's mind, though he does not say so, is Milton once again. For a moment he had seemed to be recounting his personal Fall, as his undergraduate self, environed by contagious air within the paradise of Hawkshead, came to see Nature ('this great frame of breathing elements') as a senseless idol. Instead he presents an incident that implies not just that no Fall has taken place, or could ever have taken place, but that he, Wordsworth, has been chosen as Milton's successor. The opening lines show a connection in the poet's mind that is possibly unconscious: he had passed the night dancing amid a 'promiscuous rout, / A medley of all tempers', and all four words are Miltonic in this usage.[8] The lines that follow, however, are conscious without doubt in their weighing of the language and landscape and assumptions of Wordsworth against those of *Paradise Lost*:

> Magnificent
> The morning was, a memorable pomp,
> More glorious than I ever had beheld.
> The sea was laughing at a distance; all
> The solid mountains were as bright as clouds,
> Grain-tinctured, drenched in empyrean light;
> And in the meadows and the lower grounds

---

[7] Wordsworth almost certainly has in mind the near life-sized clockwork model of a tiger savaging a white man that was housed at the East India Company when Lamb was showing him and Dorothy round London in 1802 (Owen, 'Tipu's Tiger', 379–80). The model had been made for the tyrant Tipu Sultan, and captured at the fall of Seringapatam. It is now at the Victoria and Albert Museum.

[8] As J. C. Maxwell pointed out in the Penguin *Prelude* (1971).

> Was all the sweetness of a common dawn –
> Dews, vapours, and the melody of birds,
> And labourers going forth into the fields.
>
> (Book IV, ll. 132–41)

The landscape has two levels, two imaginative worlds – Milton's celestial one, in which solid mountains turn to clouds drenched in crimson light from the empyrean, seat of the pure element of fire; and Wordsworth's own, where the sea laughs like daffodils with the pleasure of the poet, where dawn 'in the meadows and the lower grounds' is full of its normal infinite sweetness, and where 'labourers going forth into the fields' as the poet himself will now go forth, wear their biblical associations very lightly, just tenderly hinting at the fitness of things:

> And out of what one sees and hears and out
> Of what one feels, who could have thought to make
> So many selves, so many sensuous worlds,
> As if the air, the mid-day air, was swarming
> With the metaphysical changes that occur,
> Merely in living as and where we live.[9]

Wordsworth is as aware as Stevens and the rest of us just how rare it is to see a common dawn as he sees it. Indeed he takes the depth of his response, as he had taken the imaginative experiences of *1799*, Part I, to be evidence of his election:

> need I say, dear friend, that to the brim
> My heart was full? I made no vows, but vows
> Were then made for me: bond unknown to me
> Was given that I should be – else sinning greatly –
> A dedicated spirit. On I walked
> In blessedness, which even yet remains.
>
> (Book IV, ll. 142–7)

The effect of the dedication scene has been to identify the power within the self that refuses to let the poet structure his work in terms of a Fall. So strong is it, that it is felt to have been imposed from without – truly daemonic. Harold Bloom in passing defines the superego as 'the One

---

[9] Wallace Stevens, conclusion of *Esthétique du mal*.

who commands us', and this would seem a peculiarly dominant example. Wordsworth records not merely a sense of vocation (of having been
called), but a feeling that his very answer to that call had been made for
him. In the circumstances, failure to live according to the dictates of this
power would be the only Fall that could matter, and by implication even
at the time of writing (February 1804) there had still been no such
failure.

No further attempt is made in Book IV of this intermediate *Prelude*
to portray imagination impaired. The fifth, and last, Book may not have
been completed when Wordsworth decided in early March 1804 to reorganize his material and work towards a longer poem, but it must have
consisted broadly of the first third of *1805*, XIII, followed by the last
two-thirds of XI. The Climbing of Snowdon showed mature imagination at its height, and the 'spots of time' sequence demonstrated the
sources of Wordsworth's adult strength – more particularly, the sources
of the mind's power of self-restoration. It was seemingly this last factor
that led the poet to make a final attempt to introduce a Fall into his
narrative. The 'spots of time' doctrine had from the first been associated
with the invisible repair as well as the nourishment of the mind, but
merely in the context of 'trivial occupations and the round / Of ordinary intercourse'; now Wordsworth inserted between the two central
'spots' the great lines, 'Oh mystery of man, from what a depth / Proceed thy honours' (Book V, ll. 332–3), ending in their original version:

> The days gone by
> Come back upon me from the dawn almost
> Of life; the hiding-places of my power
> Seem open, I approach, and then they close;
> *Yet have I singled out – not satisfied*
> *With general feelings, here and there have culled –*
> *Some incidents that may explain whence come*
> *My restorations, and with yet one more of these*
> *Will I conclude.*
>
> (Book V, ll. 337–45)

If the poem was to end as well as begin in childhood memories chosen because Wordsworth believed them to have had a restorative effect,
it was more than ever necessary that he should demonstrate a need for
restoration. The central section in which he attempts to do so is the part

of the final Book that may never have been completed, but drafts reveal the normal short uneasy motion in the verse. Wordsworth tries successively to show 'The unremitting warfare from the first / Waged' against imagination, his own 'Sad perplexity / In moral knowledge', enslavement to analytic reason, and (most incongruous) a tendency to aesthetic judgements of Nature. But as each attempt to put a negative position prompts a positive one, we get interspersed a series of tributes to Nature for her care and protection. Both the senses and the objects of their perception have apparently been subordinated by her 'To the great ends of liberty and power', and Mary Hutchinson is offered as a type of the natural piety which it now seems that the poet has shared all along. The 'spots of time' are finally introduced by a statement that Wordsworth's imagination has never seriously been impaired. All his efforts to impose a structure go by the board as he announces:

> In truth the malady of which I speak
> Though aided by the times, whose deeper sound
> Without my knowledge sometimes might perchance
> Make rural Nature's milder minstrelsies
> Inaudible, did never take in me
> Deep root or larger action. I had received
> Impressions far too early and too strong
> For this to last: I threw the habit off
> Entirely and for ever, and again
> In Nature's presence stood as I do now
> A sensitive and creative soul.
>
> (Book V, ll. 269–79)

The Fall, it seems, had been no more than a passing phase. Early 'impressions' – 'spots of time' imprinted on the mind – had merely to reassert themselves, for all to be well.

The poet's vehemence – '*far* too early and too strong / For this to last' – carries an implication that the child's impressions were stronger for being early, closer to the hiding-places of power. Wordsworth is clearly thinking in terms of a Fall into experience, and yet he states categorically that a mind protected, or supported, by memories of primal vision contains within itself a redemptive principle which the world of experience cannot seriously affect. Once again his position is very close to De Quincey's in *Suspiria*. 'Of this, at least', De Quincey writes,

I feel assured, that there is no such thing as *forgetting* possible to the mind; a thousand accidents may and will interpose a veil between our present consciousness and the secret inscriptions on the mind. Accidents of the same sort will also rend away this veil; but alike, whether veiled or unveiled, the inscription remains forever . . .

(Ward, 91)

The great image of the palimpsest – vellum used for successive layers of manuscript, all remaining legible despite the effects of time, and efforts to erase them – shows that for De Quincey, as for Wordsworth, such inscriptions owe their power to the sense they give of an ultimate harmony:

What else than a natural and mighty palimpsest is the human brain? Such a palimpsest is my brain; such a palimpsest, O reader, is yours. Everlasting layers of ideas, images, feelings, have fallen upon your brain softly as light. Each succession has seemed to bury all that went before. And yet, in reality, not one has been extinguished. . . . The fleeting accidents of a man's life and its external shows may indeed be irrelate and incongruous; but the organizing principles which fuse into harmony and gather about fixed predetermined centers whatever heterogeneous elements life may have accumulated from without will not permit the grandeur of human unity greatly to be violated or its ultimate repose to be troubled . . .

(Ward, 169–70)

It is all, in many ways, extremely Wordsworthian. 'The grandeur of human unity' – that of the individual human consciousness, as well as of humanity in general – rests upon the oneness of disparate experience. Harmony is to be perceived through the recovery of underlying layers: 'I, the child', as De Quincey puts it elsewhere in a footnote, 'had the feelings; I, the man, decypher them. In the child lay the handwriting mysterious to *him*, in me the interpretation and the comment' (Ward, 139). The interpretation does, however, vary, and so does the optimism with which the two writers confront the Fall into experience. Both portray an education through suffering that is guided, and presided over, by beneficent powers.[10] Both seek out ways in which their writing may

---

[10] De Quincey's numinous, nebulous goddess, Levana, is very much the equivalent of the personified Nature who in *1805*, Book I, prompts the child to take the shepherd's boat on Ullswater.

express 'the mighty abstractions that incarnate themselves in all individual sufferings of man's heart' (Ward, 174). But for De Quincey suffering persists as the condition of human life – it is the source of adult
recognitions, and in itself a connection with the past[11] – whereas for the
Wordsworth of the five-Book *Prelude* recollections of early pain, fear,
discomfiture, can positively enhance the joys of a later period. The Woman
on the Hill is now for the first time followed by reminiscences of the
poet's 'time of early love' with Mary Hutchinson and Dorothy in the
summer of 1789:

> When, in the blessèd time of early love,
> Long afterwards I roamed about
> In daily presence of this very scene,
> Upon the naked pool and dreary crags,
> And on the melancholy beacon, fell
> The spirit of pleasure and youth's golden gleam –
> And think ye not with radiance more divine
> From these remembrances, and from the power
> They left behind?

'So feeling comes in aid / Of feeling', Wordsworth adds, 'and diversity
of strength / Attends us, if but once we have been strong' (*1805*, xi.
317–27). The sense that border vision can be retrieved, or at least that a
secondary imaginative strength ('O joy that in our embers / Is something that doth live') can be derived from strong impressions surviving
of the first, is deeply at odds with the structure that he has been trying
to impose upon his poem. It would have been convenient to be able to
show the 'populous plain' of Cambridge as having for a time truly impaired the imagination, or to have been able to portray some convincing
Fall in the Hawkshead Long Vacation, but a nameless force was at work
as he wrote that would not permit the unity of human grandeur greatly
to be violated. Reading back through the palimpsest of his mind –

> The days gone by
> Come back upon me from the dawn almost
> Of life . . .
>
> (*1805* xi. 333–5)

---

[11] 'Years that were far asunder', he writes in the *Confessions*, 'were bound together by
subtle links of suffering derived from a common root' (Ward, 57).

– it seemed to the poet as he was making the five-Book *Prelude* that feeling had always come in aid of feeling, and always would. He was conscious the hiding-places of his power as closing when he approached, but did not at this moment doubt that the power itself persisted.[12]

---

[12] A year later, in the very different circumstances under which the material from the five-Book poem was revised for *1805*, Book XI, he was to add the sad, self-knowing words, 'I see by glimpses now, when age comes on / May scarcely see at all' (xi. 337–8).

The Five-Book *Prelude*
of January–March 1804
(1984)

Kenneth R. Johnston

By making him appear less powerfully insightful and less socially mature, Wordsworth's dismantling of the 1799 *Prelude* made his autobiographical representation of the growth of his mind more realistic. An autobiography was not, however, what he was clearly set on writing. Although *The Prelude* is one of the most autobiographical works in English literature, none of its versions is *an* autobiography, and a great deal of confusion arises – about both the poem and the poet's life – if any version is read as literal autobiography. Since much of *The Prelude* recounts how Wordsworth did not, after all, move out into public Human Life, but came back home to the Lakes (and, he argues, to a higher conception of his life's work than society had been able to provide him), his thematic problem in dealing with Human Life correlates, in the expanding composition of the poem, with the dilemma he raises in the Introduction: the lack of a 'steady choice' of 'time, place, and manners' other than his own, suggesting that the autobiographical mode was, initially, as much a cause of blockage as it was of advancement. As suggested by the evident reasons for his failure to complete 'Home at Grasmere' in 1800, Wordsworth's problem was to generalize persuasively

Extracted from *Wordsworth and the Recluse* (New Haven, 1984), pp. 106–10.

beyond his own experience to the world at large. It was what Coleridge, sure of his man, had repeatedly said Wordsworth must do: 'I prophesy immortality to his *Recluse*, as the first and finest philosophical Poem, if only it be (as it undoubtedly will be) a Faithful Transcript of his own most august & innocent Life, of his own habitual Feelings & Modes of seeing and hearing' (Griggs, i. 1034). Notwithstanding that such descriptions of *The Recluse* seem to denote *The Prelude* as well, Wordsworth, for all his putative egotism, was less convinced of the sufficiency of this argument than Coleridge.

Therefore, in his first full resumption of 'the poem to Coleridge' in early 1804, before deciding to describe his own 'time, place, and manners' as 'a theme single and of determined bounds', he assayed to transpose the two-Part poem of 1799 into a five-Book poem organized on the theme of 'Books and Nature', or nurture and nature, education and environment. This would make his life appear normative by presenting it in the familiar classical genre of the young poet's education, resurgently popular in such widely varying late-eighteenth-century forms as Beattie's *The Minstrel*, Collins's 'Ode on the Poetical Character', and Blake's *Milton*. Wordsworth's five-Book contribution to this genre would have rounded off the 1799 version not by chronological expansion but by thematic control. It would have complemented *1799*'s emphasis on Nature with acknowledgement of the gifts of civilization and culture through formal education. The 1799 version pictures a powerfully spiritual young man, but if we did not already know he was William Wordsworth we might suppose him destined to become a philosopher, moralist, or priest, for all the poem tells us about the extent of his hopes for his poetry. But in the five-Book version we would recognize a poetical education and the start of the young poet's realization of his promise by enunciating his characteristic themes, as Pope did in his *Essay on Criticism*. In this sense, the five-Book plan represents the most fully developed stage of *The Prelude* as an actual, plausible prelude or portico to *The Recluse*.

This five-part *Prelude*, as reconstituted by textual scholars, would have contained Books I–III largely as we now know them, a Book IV containing most of the present Books IV *and* V, and a fifth concluding book that would have opened with the ascent of Snowdon and closed with the 'spots of time'. Between this fifth Book's introduction and conclusion there would have been some description of Wordsworth's imaginative impairment but no mention of the French Revolution, only some description of domestic tribulations. Thus the five-Book *Prelude* would have had a mighty finale, but the reader would have wondered why all the rhetorical power of Snowdon and the 'spots of time' was necessary when the only crises needing to be overcome were, on the evidence offered in five Books, the speaker's disaffection with college and contemporary educational theories, some rather far-fetched fears about the perishability of books, and an overstated distaste for the claims of domestic life on a poet's time.

As provisionally reconstructed by Jonathan Wordsworth and Stephen Gill, the middle section of this fifth Book gives an abstract of the impairments of imagination which Wordsworth felt interfered with his progress. The absence of any mention of the French Revolution is most striking, especially in contrast to Wordsworth's complaints about domestic cares which, functionally, must play the same role as the revolutionary books in the finished 1805 *Prelude*. He laments

> The unremitting warfare from the first
> Waged with this faculty [Imagination], its various foes
> Which for the most continue to increase.
> With growing life and burdens which it brings
> Of petty duties and degrading cares,
> Labour and penury, disease and grief,
> Which to one object chain the impoverished mind
> Enfeebled and defeated, vexing strife
> At home, and want of pleasure and repose,
> And all that eats away the genial spirits,
> May be fit matter for another song;
> Nor less the misery brought into the world
> By degradation of this power misplaced
> And misemployed, whence emanates
> Blinding cares, ambition obvious,
> And all the superstitions of this life,
> A mournful catalogue.
>
> (Book V, ll. 146–62)

Although Jonathan Wordsworth says this account of 'the degradation of social life' is more appropriate to *The Recluse*,[1] its main burden is self-pity,

---

[1] Wordsworth (1977), 18.

and is not likely to provide 'fit matter for another song' that anyone would want to read for very long. Wordsworth's care to keep his imagination safe from being 'misplaced and misemployed' bears more particularly on *The-Prelude*-as-prelude-to-*The-Recluse*, since it signifies in part Wordsworth's determination, under Coleridge's urging, to write only the greatest poetry he is capable of producing, and to resist the easy temptation of shorter poems. The *misplacement* and *misemployment* of imagination in social contexts are also the effective motive forces – as 'degrading cares' – of *The Prelude*'s residential structure. In these lines' 'warfare' imagery, we see imagination beset by internal distractions and ringed round by enemies without, which Wordsworth developed in a series of 'living pictures' intended to connect this passage about imagination's 'unremitting warfare' to the Snowdon vision. They all concentrate on moments of profound stillness at the heart of great agitation, in which heroic explorers (Columbus, Mungo Park) are shown at the very instant they move into a startlingly new, incomprehensible reality, whether of discovery, recovery from disaster, or the certain imminence of death and destruction. The bearing of these images would have been obscure in the five-Book *Prelude*, though it is easy enough to see, from the vantage of the thirteen-Book version, that these explorers are metaphors for Wordsworth, ringed round with fatal dangers as he supposed his imaginatively heroic probes into the mind of Man terribly frustrated by 'petty duties and degrading cares' and 'all the superstitions [worldly success] of this life'.

But though these apocalyptic moments culminate in 'my restorations', their metaphorical force does not correspond to any concomitantly impressive image in the text of Wordsworth's danger or impairment; 'petty cares' and 'blind ambition' are not enough, are indeed ridiculously discrepant. Though the five-Book *Prelude* 'was within easy striking distance of completion' by early March 1804, these discrepancies indicate that the distance was only quantitatively short. Wordsworth dismantled his five-Book poem very suddenly and quickly, sometime between *circa* 10 March and 18 March. It may well be that his precipitancy resulted from dissatisfaction at having left out much biographical material and his unwillingness to move on to the central philosophic message of *The Recluse*.[2] But these reasons, besides being opposite sides of the same coin (finish-*The Prelude*-as-a-way-of-not-starting-*The Recluse*), can be

[2] Ibid., pp. 20, 24.

elaborated in terms of what we see happening at the end of the five-Book poem. Or rather, what we do not see. For Wordsworth certainly had a concomitantly impressive image of his own life to match against those of Columbus, Park, Gilbert, and Dampier: it was his experience of the French Revolution and his sense of his imagination's betrayal by it.[3] Writing about this would launch him into a much different poem, far beyond the five-Book frame of 'Books and Nature', and he was unsure about his ability to represent his imagination's rescue from revolution. The 'engulphment' which threatens his metaphoric explorers is also a frequent peril to imagination in *The Prelude*, and the Revolution and finishing the poem are equal sources of it, in content and form, roughly speaking. If we phrase Wordsworth's dilemma as that of maintaining a balance between truthfulness to imagination's impairment and confidence in its restoration, his uncertainty at representing this process was part and parcel of his uncertainty of maintaining it within himself: namely, of being sure that his 'restorations' were real, actual, true, permanent, substantial – in a word, *philosophically* or *metaphysically* certain. Thus the reason for suddenly dismantling this poem, all-but-ready to send off with Coleridge, was his need to *keep on* writing to Coleridge, because only then could he believe that his writing was being read philosophically, by the one to whom 'the unity of all has been revealed'.[4] By sending Coleridge an obviously incomplete poem, Wordsworth effectively guaranteed that his work would continue to make philosophic sense – that such sense would be made of it by its primary reader – even if (and especially because) it was not the 'philosophic' poem itself. He accomplished this by removing all of the original fifth Book with its heavy rhetorical artillery, and send Coleridge something much more like the present Books I–V – something obviously open-ended. Coleridge was going away, and Wordsworth would, in effect, continue writing him the

[3] Joseph Kishel notes 'a strong thematic resemblance' between this passage and the 'upheaval of the French Revolution and Wordsworth's own spiritual crisis in the seond half of the 1805 *Prelude*' (p. 161 above).

[4] Sara Suleri, ' "Once out of Nature": The Uses of System in Wordsworth, Arnold, Yeats' (thesis, Indiana University, 1983). I am indebted at several points to Professor Suleri's thesis that the *Recluse*-as-system was a heuristic device used by Wordsworth to lend philosophical universality to *The Prelude* while at the same time ensuring – by its obvious incompleteness – that the reader (especially Coleridge) would sympathetically supply the missing connections.

verse epistle of 1798–9. But for this short-term gain in philosophic readership he would pay a heavy price, for in taking his narrative into revolutionary France he was changing not only its biographical limits but also abandoning the manageable theme of 'Books and Nature' and setting himself up for a sharp confrontation between his ongoing poem and its intended sequel, *The Recluse*.

Providence, Signs, and the 'Analogy' Passage (1989)

Mary Jacobus

The so-called Analogy passage, written in the early spring of 1804 for the brief moment when *The Prelude* was envisioned as a five-Book structure culminating in the climbing of Snowdon, represents in its own way a fracture in the text of Book XIII – as Wordsworth puts it parenthetically, '(Passage which will conduct in season due / Back to the tale which I have left behind)' (ll. 9–10). How does the 'Analogy' passage 'conduct' back to the tale which Wordsworth had left behind, given its apparently random collocation of associations and miniature narratives? Reading the passage in the light of Wordsworth's 'tale' at this point in *The Prelude* (his story of nature and imagination as each other's counterpart) may elucidate the Snowdon passage, indicating exactly how the usurping mistscape is supposed to offer an analogy to the mind. But one could also read it in the light of Wordsworth's need to deny the tropological status of metaphor. On the face of it, this series of tumultuous or disturbing scenes (a storm over Lake Coniston, a sleeping horse frozen into immobility, Columbus dipping towards the poles, Sir Humphrey Gilbert engulfed at sea before the eyes of his fellow voyag-

Extracted from *Romanticism, Writing and Sexual Difference* (Oxford, 1989), pp. 276–86.

ers, Mungo Park and Dampier anticipating their respective deaths in the desert heart of Africa and an open boat on the South Seas) appear to have little in common with the climbing of Snowdon. But read closely, they point to two underlying concerns crucial to Wordsworth's temporarily abandoned tale: not only the concern with Providence – with personal election and survival (clearly relevant to the poetic fears and aspirations associated with the composition of *The Prelude*) – but the reassurance offered by signs themselves. The 'sign' here is the Covenant, a contract of promise or redemption. Metaphoricity, figured as nature's power to transform or aestheticize itself before the spectator's gaze, becomes the guarantee provided by the Covenant. When Wordsworth alludes to the 'manner in which Nature works . . . upon the outward face of things' (ll. 10–11), we might expect in addition that the question of identity (a 'face' moulded and exalted, given distinct or separate character) will be connected with autobiography – that endowing nature with the power to 'speak' represents a symbolic displacement of the signifying power claimed by the autobiographical poet.

The element of danger common to these 'analogies' seems to point to that dangerous edge of things where either separation (signification) or loss of self (the extinction of signs) may befall the individual. The first 'living picture' which Wordsworth uses to embody his 'pleasing argument' is another landscape, this time marked by the turbulence of storm ('It was a day / Upon the edge of autumn, fierce with storm', ll. 33–34). 'Wrought into commotion', this borderline landscape ('Upon the *edge* of autumn') is indeterminate too in another way, hovering between the visible and the finally unvisualizable Sublime of Milton's war in heaven, whose 'ten thousand thousand saints' (*Paradise Lost*, vi. 767) give Wordsworth his 'Ten thousand thousand waves' (l. 40). But Wordsworth must have had another passage still more strongly in mind, Milton's account in *Paradise Lost*, Book XI, of Noah's Ark and the rainbow Covenant. When Wordsworth mentions not just a 'horse and rider stagger[ing] in the blast' but a boat that is not there ('he who looked upon the stormy lake / Had fear for boat or vessel *where none was*', ll. 45–7; my italics), the absent boat is the Ark, and its principal passenger is Noah, 'The one just man alive' (*Paradise Lost*, xi. 818), whose survival is guaranteed by the rainbow which forms the reassuring climax of *Paradise Lost*, Book XI. Milton's account of the great storm weathered by Noah, when the elements exceed their boundaries and oceanic inundation threatens the mount of Paradise itself, is in its own way a precursor of the moments of usurpation (a term presumably borrowed from Milton) which Wordsworth locates respectively in the Simplon Pass and the Snowdon landscape:

> all the cataracts
> Of heaven set open on the earth shall pour
> Rain day and night, all fountains of the deep
> Broke up, shall heave the ocean to *usurp*
> Beyond all bounds, till inundation rise
> Above the highest hills: then shall this mount
> Of Paradise by might of waves be moved
> Out of his place, pushed by the horned flood,
> With all his verdure spoiled, and trees adrift
> Down the great river to the opening gulf . . .
>
> (*Paradise Lost*, xi. 824–33; my italics)

If a link were needed to connect the vision from Mount Snowdon and the storm over Lake Coniston, this passage surely provides it. The inundating ocean, the usurpation of boundaries, and the suggestion that the Paradisal mount itself might be immersed in 'the opening gulf', all indicate that, as well as his own earlier description of sunrise in a misty Alpine landscape from *Descriptive Sketches*, Wordsworth had in mind this more threateningly apocalyptic scene.[1] He may rewrite Milton's flood as the misty apotheosis of the Snowdon landscape (a familiar feat of natural supernaturalism), but both oceans contain the same subtext. Immense natural threat is made tolerable by a sign from God.

The Covenant provides the clearest link between the storm over Coniston and the story of Noah. In Milton's rendition of Genesis, Noah.

> over his head beholds
> A dewy cloud, and in the cloud a bow
> Conspicuous with three listed colours gay,
> Betokening peace from God, and Covenant new.
>
> (*Paradise Lost*, xi. 864–7)

In the 'Analogy' passage, Wordsworth sets against the confused tumult

---

[1] See *Descriptive Sketches*, ll. 495–505.

of the storm 'A large unmutilated rainbow . . . With stride colossal bridging the whole vale' (ll. 50–2). The rainbow is described in terms at once aesthetic and visionary, as if its wholeness ('unmutilated') were set in defiance of fragmentation; as if it were a sign, not a natural phenomenon – which is what God (in Milton's account) had in any case promised that rainbows would henceforward always be:

> The substance thin as dreams, lovelier than day,
> Amid the deafening uproar stood unmoved,
> Sustained itself through many minutes space,
> As if it were pinned down by adamant.
>
> (ll. 53–6)

When, at the end of *Paradise Lost*, Book XI, Adam asks for an explanation of 'those coloured streaks in heaven',

> serve they as a flowery verge to bind
> The fluid skirts of that same watery cloud,
> Lest it again dissolve and shower the earth?
>
> (*Paradise Lost*, xi. 879, 881–3)

the Archangel Michael tells him that the rainbow is God's 'Covenant never to destroy / The earth again by flood, nor let the sea / Surpass his bounds' (xi. 892–4), and that all future rainbows will be a reminder of his promise. With this passage in mind, Wordsworth hardly needed to invoke the Covenant explicitly to make his point – that the airy substance of the rainbow not only defends the Coniston landscape against dissolution into chaos, but that, as the Noah or chosen son of *The Prelude*, he himself is promised immunity from destruction. Moreover, the rainbow has another function. It ensures that Wordsworth's tropes will be read not as metaphors but as adamantine analogies ('As if it were pinned down by adamant'). The ultimate reassurance provided by the rainbow Covenant lies in betokening a natural, hence God-given, sign system – a divine language that guarantees the subject's relation to signification. Just as metaphor is adamantine sign, so the fixture of signs preserves their user from mutilation.

The sleeping horse in the passage that follows shares with the Snowdon landscape and the adamantine rainbow a seeming capacity for natural self-transmutation:

With one leg from the ground the creature stood,
Insensible and still; breath, motion gone,
Hairs, colour, all but shape and substance gone,
Mane, ears, and tail, as lifeless as the trunk
That had no stir of breath. We paused awhile
In pleasure of the sight, and left him there,
With all his functions silently sealed up,
Like an amphibious work of Nature's hand,
A borderer dwelling betwixt life and death,
A living statue or a statued life.

(ll. 64–73)

Once more, Wordsworth attributes to nature the ability to cross into the aesthetic realm. This is poetry in stillness not motion ('a living statue or a statued life') which asks implicitly, like Keats's urn, if the price of aesthetic or figurative arrest may be empirical death – not, perhaps, a problem for a horse, but (potentially at least) a problem for the autobiographical poet. The obvious link here would be with the power of the imagination to dissolve, diffuse, dissipate, in order to recreate ('to one life impart / The functions of another', ll. 24–5) which Wordsworth illustrates in the 'Preface' of 1815 with his lines about the Leech Gatherer.[2] But is there, perhaps, another route to go? Wordsworth's very aestheticizing of the horse suggests a concern with the figural in its own right. The sleeping horse is 'amphibious' because neither dead nor alive, literally a figure for figurality, 'all his functions silently sealed up'. Paul de Man, writing of the deaf dalesman in *The Excursion*, argues for the way in which figuration involves a similar sensory privation, or stilling of the audible and sensible world. In de Man's words, 'the story of a deaf man who compensates for his infirmity by substituting the reading of books for the sounds of nature' constitutes 'a discourse that is *sustained* beyond and in spite of *deprivation*' – an allegory (like other figures of deprivation in *The Prelude*) of Wordsworth's own figurative mutilation or deprivation and his attempt at self-restoration through the figure of reading called autobiography.[3] We might recall that Wordsworth in Book I of *The Prelude* writes of his want of poetic power – his timorous procrastination – as a similar functional privation or blankness ('a more

---

[2] See e.g. *Borders of Vision*, 2–3.
[3] See 'Autobiography as De-Facement', in *The Rhetoric of Romanticism* (New York, 1984), pp. 72–4.

subtle selfishness, that now / Doth lock my functions up in blank reserve', i. 247–8). What does Wordsworth's inability to get launched on his autobiographical poem have in common with a sleeping horse? The answer may well be a suspension of lived, empirical existence ('Ah, better far than this to stray about / Voluptuously through fields and rural walks', i. 252–3) – paradoxically, the very suspension enjoined by figurality. Striving to make oneself a figure for oneself (a living figure or a figured life) both holds, and holds at bay, the threat embodied by the figural, that of becoming 'A borderer dwelling betwixt life and death', neither fully alive nor entirely divested of life, but consigned to the hinterland of figuration.

Wordsworth's chief defence against the figural privation which constitutes him as an autobiographical subject is his insistence that nature too is an artist, composing 'living pictures' (l. 32) of its own ('those I mean / Which Nature forces on the sight when she / Takes man into the bosom of her works', ll. 74–6). Just to muddy the waters, he adds: 'Books are full of them' (l. 79). If nature's living pictures are to be found especially in books, then who is to say where nature ends and figuration (reading and writing) begins? In the miniature narratives that follow, Wordsworth returns to the imminent (and immanent) danger of extinction which gives both the Snowdon episode and the Coniston storm their undertow of threat while also, by a compensatory movement, provoking their persistent appeal to Providence. Columbus, Gilbert, Park, and Dampier are figures of solitary voyagers confronting impossible odds in their quest for new worlds or, like Park, in his journey of exploration into the interior of Africa. Survival is the issue, although for the first of these travellers, Columbus and his crew, loss of bearings – the disorientation of no longer knowing where they are in relation to a hitherto fixed point – figures the momentous of the voyage of discovery.

> When first, far travelled into unknown seas,
> They saw the needle faltering in its office,
> Turn from the Pole.
>
>   (ll. 82–4)[4]

In a narrative suggestive of 'The Ancient Mariner', Columbus has recently endured extremes of heat and drought from which he is only

---

[4] References to the analogy passage are to the text at Norton *Prelude*, 496–9.

delivered by seemingly miraculous rain and mist.[5] Despite his personal
privations, he yet has time to observe a moment when nature's laws
appear to be suspended, and the old world loses its direction in the new.
The needle falters, the North Star seems to change its altitude as the
ship shifts in relation to the Pole. That faltering, uncertain moment
makes Columbus (and Wordsworth with him) an observer of nature's
estranging effects – for Columbus at least, at considerable personal risk.
It is as if Wordsworth wants to suggest the power of nature's waters to
turn round, as well as orient, the minds of its inmates, gesturing here
towards the defamiliarization which nature itself can effect. Just as the
spectacle of the Blind London Beggar makes the 'mind . . . turn round
/ As with the might of waters' (*Prelude*, vii. 616–17), so the thought of
Columbus dipping down towards the Pole becomes an apprehension, at
once privative and sublime, 'of the utmost that we know / Both of
ourselves and of the universe' (vii. 619–20).

   The motif of personal extinction, whether actual or threatened, links
the remaining travel narratives. In the case of Sir Humphrey Gilbert,
Wordsworth tells of an engulfment accompanied by personal confidence
(or carelessness) about survival so immense as to seem to the awed onlookers like exemplary Christian faith. This is the spectacle presented to
Gilbert's followers in a second ship,

> When they beheld him in the furious storm
> Upon the deck of his small pinnace sitting
> In calmness, with a book upon his knee –
> The ship and he a moment afterwards
> Engulphed and seen no more.
>
> (ll. 90–4)[6]

---

   [5] See F. Columbus, *The Life of the Admiral Christopher Columbus by his Son Ferdinand*,
trans. B. Keen (New Brunswick, 1959), p. 179.

   [6] Wordsworth's source is Edward Haie's report of Sir Humphrey Gilbert's voyage from
Hakluyt's *Principall Navigations*; see *The Principall Navigations, Voyages, Traffiques and
Discoveries of the English Nation* (8 vols.; New York and London, 1907), vi. 35–6: '. . .
giving foorth signes of joy, the Generall sitting abaft with a booke in his hand, cried out
unto us in the Hind (so oft as we did approch within hearing) We are as neere to heaven
by sea as by land . . . The same Monday night . . . the Frigat being ahead of us in the
Golden Hinde, suddenly her lights were out, whereof as it were in a moment, we lost the
sight, and withall our watch cryed, the General was cast away, which was too true. For in
that moment, the Frigat was devoured and swallowed up of the Sea.'

In Wordsworth's startling *mise-en-abyme*, Gilbert goes down reading ('a book upon his knee') with all the obliviousness of a man drowning in his own text. By using a book-derived episode about a figure immersed in a book as an analogy for nature's 'living pictures', Wordsworth may in the end be saying not just that reading (like writing) risks putting an end to the empirical life of the reader-writer, but that nature too is a book in which we can drown, as in any other sea of signs. One spin-off would be to deconstruct the traditional distinction between nature as original and book as representation, offering instead the (equally traditional) analogy between the Book of Poetry, or Revelation, and the Book of Nature on which Wordsworth draws in Book V with the Arab Dream.[7] The function of this analogy is ultimately stabilizing. If both nature and books are texts, textuality can thereby be deprived of its dangers – specifically, of its risk to the empirical self confronting the perils of figuration. Nature becomes a benign instance of the figurality of all things. Looked at like this, Gilbert's engulfment might be read as Wordsworth's counter-argument to himself for safety in textuality, as a kind of lifeline; hence Gilbert's sublime indifference to his fate. With just such confidence Wordsworth presumably wished to confront his own engulfment at the end of *The Prelude*.[8]

The last two travel narratives involve an explicit imagining or anticipation of one's own death. They therefore enact the threat to consciousness represented by the drowning of Gilbert, while at the same time reassuring us of the explorer's ultimate survival. Wordsworth's perspective resembles that of the onlookers as Gilbert's ship goes down ('Like spectacle / That traveller yet living doth appear / To the mind's eye', ll. 94–6); he himself remains only a witness, by definition spared the same fate. Yet it seems also that the convergence of his own and another's consciousness is the basis for his identification, with Mungo Park at

---

[7] See *Prelude*, v. 99–109.

[8] Joseph F. Kishel notices the oddity of this passage – 'We read Wordsworth, and he tells us that he has read the story of Gilbert's drowning. In the story, Gilbert himself sits calmly on the deck of his endangered pinnace, reading yet another book' – but suggests only that 'This Chinese puzzle of distanced observers leaves us with a strong sense that Wordsworth is grappling with but not solving questions of conscious artistic control'; see 'The "Analogy Passage" ', p. 162. Kishel's argument (designed to counter Hartman's 'apocalyptic' reading of the Snowdon episode) focuses on the question of Wordsworth's conscious or unconscious struggle for artistic distance at a turbulent moment in his career.

least. Park, the 'traveller yet living', left a graphic account of what he took to be his last moments in the desert:

> as I was now too faint to attempt walking, and my horse too much fatigued to carry me, I thought it but an act of humanity, and perhaps the last I should ever have it in my power to perform, to take off his bridle and let him shift for himself; in doing which I was suddenly affected with sickness and giddiness; and falling upon the sand, felt as if the hour of death was fast approaching. 'Here then, thought I, after a short but ineffectual struggle, terminate all my hopes of being useful in my day and generation: here must the short span of my life come to an end.' – I cast (as I believed) a last look on the surrounding scene, and whilst I reflected on the awful change that was about to take place, this world with its enjoyments seemed to vanish from my recollection. Nature, however, at length resumed its functions; and on recovering my senses, I found my self stretched upon the sand, with the bridle still in my hand, and the sun just sinking behind the trees.[9]

Wordsworth omits all but the briefest summary of Mungo Park's thoughts on his impending death ('overcome with weariness and pain . . . Sunk to the earth', ll. 98–100), focusing instead on his awakening to find his horse by his side and his arm still within the bridle, 'the sun / Setting upon the desart', 102–3). But Park's 'hopes of being useful in [his] day and generation' must have resonated with Wordsworth's own literary ambitions, if nothing else, while Park's graphic account of the extinction and revival of consciousness takes him from self-loss to a sense of providential self-recovery – from engulfment and back again, as if he had stepped over the brink of Snowdon's 'deep and gloomy breathing place' and returned to solid land; or as if Gilbert had only momentarily appeared to go under.

In telling Dampier's story, Wordsworth remains similarly on the brink, casting himself as reader: 'Kindred power / Was present for the suffering and distress / *In those who read the story*' (ll. 103–5; my italics). Wordsworth seems to be offering something like a theory of the Sublime of reading, in which the power of 'suffering and distress' to produce pleasure depends on the readers' own immunity from the threat of

---

[9] M. Park, *Travels in the Interior Districts of Africa . . . in the Years 1795, 1796 and 1797* (2nd edn, London, 1799), p. 177.

bodily destruction. With Dampier's story of imminent death by water we come full circle to the missing Ark on Lake Coniston. As Dampier writes,

> The sea was already roaring in white Foam about us; a dark Night coming on, and no Land in sight to shelter us, *and our little Ark in danger to be swallowed by every Wave*; and what was worst of all, none of us thought ourselves prepared for another World. The reader may better guess, than I can express, the confusion that we were all in. I had been in many Imminent Dangers before now ... but the worst of them all was but a play-game, in comparison with this.[10]

Dampier is by no means the one just man assured of personal salvation; on the contrary, his 'lingering view of approaching Danger' – danger that comes on 'with such a leisurely and dreadful Solemnity' – provides ample time for reflection (as Wordsworth puts it, 'Bitter repentance for his roving life', l. 115), and also for interpreting the signs (Wordsworth's apocalyptic 'portents of the broken wheel / Girding the sun', ll. 108–9). In his deliberate appeal to the reader ('The reader may better guess, than I can express, the confusion that we were in'), Dampier draws attention to the drama of providential survival. Even in the midst of the storm, he has time to 'call to mind the many miraculous Acts of God's Providence towards [him]', and to negotiate the threat of death (in Wordsworth's phrase) 'by prayer and trust in God' (l. 117). The reader who identifies with Dampier's peril without actually undergoing it becomes the guarantee of his survival; as in the case of Mungo Park, we know that if Dampier had perished, there would have been no travel narrative.[11]

Is this, perhaps, the significance for Wordsworth of these exotic 'analogues' in which a solitary consciousness encounters death – not so much their representation of sublime effects or momentous states of mind, as the fact that they guarantee the tale-teller's immortality or, at least, his continued empirical existence? Dramas involving risky survival may be especially liable to come to mind as a long poem reaches its end. We

[10] W. Dampier, *A New Voyage Round the World* (2nd edn, London, 1697), p. 496; my italics.

[11] As Theresa M. Kelley points out, however, Park – like Dampier – was later to lose his life; see *Wordsworth's Revisionary Aesthetics* (Cambridge, 1988), p. 130.

know, in fact, that Wordsworth had a change of plan and continued to expand *The Prelude* beyond this briefly glimpsed ending – as if he was unable to confront the cessation of his own tale ('the tale which I have left behind', l. 9), and with it, his extinction as an autobiographical figure within the poem. Park and Dampier become the sign of a continued life in writing and even beyond – surviving to travel on past the vividly anticipated endings to their stories. If Wordsworth himself briefly appears to us between the lines as a kind of Ancient Mariner, unable to arrest his own narrative and forced to retell his tale to whoever will listen, this is no more than to say that the compulsion to narrate always involves a compulsion to repeat, and that the compulsion to repeat simultaneously signifies and averts death. These narratives of averted endings offer signification itself as a token of survival in the face of the overwhelming dangers of textual exploration. The text becomes rainbow as well as sea, promising adamantine firmness as well as oceanic usurpation. Converted from a shifting sea of tropes to a fixed system of analogy, both nature and figuration lose their dangers and the writer can continue his voyage of exploration, buoyed up by the very signs which had earlier threatened to engulf him.

Appendix I: The Analogy Passage

Mary Wordsworth copied *Five-Book Prelude* Book V, lines 1–65, into MS W folios 36r–37r, probably some time in early March 1804. Wordsworth made some corrections to the copy and continued the draft, beginning in fair copy, on the following verso (37v). The new lines commented on the climbing of Snowdon, 'tracing this analogy betwixt / The mind of man and Nature'. Considerable care was taken over them; they were subjected to extensive revision, and lines 74–116 of the text below were recopied. But Wordsworth seems finally to have lost heart, and eliminated them from the poem. He turned to a fresh recto (43r), and started again with the draft at Book V, line 66, of the present text.

The analogy passage has been in print longer than any other lines written specifically for the *Five-Book Prelude*, and as a result has attracted a good deal of critical attention[1] – an irony, given that it never formed part of the completed poem. It has been in print as long as the *Thirteen-Book Prelude*, having been included by Ernest de Selincourt in his Clarendon edition of 1926.[2] It remained available in that form until Jonathan Wordsworth produced a markedly different version for the Norton *Prelude*.[3] Readers will find the present text to be closer to de Selincourt than to the Norton, because, like de Selincourt, I have preferred the later copy of lines 74–116 to the earlier draft, and, where the Norton generally attempts to retrieve deleted readings in an effort to provide readers with

[1] See Introduction, pp. 22–4.
[2] *The Prelude or Growth of a Poet's Mind*, ed. Ernest de Selincourt (Oxford, 1926), pp. 600–5.
[3] Norton *Prelude*, pp. 496–9.

the base text of the passage, de Selincourt and I have followed the principles set out on pp. 25–6, above. This is the only way of producing a text
embodying the poet's latest revisions. Where Norton can be said to present
the passage in something approaching the shape in which it was first drafted,
the present version is much closer to the form it would have taken had it
been retained in the *Five-Book Prelude*.

> Even yet thou wilt vouchsafe an ear, oh friend,[1]
> And something too of a submissive mind,
> As in thy mildness thou I know hast done,[2]
> While with a winding but no devious song
> Through [   ][3] processes I make my way   5
> By links of tender thought.[4] My present aim
> Is to contemplate for a needful while
> (Passage which will conduct in season due
> Back to the tale which we have left behind)[5]
> The diverse manner in which Nature works   10
> Ofttimes upon the outward face of things;
> I mean so moulds, exalts, endues, combines,
> Impregnates,[6] separates, adds, takes away,
> And makes one object sway another so,[7]

[1] *oh friend* Coleridge.

[2] An alternative reading appears in the manuscript: 'As to this prelude thou I know hast done'.

[3] There is a gap in the draft at this point that was never filled.

[4] *links of tender thought* a reference to the associations by which the imagination is formed, and the poem as a whole put together.

[5] Although the passage was not completed, Wordsworth makes clear from the outset that it was designed to take him back to the Snowdon scene.

[6] *Impregnates* Wordsworth is recalling Milton's description of the Holy Spirit in *Paradise Lost*, i. 19–22:

> thou from the first
> Wast present, and with mighty wings outspread
> Dove-like sat'st brooding on the vast abyss
> And madest it pregnant.

[7] *I mean so moulds . . . another so* Nature performs a function akin to the secondary imagination, analogous to the artist's act of creation. See the discussion of imagination in the 1815 Preface, and Coleridge's definition of the primary and secondary imaginations in *Biographia Literaria* (*Romanticism*, 476–9, 574).

By unhabitual influence or abrupt,[8]   15
That even the grossest minds must see and hear
And cannot choose but feel.[9] The power which these
Are touched by, being so moved, which Nature thus
Puts forth upon the senses (not to speak
Of finer operations), is in kind   20
A brother of the very faculty
Which higher minds bear with them as their own.
These from their native selves can deal about
Like transformation, to one life impart
The functions of another – interchange,[10]   25
Trafficking with immeasurable thoughts.[11]
Oft tracing this analogy betwixt
The mind of man and Nature, doth the scene
Which from the side[12] of Snowdon I beheld
Rise up before me, followed too in turn   30
By sundry others, whence I will select
A portion, living pictures, to embody
This pleasing argument.
                             It was a day
Upon the edge of autumn, fierce with storm;
The wind blew through the hills of Coniston   35
Compressed, as in a tunnel; from the lake
Bodies of foam took flight, and the whole vale
Was wrought into commotion high and low –
Mist flying up and down, bewildered showers,
Ten thousand thousand waves,[13] mountains and crags,   40
And darkness, and the sun's tumultuous light.

---

[8] *By unhabitual influence or abrupt*   using powers exerted rarely or suddenly.

[9] *That even the grossest minds . . . choose but feel*   For Wordsworth and Coleridge it was necessary to the project of *The Recluse* that everyone, however untutored, be susceptible to the redemptive power of the imagination.

[10] *interchange*   The alternative reading in the manuscript is 'shift, create'.

[11] The favoured beings of whom Wordsworth writes are capable of transferring the qualities of one object to another – just as the mist 'usurps' the features of the sea. This process works in both directions, creating an 'interchange' of characteristics.

[12] *side*   An alternative reading in the manuscript is 'breast'.

[13] *Ten thousand thousand waves*   a Miltonic formulation; see *Paradise Lost*, v. 588: 'Ten thousand thousand ensigns high advanced'.

Green leaves were rent in handfuls from the trees,
The mountains all seemed silent, din so near
Pealed in the traveller's ear, the clouds ran wild,
The horse and rider staggered in the blast,[14]   45
And he who looked upon the stormy lake
Had fear for boat or vessel where none was.[15]
Meanwhile, by what strange chance I cannot tell,[16]
What combination of the wind and clouds,
A large unmutilated rainbow stood   50
Immoveable in heaven, kept standing there,
With a colossal stride[17] bridging the whole vale.
The substance thin as dreams,[18] lovelier than day,
Amid the deafening uproar stood unmoved,
Sustained itself through many minutes space,   55
As if it were pinned down by adamant.
     One evening, walking in the public way,[19]
A peasant of the valley where I dwelt
Being my chance companion, he stopped short
And pointed to an object full in view   60
At a small distance. 'Twas a horse, that stood
Alone upon a little breast of ground
With a clear silver moonlight sky behind.
With one leg from the ground the creature stood
Insensible and still; breath, motion gone,   65
Hairs, colour, all but shape and substance gone,

[14] Ll. 40–5 rework Virgil's less violent account of the north wind, *Georgics*, iii. 196–204.

[15] *boat or vessel where none was*   Jacobus suggests that the boat is Noah's ark, and that this episode refers to Milton's account in *Paradise Lost*, Book XI, of the ark and the rainbow covenant (see pp. 188–9).

[16] For a moment Wordsworth catches the conversational tones of the *Lyrical Ballads*; cf. 'The Idiot Boy', 389; 'The Thorn', 214; and 'Anecdote for Fathers', 39: ' "I cannot tell, I do not know" '.

[17] *With a colossal stride*   an echo of Cassius's account of Caesar: 'Why, man, he doth bestride the narrow world / Like a Colossus' (*Julius Caesar*, I. ii. 135–6).

[18] *The substance thin as dreams*   There is an echo of Prospero's comment, 'We are such stuff / As dreams are made on', and a more general reminiscence of the entire speech (*Tempest*, IV. i. 148–58).

[19] Ll. 57–73 are discussed within the larger context of Wordsworth's poetry by Jonathan Wordsworth, *Borders of Vision*, ch. 1.

Mane, ears, and tail as lifeless as the trunk
That had no stir of breath. We paused awhile
In pleasure of the sight, and left him there
With all his functions silently sealed up,   70
Like an amphibious work of Nature's hand,
A borderer dwelling betwixt life and death,
A living statue, or a statued life.
    To these appearances which Nature thrusts
Upon our notice – her own naked work,   75
Self-wrought, unaided by the human mind –
Add others more imperious,[20] those I mean
Which on our sight she forces, calling man
To give new grandeur to her ministry,[21]
Man suffering or enjoying. Meanest minds   80
Want not these monuments,[22] though overlooked
And little prized, and books are full of them:
Such power – to pass at once from daily life,
And our inevitable sympathy
With passions mingled up before our eyes –   85
Such presence is acknowledged when we trace
The history of Columbus.[23] Think of him
And of his followers when, in unknown seas
Far travelled, they first saw the needle take
Another course and, faltering in its office,   90
Turn from the Pole.[24] Such object doth present

---

[20] *imperious* dominating, imposing. Wordsworth is discussing phenomena that do not require the transforming power of imagination to impress themselves on the human mind. As elsewhere in *The Prelude*, they can entail 'suffering' – i.e., the fostering influence of pain and fear (see Book I, l. 438).

[21] *ministry* guidance, as at Book I, l. 368.

[22] *monuments* evidence of Nature's power.

[23] Wordsworth knew about Columbus primarily from Ferdinand Columbus, *The History of the Life and Actions of Admiral Christopher Columbus* (1571), probably from its appearance in Awnsham and John Churchill, *A Collection of Voyages and Travels* (1704), known to him from Hawkshead days, and in Wordsworth's possession at Rydal Mount (Shaver, 54; *WR* ii. 109).

[24] The north star seems to change altitude as the ship shifts in relation to the Pole. De Selincourt quotes the passage in Ferdinand Columbus's *Life* to which Wordsworth refers:

(To those who read the story at their ease)
Sir Humphry Gilbert, that bold voyager,
When after one disastrous wreck he took
His station in the pinnace, for the sake   95
Of honour and her crew's encouragement,
And they who followed in the second ship,
The larger brigantine which he had left,
Beheld him while amid the storm he sate
Upon the open deck of his small bark   100
In calmness with a book upon his knee –
To use the language of the Chronicle,
A soldier of Christ Jesus, undismayed –
The ship and he, a moment afterwards,
Engulfed, and seen no more.[25]

                      Like spectacle   105
Doth that land-traveller,[26] living yet, appear
To the mind's eye, when, from the Moors escaped,

'He also perceived, that at night the compass vary'd a whole point to the NW., and at break of day it came right with the Star. These things confounded the Pilots, till he told them the cause of it was the compass the star took about the Pole, which was some satisfaction to them, for this variation made them' apprehend some danger in such an unknown distance from Home and such strange Regions'.

[25] Wordsworth refers to the narrative in Hakluyt's *Principal Navigations, Voyages, and Discoveries of the English Nation* (1589) (see *WR* ii. 195), in which Gilbert is described as remaining with his frigate, despite its battered state, out of loyalty to his crew, rather than joining the survivors in the Golden Hinde: 'Munday the ninth of September, in the afternoone the Frigat was neere cast away, oppressed by waves, yet at that time recovered: and giving foorth signs of joy, the General sitting abaft with a booke in his hand, cried out unto us in the Hind (so oft as we did approach within hearing) We are as neere to heaven by sea as by land. Reiterating the same speech, well beseeming a souldier, resolute in Jesus Christ, as I can testifie he was. The same Monday night, about twelve of the clocke, or not long after, the Frigat being ahead of us in the Golden Hinde, suddenly her lights were out, wherof as it were in a moment, we lost the sight, and withall our watch cryed, the Generall was cast away, with was too true. For in that moment, the Frigat was devoured and swallowed up in the Sea'.

[26] *that land-traveller*   Mungo Park (1771–1805), in whose travels to the river Niger in West Africa, 1795, Wordsworth was much interested (see *WR* ii. 309). In his *Travels* (1798), Park described how he fainted as he tried to release his horse from its bridle: 'Nature however at length resumed its functions, and on recovering my senses I found myself stretched upon the sand with the bridle still in my hand, and the sun just sinking behind the trees'.

Alone and in the heart of Africa,
And, having sunk to earth, worn out with pain
And weariness that took at length away   110
The sense of life, he found when he awaked
His horse in quiet, standing at his side,
His arm within the bridle, and the sun
Setting upon the desert. Kindred power
Is with us, in the suffering of that time,   115
When, flying in his Nicobar canoe
With three Malayan helpers, Dampier saw
Well in those portents (the broken wheel
Girding the sun,[27] and afterwards the sea
Roaring and whitening at the night's approach),   120
And danger coming on – not in a shape
Which, in the heat and mettle of the blood,
He oft had welcomed, but considerate,[28]
With dread and leisurely solemnity.
Bitter repentance for his roving life   125
Seized then upon the vent'rous mariner,
Made calm at length by prayer and trust in God.[29]
Meanwhile the bark went forward like an arrow
Shot from a bow, the wind for many hours
Her steersman, but a slackening of the storm   130
Encouraged them at length to cast a look
Upon the compass, by a lighted match
Made visible, which they in their distress
Kept burning for the purpose. Thus they fared,

[27] In his *New Voyage round the World* (1697), William Dampier described how, having left Nicobar for Achin in a canoe, accompanied by three Englishmen, four Malayans, and a Portuguese half-caste, they had 'a very ill presage, by a great Circle about the Sun (five or six times the Diameter of it) which seldom appears, but Storms of Wind and much Rain ensue'.

[28] *considerate* Wordsworth means that danger imposes itself on Dampier through considerate and sober reflection on the past (see next note). The deleted reading at this point is 'deliberate'.

[29] Dampier relates how 'the Sea was already roaring in a white Foam about us', and goes on: 'I must confess that my courage failed me here: and I made very sad reflections on my former Life, and looked back with Horrour and Detestation on Actions which I before detested, but now I trembled at the remembrance of.'

Sitting all night upon the lap of death   135
In wet and starveling[30] plight, wishing for dawn,
A dawn that came at length, with gloomy clouds
Covering the horizon, the first glimpses
Far from the horizon's edge, high up in heaven –
High dawn, prognosticating winds as high.[31]   140

---

[30] *starveling*   perishing with cold and hunger – a rare usage, which Wordsworth borrows from Dampier: 'In this wet starveling plight we spent the tedious night'. Wordsworth borrowed the same phrasing for *The Waggoner* (1806), 809: 'And Babes in wet and starvling plight'.

[31] Wordsworth follows Dampier very closely: 'At length the Day appeared, but with such dark black Clouds near the Horizon, that the first Glimpse of the Dawn appeared 30 or 40 Degrees high, which was dreadful enough: for it is a common Saying among Seamen, and true, as I have experienced, that a high Dawn will have high Winds, and a low Dawn small winds'.

Appendix II: Schedule of Manuscripts

The present text of the *Five-Book Prelude* is reconstructed on the basis of the two extant manuscripts and analogous passages in drafts for other versions of the poem. A complete schedule of textual sources is presented below, integrated with notes on the text.

MS V (DC MS 22): Dorothy Wordsworth's fair copy of The *Two-Part Prelude*, dating from late November–early December 1799. It provided the source for parallel passages in the *Five-Book Prelude*, January–March 1804. Survey, transcription and photographs available at Cornell *Prelude 1798–9*, 221, 258–65.

MS WW (DC MS 43): Twenty-three disjoined leaves from a pocket notebook used first by Dorothy Wordsworth on the Scottish tour of autumn 1803, then by Wordsworth for drafting part of the *Five-Book Prelude*, January–March 1804. The notebook also contains some drafts for Books VI and VIII of the *Thirteen-Book Prelude*. This very difficult manuscript is best approached with the help of the infra-red photographs and transcriptions available at Cornell *13-Book Prelude*, i. 329–66, ii. 237–61.

MS W (DC MS 38): Mutilated notebook used for assembly of Books III, IV and V of the *Five-Book Prelude* in February–March 1804. As Jonathan Wordsworth has observed, it was probably filled before abandonment of the scheme, with no indication of the reorganization of Books IV and V that had taken place by 18 March. Photographs and transcriptions of the relevant materials can be found at Cornell *13-Book Prelude*, i. 367–430, ii. 262–313.

MS M (DC MS 44): Mary Wordsworth's fair copy of the *Thirteen-Book Prelude*, Books I–V, completed and sent to Coleridge by 18 March.

Some photographs available at Cornell *13-Book Prelude*, i. 431–7.

MS Z (DC MS 49): Notebook containing Books XI and XII of *Thirteen-Book Prelude* dating from February to early May 1805. See the survey, transcriptions and photographs at Cornell *13-Book Prelude*, i. 597–626, ii. 429–66.

MS A (DC MS 52): Fair copy by Dorothy Wordsworth of *Thirteen-Book Prelude*, dating from late November 1805–February 1806. Survey, transcriptions and photographs available at Cornell *13-Book Prelude*, i. 630–1162, ii. 471–993.

Books I–III: These lines do not survive in any of the *Five-Book Prelude* MSS. Text drawn entirely from MS M, fair copy entered less than a week after abandonment of the five-Book scheme.

Book IV, 1–85: These lines do not survive in any of the *Five-Book Prelude* MSS. On the basis of what does survive, it may be conjectured that it consisted of some version of *Thirteen-Book Prelude*, iv. 121–80 and 222–46. These lines are edited from MS M, 162r, 162v, 163r, 164r.

IV, 86–185: The source is *Five-Book Prelude* MS W, 2v, 4v, 5v, 6v, 2v, 3v, 4v.

IV, 186–321: The encounter with the discharged soldier was composed originally at Alfoxden in late January 1798 (see Cornell *LB* 277–82). It was not transcribed in the *Five-Book Prelude* MSS, but was intended to follow at this point. The text is edited from MS M, 166v, 167r, 167v, 168r, 168v, 169r.

IV, 322–70: The source is *Five-Book Prelude* MS W, 20v, 21r, 21v, 22r.

IV, 371–7: In *Five-Book Prelude* MS W, the Infant Prodigy passage was meant to follow these lines. But there is no introduction to it in the notebook. Jonathan Wordsworth conjectures that *Thirteen-Book Prelude*, v. 223–9, may have been composed for this purpose. Although there is no evidence for it, the lines are required for the transition, and they are edited here from MS M, 174r, 174v.

IV, 378–458: The source is *Five-Book Prelude* MS W, 29r, 29v, 30r, 30v.

IV, 459–526: At this point a leaf or leaves were removed from the notebook, containing material analogous to *Thirteen-Book Prelude*, v. 377–445. These lines are drawn from MS M, 177r, 177v, 178r.

IV, 527–96: The source is *Five-Book Prelude* MS W, 26r, 26v, 27r, 27v. It should be pointed out that Reed's numbering of these leaves is incorrect (his numbering runs from 31–2).

IV, 597–710: Leaves were removed at this point in the notebook, probably containing material analogous to *Thirteen-Book Prelude*, v. 516–629. This material is supplied from MS M, 180r, 180v, 181r, 181v, 182r.

IV, 711–23: The source is *Five-Book Prelude* MS W, 33r, 33v.

Book V, 1–108: The source is *Five-Book Prelude* MS W, 36r, 36v, 37r, 43r (ll. 68–72), 37v (ll. 73–8), 38r, 43r, 43v.

V, 108–33: At this point the draft becomes too fragmentary to provide retrievable text. This material corresponds to *Thirteen-Book Prelude*, xiii, 128–53, edited from MS A, 328r, 329r.

V, 134–71: The source is *Five-Book Prelude* MS W, 45r, 47r, 46r (ll. 146–8), 46v, 47r.

V, 172–201: At this point the draft becomes too fragmentary to provide retrievable text. This material corresponds with *Thirteen-Book Prelude*, xi. 108–37, edited from MSS Z and A: MS Z, 6v (ll. 172–84), 7r (ll. 185–92); MS A, 296r (ll. 193–201).

V, 193: The MS Z draft continues from this point in the 'Black Book', a MS now apparently lost.

V, 202–79: The source is *Five-Book Prelude* MS W, 49v, 51v, 52v, 53r, 12r, 12v, 13v.

V, 279: It is clear from the directions given in the draft that the spots of time were meant to follow at this point; they were not, however, copied out in the MS, probably for lack of pages. What evidence there is indicates that the spots of time were copied directly from the *Two-Part Prelude*, and had not yet reached the form in which they appear in MS Z, which followed MS W.

V, 280–6: The source is *Two-Part Prelude* MS V, 8r.

V, 287–91: The source is *Five-Book Prelude* MS W, 13v – one of several pieces of evidence that indicate the position of the spots of time within the poem. The phrasing 'While I was yet an' (l. 291) indicates that at the time MS W was drafted this passage was closer to the *Two-Part Prelude* text than to MS Z, the next extant stage of work on it.

V, 291–319: The source is *Two-Part Prelude* MS V, 8r, 8v.

V, 319–45: The source is *Five-Book Prelude* MS W, 50v, 51r. The MS W draft of the *Five-Book Prelude* ends at l. 345. The catch-words 'One

Christmas-time' are sufficient to indicate that the waiting for the horses episode was to conclude the poem. I have drawn the remaining text from the *Two-Part Prelude* on the grounds that what little evidence there is suggests that the revisions found in subsequent drafts towards the *Thirteen-Book Prelude* had not yet been made.

V, 346–89: The source is *Two-Part Prelude* MS V, 8v, 9r, 9v.

Index